CASE STUDIES IN
CULTURAL ANTHROPOLOGY

GENERAL EDITORS
George and Louise Spindler
STANFORD UNIVERSITY

THE TIWI OF NORTH AUSTRALIA

The Tiwi Islands

THE TIWI
OF
NORTH AUSTRALIA
THIRD EDITION

C.W.M. HART
ARNOLD R. PILLING
Wayne State University
JANE C. GOODALE
Bryn Mawr College

HOLT, RINEHART AND WINSTON, INC.

NEW YORK • CHICAGO • SAN FRANCISCO • PHILADELPHIA

MONTREAL • TORONTO • LONDON • SYDNEY • TOKYO

Cover photo: *Stanley Munkara, an Aborigine from Tikilaru, Bathurst Island, Northern Territory, dressed for his part in a* pukamani *dance. Photo by Joe Brian, Australian Information Service, "some years" before 1987. In 1987, Stanley Munkara was a member of the Tiwi Land Council, a unit approximating a Tiwi tribal council.*

Library of Congress Cataloging-in-Publication Data
Hart, C. W. M. (Charles William Merton),
   The Tiwi of North Australia.
   (Case studies in cultural anthropology)
   Bibliography: p.
   Includes index.
   1. Tiwi (Australian people) I. Pilling, Arnold R.
II. Goodale, Jane C. III. Title. IV. Series.
DU125.T5H37 1988   306'.0899915   87-7510

ISBN 0-03-012019-5

890 016 987654321

Holt, Rinehart and Winston, Inc.
The Dryden Press
Saunders College Publishing

To all the Tiwi
of past and present generations,
from whom Hart, Pilling, Goodale,
and several generations of university students
have already learned so much.

NGINI NGATI NGAUWILA TIWI, AMPI PATJUANI AMANTIA AMPI NGARIMU.

[This   one   (to)   all   Tiwi,   from deceased (time)   and   from   alive   (time).

NGAWA   URATIRIMA   NGINTIRIKIRIMI   NGINUKI   TURA,

We   three (who have)   made   this   book,

NGIMPI NGATI   KURUWANI   NGINI   NGITI MUANUALUWA.

we   (as)   one   thank (with) this (for)   us   teaching.]

Foreword

ABOUT THE SERIES

These case studies in cultural anthropology are designed to bring to students, in beginning and intermediate courses in the social sciences, insights into the richness and complexity of human life as it is lived in different ways and in different places. They are written by men and women who have lived in the societies they write about and who are professionally trained as observers and interpreters of human behavior. The authors are also teachers, and in writing their books they have kept the students who will read them foremost in their minds. It is our belief that when an understanding of ways of life very different from one's own is gained, abstractions and generalizations about social structure, cultural values, subsistence techniques, and the other universal categories of human social behavior become meaningful.

ABOUT THIS CASE STUDY

For the 1960 edition of this case study we wrote: "A vivid picture of Tiwi life, as viewed from within the culture, emerges in this book. The reader is not made an outsider, left to peer into a dimly understood, formalized, alien way of life. Rather, he is taken inside the family group, by the night's campfire. He becomes a witness to angry quarrels, a participant in involved machinations aimed at success—as defined by the Tiwi. He comes to know individual Tiwi as real people." These statements still hold true. This new edition brings the picture up to date, but it does not destroy these values of immediacy and intimacy.

There are new dimensions in this edition of *The Tiwi*. During the 57 years between Hart's fieldwork in 1928–1929, Pilling's in 1953–1954, and Goodale's in 1954, 1962, 1980–1981, and 1986–1987 much has changed. Nevertheless, Tiwi culture persists. Adaptations have been made to the exigencies of life created by the Anglo-European presence and the changing times in which we all participate. But the past and the present have folded together into a synchronic whole that is by no means lacking in coherence.

Once again the Tiwi are owners of their own land. This has ramifications that Jane Goodale pursues in her chapter at the end of the study. Electricity, gasoline engines, boats, firearms, packaged and processed foods have become a part of their lives. Tiwi men and women have become national figures in the Australian consciousness. And yet, traditional rituals persist and hunting

vii

and gathering still produce important subsistence much preferred to store-bought items that are often fed to dogs or used as bait.

This new edition of the Tiwi is notable both for the length of time the culture has been under observation by anthropologists and for the fact that three anthropologists studying the same people have collaborated in the reporting of their observations. The larger part of the main text has been written by Hart and left, with minor editing, as it stood in the original edition. Pilling has added significant material throughout, and has only occasionally edited Hart's commentary. Goodale's contribution is contained in one chapter at the end of the study. The reader will be able to detect subtle differences in style and stance in the writings of the three authors. Hart was writing from a period of fieldwork in the late 1920s and an authorship from the late 1950s. He was, of course, not influenced by the feminist, semiotic, symbolic, or reflexive developments characterizing cultural anthropology in the past decade. His descriptive analysis of Tiwi life, and particularly that of the contractual negotiations, is good social anthropology constructed from the male point of view. Jane Goodale has written *Tiwi Wives* (1971) from the female point of view among the Tiwi. The two analyses are complementary.

ABOUT THE AUTHORS

C. W. M. Hart

Charles William Merton Hart (1905–1976) was born in Melbourne, Australia, and did not become an American citizen until 1953. He was already a law student at the University of Sydney when the eminent anthropologist Radcliffe-Brown began teaching at Sydney in 1925, and Hart was among the first of the young Australians to become a full-time anthropology graduate student. In 1930, on a Rockefeller Travelling Fellowship, he spent a summer studying at the University of Chicago with Edward Sapir and Robert Redfield, and then went on to the London School of Economics to work toward his doctorate with Charles G. Seligman and Bronislaw Malinowski. Looking for a job in 1932, the darkest year of the Great Depression, the only teaching job in anthropology that was then available in the whole British Empire (then at its height) was at the University of Toronto in Canada, where he taught from 1932 to 1947. In the latter year he moved to the University of Wisconsin at Madison where he was Professor of Anthropology until 1959. In that year he took on the task of founding the first chair of Social Anthropology in the University of Istanbul and stayed in Turkey for 10 years. After returning from Istanbul, he joined the faculty at Wichita State University, where he taught part-time until his death.

Hart observed the Tiwi in 1928 and 1929, and shortly thereafter gave these people their modern tribal designation. Aside from his contribution of Chapters 1 through 4 of the present volume, he wrote an overview of Tiwi ways in 1930, "The Tiwi of Melville and Bathurst Islands"; a 1931 paper on their traditional naming patterns; a 1954 piece on variation in Tiwi personality,

Photo 1. C. W. M. Hart among the Tiwi, in 1928–1929. This is the only known image of Hart to survive from his life on Bathurst Island.

"The sons of Turimpi"; a 1955 chapter titled "Contrasts between prepubertal and postpubertal education," in *Education and Anthropology*, edited by George Spindler, which includes a lengthy comment on and partial analysis of Tiwi initiation; a 1970 paper, "Some factors affecting residence among the Tiwi"; and a 1974 chapter titled "Fieldwork among the Tiwi, 1928–1929," in George Spindler's *Being an Anthropologist: Fieldwork in Eleven Cultures*, appearing in this edition of *The Tiwi of North Australia* as Chapter 8.

Arnold R. Pilling

Arnold R. Pilling (1926–   ), a Californian, studied at the University of California, under Robert H. Lowie and Robert F. Heizer; at the University of Colorado, under Omer C. Stewart; and at the University of London, under C. Daryll Forde, John Barnes, and V. Gordon Childe. He was a Fulbright Fellow to Australia in 1953 and 1954 and spent most of that time studying the culture of the Tiwi. He has more recently carried out extensive fieldwork among the Yurok and Chilula Indians and their neighbors of northwestern California, and is the author of the "Yurok" article in *The Handbook of North American Indians* and, with Patricia L. Pilling, a 1970 paper on cultural brokers among these Indians. He also wrote a classical 1972 article on dating photographs. Pilling is professor of anthropology at Wayne State University in Detroit and director of its Museum of Anthropology. He served as organ-

Photo 2. Pilling near Bathurst Island Mission, in October 1953; he was just returning from a day interviewing in the bush. This is the only surviving image of Pilling taken during his 1953–1954 fieldwork.

izing secretary-treasurer of The Society for Historical Archaeology in the late 1960s, and has published on the archaeology, historical archaeology, and ethnohistory of Detroit and Michigan.

Aside from his contribution of the Introduction and chapters 5 and 6 of the present volume, he has written a 1958 summary of Australian archaeology; a 1962 book on sources relating to Australian aborigines; a 1962 article titled "A historical *versus* a non-historical approach to social change and continuity among the Tiwi"; a 1965 work on the Tiwi as an Australian minority; a 1968 paper titled "Southeastern Australia: level of social organization," in which he outlines Tiwi social units; and has edited, with Richard A. Waterman, a 1970 book on change among Australian aborigines, which includes a chapter on changes in Tiwi language.

Jane C. Goodale

Jane C. Goodale (1926–   ), a Bostonian by birth, studied anthropology at Radcliffe College and the University of Pennsylvania. Since 1960 she has taught at Bryn Mawr College, where she is Professor and was chairman of the department. During 1986–1987 she was visiting Principal Lecturer in Anthropology at the Darwin Institute of Technology. Goodale lived among the Tiwi of Milikapiti in 1954, briefly in June 1962, for 16 months in 1980–1981, and visited them frequently in 1986–1987. Her Tiwi studies have, at

Photo 3. Jane Goodale, in 1986, at the Milikapiti Sports and Social Club, with three of her chief female informants and kin. Left to right: Paddy Henry, Happy Cook, Mary Elizabeth Moreen, Jane Goodale, and Polly Miller.

one time or another, been funded by the National Geographic Society, National Institute of Mental Health, National Science Foundation, American Council of Learned Societies, Bryn Mawr College, and the University of Pennsylvania Museum. Goodale has also carried out fieldwork in Papua New Guinea in 1962, 1963–1964, 1967–1968, and 1973, resulting in articles on the Kaulong people of Southern West New Britain Province, including papers with her coinvestigator Ann Chowning, who studied the neighboring Sengseng.

In addition to Chapter 8 in the present volume, her publications on the Tiwi include a 1955 overview, "Melville Island"; a 1957 article on Tiwi duck hunting, " 'Alonga bush'—a Tiwi hunt"; a 1959 paper on Tiwi mourning, "The Tiwi dance for the dead"; another paper that year, "The Tiwi women of Melville Island, Australia"; a 1960 account, "Sketch of Tiwi children"; another 1960 paper on Tiwi funeral customs; a 1962 paper, "Marriage contracts among the Tiwi"; a 1963 paper on the kulama ceremony, "Qualifications for adulthood: Tiwi invoke the power of a yam"; a 1966 contribution, written with Joan D. Koss, "The cultural context of creativity among Tiwi"; a 1970 chapter on Tiwi ceremonial change; her well-known 1971 book Tiwi Wives; a 1982 article "Production and reproduction of key resources among the Tiwi of North Australia"; and a 1985 paper, "Aboriginal Women and Development."

George and Louise Spindler
Series Editors
Calistoga, California

Preface to the Third Edition

Since *The Tiwi of North Australia* was first published in 1960, it has become a classic among ethnographic monographs, not only for the vividness of the ethnographic account of traditional culture, but also for its approach to the documentation of culture change. More than a generation of college and university students have come to know of hunting and gathering peoples through this book, as well as how such societies have changed under pressures from outsiders.

In the early 1980s, Jane C. Goodale, whose book *Tiwi Wives* had made her an expert on the Tiwi probably as well-known as Hart and Pilling, returned to investigate recent changes among the Tiwi. Hart having died in 1976, Pilling had become the only surviving author of the 1960 *Tiwi of North Australia*. Pilling decided that a further updating by Goodale, telling how the Tiwi were living in the 1980s, would interest a new generation of students and teachers of anthropology. Such a book would also be a first in anthropology, because it would bring together the observations of three different anthropologists, looking at essentially the same people at three different periods.

Goodale readily accepted the invitation to join Hart and Pilling as a third participant/observer, reporting upon her fieldwork of 1980 and 1981. Delays ensued and Goodale returned to Darwin and the Tiwi for further fieldwork in 1986 and 1987. The monograph that follows is by three authors and derives from four periods of observation of the Tiwi between Hart's visit of 1928–1929, through Pilling's stay of 1953–1954, and Goodale's trips of 1954, 1962, 1980–1981, and 1986–1987.

The Introduction to the Third Edition retains the outline and some of the content as it was written by Hart for the 1960 edition. It has been drastically altered in places by Pilling, however, who brings its thinking in line with recent knowledge of Australia's prehistory. Chapters 1, 2, 3, and 4 are essentially as they were written by Hart in 1959; however, both he and recently Pilling have made minor changes in the text to improve its accuracy and update its content. Pilling has also added a section in Chapter 4, which details the pre-Mission pattern of sneak attacks. The dropping of this pattern was part of a drastic alteration of Tiwi society, which occurred even before missionaries arrived among the Tiwi. Chapter 5 is basically as Pilling wrote it in 1959. Chapter 6 remains little changed from its 1960 version, except for the section "Tiwi and the Australian Nation," which has been updated into the early 1970s. Chapter 7 is Goodale's new account of the Tiwi as she has seen them in 1954, 1980–1981, and 1986–1987.

Chapter 8 has been appended as an additional window into lifeways now past. It is an essay published in 1974 in which Hart documents his memories at that late date of what fieldwork was like over 50 years ago.

The contrasts and similarities to Jane Goodale's experience among the Tiwi, as she describes it in her chapter, provide us with insights about how both the Tiwi and we have changed.

The Tiwi are owed much by all three authors of this monograph. The Tiwi have been gracious hosts and friends to anthropologists and other outsiders for more than 50 years.

A.R.P.

Contents

List of Illustrations

CASE STUDIES IN
CULTURAL ANTHROPOLOGY

GENERAL EDITORS

George and Louise Spindler

STANFORD UNIVERSITY

THE TIWI OF NORTH AUSTRALIA

Introduction:
The Australian Aborigines

THE PEOPLING OF AUSTRALIA

Though European seafarers, particularly the Portuguese and the Dutch, had sighted and even landed upon the shores of Australia at much earlier dates, the first real knowledge of Australia and what it contained was brought back to Europe by the great English explorer, Captain James Cook, as a result of his voyage of 1769–1771. During that voyage, Cook surveyed and mapped most of the long eastern coastline of the island continent, and because he was a keen scientist himself and also had on board several naturalists, including the noted botanist Sir Joseph Banks, the wonders of the new country—its peculiar flora and fauna and its strange human inhabitants—were carefully examined and described for the first time. We may therefore fix the bringing of the Australian native peoples to the attention of the Western world as dating from Cook's visit during 1770.

By that date, most of the rest of the world was known and at least some rough notions of what the existing races looked like were held by educated Europeans. Captain Cook and the naturalists with him were therefore quick to realize that the Australian natives, in both their physical appearance and way of life, were distinct from any people elsewhere. Dark skinned and wide nosed as they were, their low brows and wavy hair (including luxuriant beards) clearly differentiated them from African Blacks, while their culture distinguished them from the islanders of the Pacific. Physical type different from anybody else, culture technologically primitive—these were the two predominant impressions that the Australian natives made on the first Europeans to associate with them and they are still, to modern anthropologists, the two basic features that must be used when trying to place the Australians within the racial and cultural history of humanity.

Why the Australians—when finally discovered by the Europeans—should be so different in physical type and culture compared with most of the world is usually explained by employing the same concept that scientists use to account for the existence in Australia of eucalyptus trees, kangaroos, koala bears, and the duck-billed platypus—namely, the long isolation of these forms that were thought elsewhere to have either died out or changed into something a little more modern. Australia is a large and geologically an ancient country, but in relation to other large masses on the earth, it is very "cut-off" and

Photo 4. Mangroves as they look close up. It is likely that the first Australians left such a landing among the mangroves, when they pushed off for what became a storm-tossed voyage to the Australian mainland. In the present view are members of the Tiwi Rangwila group whom Pilling visited in the bush during August 1954, as their dugout canoes appeared while being loaded.

remote. Recent white settlement in Australia has built up large modern cities that are similar in many respects to those in America. During World War II, American troops visiting these Australian cities were astonished to find so many of their cherished American institutions—department stores, drug-stores, movie theaters—located in a country "so far from everywhere." Its isolation accounts for the preservation in Australia of plants, animals, and a native race which, deprived of contact with the rest of the world until recently, developed or retained characteristics that are unique in the modern world.

Most of what we can say about the first entry of humans into Australia is rather speculative. Early humans lived at least as near to Australia as Java, Java actually being part of the Asia land mass at several low water periods in the Pleistocene. From Java one can see, even today, from one island high point to the next island, all the way from Java to Timor and Roti to the southwest. However, some water craft has always, even at the lowest water, been necessary to allow humans to cross the passages between the Indonesian islands, as well as those between the Indonesian islands, Australia, and New Guinea.

How many years ago the first humans reached Australia can be inferred from evidence available by the 1980s. In the early 1950s, the scientific dating technique called "radiocarbon dating" was developed. It was also in this period that the first formally trained archaeologist was appointed at an Australian university.[1] By the early 1960s, several more archaeologists had been appointed at Australian universities, and stratigraphic archaeology, supplemented by radiocarbon dating, began to move the study of Australia's human prehistory into the same realm of scholarly research as that being carried out on other continents. By 1970, researchers working at Lake Mungo, in New South Wales, in the region of the junction of the Darling and Murray rivers, had reported evidence of human activity associated with a radiocarbon date at least as early as 30,780 ±520 years.[2] By 1981, cultural material had been recovered in association with carbonized wood bearing a radiocarbon date of 39,500 +2,300/−1,800 years ago.[3]

Recent writings on low water periods relevant to the history of humans in Australia state that about 17,000 years ago, the ocean was about 160 meters below its present level. Possibly some elements of the ancestry of Australians and/or Tasmanians arrived at that time. The sea was at least as low as 30 meters below its present level throughout the period from about 6,500 years ago and 80,000 years ago. A second maximum low water stand, again at some 160 meters below present sea level, occurred about 53,000 years ago.[4]

Use of recent maps of the area between Timor and Australia[5] and the formula for how far one can see from a high point[6] establish that, at 160 meters below present sea level, an observer could see from high areas of Timor to an island shoal reaching within 29 meters of present sea level about 55 miles off the southeast shore of Timor and to a long underwater ridge reaching to within 14 meters of modern sea level about 85 miles southeast of the same part of Timor, as well as from the island to the ridge. The latter ridge arcs out from Sahul as the massive continent that includes present-day Australia, New Guinea, Tasmania, and the undersea shelf known as the Sahul Banks reaches its northwestern edge about 400 miles west of Bathurst Island.[7] The attraction of such distant shores would possibly have been enhanced for the first migrants toward Australia when dense smoke rose from lightning-caused bushfires raging through 10-foot-tall, rank, virgin, bamboolike grass that had desiccated in the tropical dry season. To the migrants these islands on the edge of Sahul may have seemed like others in a long series.

However, data are not sufficient to establish that humans could have seen,

---

[1] This first trained archaeologist was D. J. Mulvaney, appointed in the History Department at the University of Melbourne in 1953 (White and O'Connell, 1982: 29).

[2] This sample is known as ANU-680. See Bowler et al., 1970.

[3] Sample SUA-1500, as cited by White and O'Connell, 1982: 221.

[4] White and O'Connell, 1982: 15.

[5] The maps used in reaching conclusions about what a person on high points in Timor could see of islands to the south of Timor are National Geographic Society, 1981: 216 and U.S. Army Map Service, 1963a-b, 1964.

[6] Raisz, 1962: 152 gives the formula for calculating the distance one can see from an outlook: r being being the number of miles to the horizon:

$$r = 1.065\sqrt{3/2 \text{ height in feet}}$$

It is noted by Raisz that when one is attempting to tell whether one can see from one outlook to another, one calculates the distance one can see at each outlook and adds the two distances together.

[7] A discussion of various routes by which the early migrants might have reached Sahul has been published by Birdsell, 1977.

Photo 5. The "bush," the sort of tree cover found as part of the savanna of most Tiwi country, here shown as it appears after the grass cover has been burned off. In the foreground is a temporary daytime camp in which a Tiwi sail was being used as a shade by an afternoon napper, during November 1953.

during 160 meter low water periods, from one island high point to the next island, all the way from Asia to Australia. Presently available soundings on the Sahul shelf stretching between the Sahul Banks and modern Australia do not show any combination of former islands that would have allowed sightings from the 14-meter ridge onward. Further soundings on the Sahul shelf may alter this situation, just as the data newly available between 1975 and 1981 altered the outline of the edge of Sahul in this area near Timor.[8] But for now, even as when the first edition of *The Tiwi* was written in 1959, Australia's first migrants can most appropriately be thought of as having arrived after having their simple coastal water craft accidently pushed many miles eastward during a major storm.

What were these water craft like 53,000 years ago, even 40,000, or 18,000 years back? No illustration or boat part lasts from so early an era. Our best evidence concerning the early Sahul water craft comes from those of Australian aborigines as they were used in the 19th and early 20th century. These craft could only be called "canoes" out of courtesy—they were incredibly frail. They consisted of a single sheet of bark bent roughly into the shape of a boat, laced together at the ends, caulked with wild honeycomb or some vegetable gum; their sides were held apart by a few sticks. Such "canoes"

[8] Compare National Geographic Society, 1975: 164 to 1981: 216.

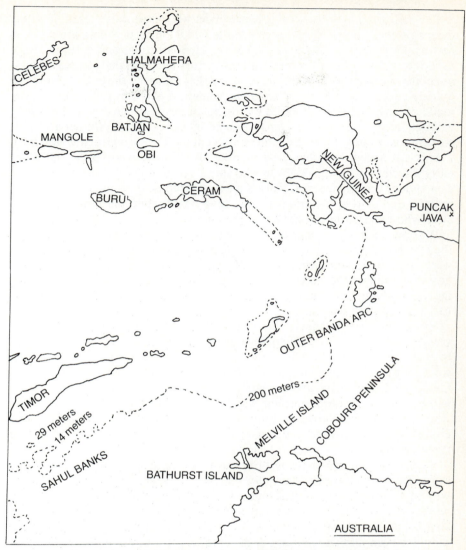

Figure 2. Obi, Ceram, Halmahera, New Guinea, Timor, Sahul Banks, Australia, and adjacent islands. Adapted from National Geographic Society, 1981.

were little better than rafts; even in calm water they were likely to swamp, capsize, or disintegrate, and the only thing that can be said for them is that when swamped or capsized, the bark would still float, enabling the occupants to cling to the remains, at least briefly. Hanging on to a swamped sheet of bark is not an activity that merits the name seafaring, and in the shark-infested waters around the Australian coastline and in the crocodile-infested northern rivers it was not conducive to survival.

The sail was unknown to the Australians who used these craft; the only means of propelling such a vessel was the paddle and, as Pilling found when he traveled briefly in 1954 on a makeshift Tiwi raft, tides and currents. Such canoes were in use in the early twentieth century here and there in Australia—including among the Tiwi of North Australia—because these craft could be quickly constructed. But by the 1950s, when the natives used canoes, those made of bark had been replaced by the dugout canoe.[9] No Australian would willingly have ventured very far from land in a bark canoe, although 14 mile stretches were negotiated by nineteenth century Tiwi using such water craft.

It is not known whether Tiwi or other Australian Aborigines—let alone early travelers to Sahul—knew how to steer their water craft by using a paddle as a rudder oar in currents. This is an ethnographic question which ethnographers and/or oral historians should investigate while there are still a few alive who traveled in the coastal bark canoes.

We now realize that much as the peopling of the Americas occurred without the first occupants even knowing they had moved into a new continent—they were crossing a "land bridge" half the width of the United States—so to the first Australians, the hazardous raft/canoe trip to the Australian coast was much like many that had occurred before, just another time that a frail craft had been pushed eastward by a storm to a distant island.

When the first occupants arrived on the shores of Australia, their sea voyages were over, for they possessed no boats or sails to carry them onward to the far-off Pacific Islands. These first occupants had to make the best of what they had brought and that which they found. They moved into the large, unoccupied land mass before them, and their descendants remained there without much alteration in their way of life for succeeding millennia. Those who stayed near the coast or found rivers to settle along retained the use of crude bark canoes, whereas those who reached the desert interior forgot about them entirely.

Such a pattern of reasoning brings us to a final question: Why were these Australians left isolated from the influence of later migrants who came by way of the same series of islands? The answer is that all later migrants—whose descendants we know today as Melanesians, Polynesians, or Micronesians—had much better canoes and an extensive knowledge of sailing when they left Asia. Hence they could far better control where they went and had greater freedom to move on further if they did not like an area where they had landed. Evidence seems to suggest that the bulk of these later peoples, and certainly the Melanesian peoples, came from the direction of Southeast

---

[9] Lloyd Warner (1937) and others have discussed the origin of the dugout canoes of the north coast of Australia. This type of canoe seems first to have been used on the Arnhem Land coast by Malay visitors, possibly as early as the late eighteenth century. It is not known how long it was before Arnhem Land aborigines began to make them. Pilling (1958: 304–306) reports that a Malay dugout was known among the Tiwi as early as the 1860s; however, this craft—a highly valued possession of the Tiwi near Milikapiti—apparently had drifted from the area of modern Indonesia on to the north coast of Melville Island. Tiwi did not make their own dugout canoes before the twentieth century. Timalarua, the Tiwi canoe maker known by Hart (see p. 52 herein), was probably among the first, if not *the* first, Tiwi dugout maker.

Asia around the *northern* side of New Guinea and therefore never approached the northern coasts of Australia at all, being carried on past the eastern end of New Guinea toward the Solomons and the New Hebrides. If any such later peoples did sight or land on the northern coast of Australia, they stayed only briefly, leaving no trace, probably because the region appeared uninviting. More recently, others have also found the northern coastline of Australia unattractive; these include the Japanese Navy, in World War II, which carefully bypassed it and followed the route of the Melanesians along the northern shores of New Guinea, through the Bismarcks and the Admiralties toward the Solomons and Guadalcanal. Thus the early Australians were left in isolated possession of a continent during the 30,000 or more years following their arrival.

For those who maintain that human progress is an inevitable movement, it should be noted that all the evidence indicates that during those long centuries the Australians remained at almost the same technological level as they were when they first landed.

AUSTRALIAN CULTURE WHEN THE EUROPEANS CAME

The continent of Australia varies a good deal in such matters as climate, rainfall, and amount of vegetation, but in general it may be said that well over half of it is country in which keeping alive is fairly easy, even for people of such a low level of culture as that represented by the first Australians. In particular, there were no dangerous animals (except snakes), and much of the climate being like that of Southern California, the country was mostly free of tropical jungles and the diseases that are associated with them. For a hunting and gathering people, the main problem of existence in Australia was lack of water, as indeed it still is today, despite modern technology. At least one-third of the continent, comprising about a million square miles, is arid desert or semidesert where rain rarely falls, and the so-called river beds are bone dry for years at a stretch.[10] Elsewhere there are well-watered areas that provide an adequate food supply for a hunting and gathering people. The Murray River Valley in the southeast and the coastal strips along the east, southeast, and north coastlines are the best watered regions, and these were the areas that supported the largest native populations when the white man arrived. But even in such favorable tracts the population was spread very thin. The best estimate of size of the native population for the whole continent before the arrival of Europeans is that within the total area of approximately 3 million square miles there lived slightly above a quarter of a million people, giving an average density of one person to every 12 square miles.

[10] It rained in Alice Springs in Central Australia on New Year's Eve, 1929–1930. According to their parents, white children 6 to 7 years old were then seeing rain for the first time in their lives.

The density was lowest in arid areas, and is estimated to have been so low that, in some instances, more than 50 square miles were required to support one person.[11] The population density for the livable parts of Australia is estimated at about one person to 6½ square miles, and for the best-watered sections as about three persons to every 10 miles.[12] Some detailed corroboration for this last figure is supplied by the Tiwi of Melville and Bathurst Islands who are dealt with at length in this monograph. The Tiwi are one of the few tribes occupying a well-watered and favorable environment for hunting and gathering who have been left in continuous occupation of their native habitat down to the present day. A careful and exhaustive census of them (by Hart) in 1928–1929 showed that the approximately 2,900 square miles comprising the two islands were occupied and used by 1,062 people.

Thus between the time of their first arrival and approximately 1770 when the white men first got to know them, the original occupants had multiplied to a population of between 250,000 and 275,000. This relatively small number (for the size of the continent) was thinly spread over most of the land, but was more numerous in the areas where the water supply was good and where the natives had available adequate sources of meat—marsupial, reptile, and bird—and fish, as well as a considerable quantity of wild plant foods.

Basically, all Australian tribes had cultures of the same general type, although local variation had developed as the original emigrants spread out into different geographical environments and their descendants lost contact with each other. The question of how many tribes there were at the beginning of white settlement is almost impossible to answer because "tribe" in Australia meant little more than a group of bands with a language which they viewed as distinct. There were at least 500 languages (all belonging to the same linguistic family, but most of them mutually unintelligible), which in the total population of a quarter of a million gives an average of about 500 speakers for each linguistic group. This seems a low figure for a so-called "tribe" and is probably brought about by the large number of very small linguistic units ("tribes") that early writers report in some areas such as coastal New South Wales and parts of Victoria. Certainly the linguistic units ("tribes") that survived down to modern times and could therefore be studied by twentieth-century anthropologists, such as Arunta, "Murngin,"[13] and Tiwi tribes, were considerably larger than 500 people, but probably even the biggest "tribes" did not exceed 2,000 in population.

Scattered in small local groups (bands) over enormous areas of country and armed only with boomerangs, crude stone-pointed spears, and spear throwers, the Australian natives were in no position to resist the white settlers.

---

[11] Tindale, 1974: 31.

[12] Radcliffe-Brown, 1930.

[13] In 1937, when Warner published his classical work on Arnhem Land aborigines, he called them "Murngin"; today, this same group is known as the "Yolngu."

They were simply brushed aside by the early British colonists[14] who began arriving in 1788, and in the course of the next century and a half, the natives disappeared entirely from much of the landscape. Because the British settled first in the well-watered fertile areas of the east and southeast, it was the tribes of these regions who disappeared earliest, so that in the present state of Victoria, which once contained a comparatively dense native population, a full-blood aborigine at the present time is about as rare as a full-blood Indian in Massachusetts and for much the same reasons.

White settlement in Australia since Cook's arrival in the fertile southeast corner has tended, however, to be very localized and uneven. The lack of water in the desert and semidesert areas has continued to hamper or inhibit white occupation. Moreover, even in some places where the rainfall is relatively high, such as the northern and northwestern coastlines, isolation has continued to make these regions unattractive to any heavy white intrusion. In American terms, such lands have remained until the present day as frontier areas ("The Outback" is what the Australian city dwellers call them) and in such regions the native or aborigine ("abo" in Australian slang) can still be found, often in surprisingly large numbers and in many cases still practicing and adhering to many of the traditional customs of his ancestors. In the central desert regions the western neighbors of the Arunta continue to practice something not far removed from their aboriginal tribal life on land which the white man regards as useless for settlement purposes. Further north, in the area called Arnhem Land, on the western side of the Gulf of Carpentaria, there exist enormous stretches, which until relatively recently were inaccessible, although the country is not at all hopeless. There the natives tribes such as the Yolngu still retain much of their traditional culture. Similarly, to the west of Arnhem Land, along the coastline and on islands lying offshore, isolation and lack of white settlement have permitted a number of tribes to continue down to the present time relatively untouched by European influences. Because the annual rainfall along the northern coast is appreciable and reliable, some of these tribes live in country that is much more favorable to hunters and gatherers than is the desert area inhabited by the Arunta and their neighbors. Among these north-coast tribes the people occupying Melville and Bathurst Islands and who call themselves Tiwi have been studied by Hart in 1928–1930; by Pilling in 1953–1954; and by Goodale in 1954, briefly in 1962, 1980–1981, and 1986–1987; as well as others. The account that follows is presented with two main objectives in view: first, to explain how this Australian culture operated as a going concern in aboriginal times and, second, to analyze what has happened to it as it has been brought into the modern world.

---

[14] There is an interesting link between American history and the first white settlement in Australia. Prior to the Revolutionary War, Great Britain deported her worst criminals to convict settlements in the colony of Georgia. After American independence, she had to find a new dumping ground to relieve the overcrowding in the British jails and established her new convict settlement at Botany Bay near the present city of Sydney on the east coast of Australia.

1/Tiwi Marriage

CULTURAL ISOLATION

People who live in the congested cities and towns of the modern world have difficulty in realizing how different life can be at the hunting and gathering level of human existence. The basic fact about the life of hunters and gatherers is the thinly spread-out manner in which they live and the isolation of families and households from each other. In the case of the Tiwi, these conditions of isolation and dispersal were accentuated by their island habitat. Melville and Bathurst Islands lie off the northern coast of Australia some 50 to 80 miles from Darwin, which is the administrative capital of the empty north. They are separated from the mainland by about 25 miles at the narrowest part. This distance is slightly greater than the distance that separates England from France at the Straits of Dover, and just as the dim outline of coastal France can be seen from England on clear days, so the dim outline of the Australian mainland can be seen from the southern edges of the islands. Three small islands are stepping stones between Melville Island and the mainland, leaving gaps of no more than 14 miles for the Tiwi to cross. The transit was a hazardous one in the frail bark canoes of nineteenth-century Tiwi. Tradition indicated that contact of Tiwi with mainland aborigines was minimal before 1890; there was only an occasional raid by Melville Island Tiwi in order to capture a wife. To the Tiwi of Bathurst Island, the dimly seen coastline of Australia was *Tibambinum*, the home of the dead, to which all Tiwi souls went after death.[1] It follows from this that the Tiwi of Bathurst Island regarded the inhabited world as composed of their own two islands, and on those islands they lived a self-contained and exclusive existence. Occasionally outsiders appeared, either castaways from surrounding areas, including presumably the Australian mainland, and in recent centuries, fishing boats and pirates from Indonesia, loosely called "Malays" in the literature. To such visitors from outside, the Tiwi were consistently and implacably hostile. Their own traditions and what little written history there is of "Malay" penetration into the Arafura Sea both tell the same story. Outsiders who

---

[1] Goodale notes that from 1954 onward at Milikapiti Tiwi believed that their souls continued, after death, to stay around the grave site.

landed on the islands were massacred or vigorously resisted. Whether they were classified as *Malai-ui* ("Malays") or *Wona-rui* (Australian aborigines from the mainland) they were not Tiwi and hence not real people, or at least not human enough to share the islands with the chosen people who owned them.

Thus, the word "Tiwi" did not mean "people" in the sense of all human beings, but rather "we, the only people," or the chosen people who live on and own the islands, as distinct from any other alleged human beings who might show up from time to time on the beaches. This exclusion of outsiders from real "us-ness" and hence from real "human-ness" was continued when the Europeans began to arrive in the early nineteenth century, and certainly as late as 1930 the Tiwi continued to call and think of themselves as Tiwi, *the* people, and to use other words for all non-Tiwi, whether they were mainland aborigines, Malay fishermen, Japanese pearl-divers, French priests, or British officials, who penetrated into their exclusive little cosmos.[2]

Their firm tradition that the 25 miles of ocean were adequate to isolate them from the mainland is confirmed by certain objective distributional evidence. Several characteristic features of mainland native technology were absent on Melville and Bathurst Islands, notably the spear thrower and the curved (or return) boomerang. To anthropologists, the idea of an Australian tribe lacking spear throwers and curved boomerangs is almost a contradiction in terms, and the only feasible explanation is isolation and hence failure of these mainland traits to diffuse to the islands.[3]

That no culture stands absolutely still in its technology no matter how isolated it may be is suggested by the fact that the Tiwi, although lacking the spear thrower and curved boomerang of the mainland, elaborated their wooden spears to a complexity of design and a degree of decoration unknown to the mainland, and also developed a much greater assortment of straight throwing sticks, made of hardwood, than any mainland tribe. Moreover, their carved and elaborately painted grave posts are unique among Australian tribes, and point up both the Tiwi isolation from the mainland and the favorable food situation, which permitted the leisure time necessary to manufacture the elaborate posts as well as the elaborate ceremonial spears. In the nontechnological aspects of their culture we find in many respects the same absence of mainland traits and the same elaboration of traits that were distinctively or even uniquely Tiwi. Male initiation ceremonies on the mainland focus upon circumcision or subincision or both; neither custom was practiced by the Tiwi, who instead included in their initiation ritual the forcible plucking out of the pubic hair of the novice. The degree of plural marriages achieved under their

---

[2] In 1986, Goodale recorded for a first time the word *purntubula*, which her informant translated as "all the people; same as 'tiwi,' but old name from 'palinari' [long ago] time of Purukupati." It was suggested that a corporate trust formed in 1986 by the TLC should be known as Purntubula Pty. Ltd.

[3] A toy spear thrower, played with by children, was in use, but this may be the result of post-white contact. Its native name—*pani*—seems most un-Tiwi, and a likely guess is that it was introduced by Cooper's mainlanders, being accepted as a toy for children but scorned as childish by the adult men.

marriage rules was far greater than anything reported for the mainland; the absolute prohibition of any female, regardless of age, being without a husband was unkown elsewhere in Australia; certain features of the kinship system fail to conform to any of the mainland norms, and so on. Wherever we look in their culture we get the strong impression of an Australian tribe that was able to develop within the general Australian type of culture a number of distinct features, some of them unique, while at the same time lacking entirely other features that were widespread on the mainland. Tiwi isolation from the mainland explains the differences and the lacks; their favorable environment explains why they were able to develop certain traits along their own unique lines.

THE TRIBE AND THE BANDS

Because they were isolated and few outsiders came near them, they did very little as a united tribe. Everybody on the two islands was a Tiwi, and the Tiwi world stopped at the water's edge. Fuzziness on the edges of tribal territory—a chronic headache to anthropologists working with mainland tribes—did not exist, nor did the problem of marriage outside the tribe. All Tiwi, of course, spoke the same language and practiced the same customs and regarded themselves as *the* people; these were almost the only respects in which they could be said to do anything as a tribal unit. There was no tribal government, there were no tribal officials, and no occasions that required the whole tribe to assemble together as a collective entity. For daily and yearly living, the important group was the band or horde,[4] of which there were nine. The total area of the two islands is about 3,000 square miles, but some of this is swampy, some of it waterless, some of it mosquito-infested mangrove jungle, and the suitability of the rest for native living varies a good deal. Hence, the actively used and lived-in areas for each band probably averaged about 200 square miles each and, in any case, there was not a very close relationship between band size and area occupied. Details of band size at various times are given in a later chapter, but, typically, Tiwi bands probably varied in size between 100 and 300 people.

The band was the territorial group with which a man most closely identified himself. Though the band lived from day to day spread out over a wide area and a man might not see many of his fellow band-members for weeks at a time, the average Tiwi thought of the 200 or 300 square miles of band territory as his own "country" and of his fellow members as his own people. This is why the tribal name—Tiwi—so seldom needed to be used at home on the islands. It did not identify one group as distinct from another, because all

---

[4] Radcliffe-Brown, the great authority on Australian tribal society, tried to introduce the word "horde" for the Australian local group, but probably because of its suggestion to the popular mind of a dense concentration of people, it has never become established and in these pages we have used the more neutral word "band."

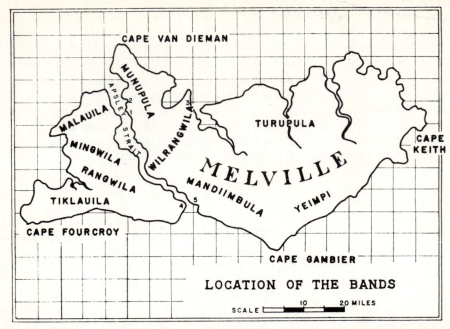

Figure 3. White Locations: 1. Fort Dundas; 2. Garden Point in 1954, Pularumpi in 1980; 3. Snake Bay in 1954, Milikapiti in 1980; 4. Site of Roman
Catholic Mission, Nguiu Shire since before 1980; 5. Paru, site of Joe Copper's
house, site of outstation since before 1953.

locals were Tiwi. Just as in New York suburb one does not say that there are
some Americans in the house next door, but may say that there are some
Texans or some Californians or some people from Michigan next door, so a
Tiwi, seeing a group of visitors arriving in his band territory, would immediately identify them as Malauila or Rangwila or by whatever band they
belonged to. A father would say casually, "I have betrothed my daughter to
a Tiklauila" or "My wife is a Munupula woman"; a mourner would say, "He
died when visiting the Munupula and therefore we will have to go to Munupi
for the funeral"; an old man would reminisce about being brought up as a
youth by his mother's brother, who was a Turupula, and the good times he
had in Turupi; and another would recount details of big battles between the
Munupula and the Malauila. All of these were band names or band territories.
The nine bands thus acted, psychologically, as small tribelets or semisovereign
groups, because it was with one of them that every Tiwi most closely identified in his day-to-day life on the islands. It is only when, as nowadays, he
leaves the islands to go to work for the white man in Darwin that he has
to think of himself as a Tiwi, because there he mingles with men of other
tribes. Even then, work and residence in the white man's town does not entirely obliterate band identification. A Tiklauila in Darwin prefers to work

with and to consort in the evenings with other Tiklauila, and Malauila with Malauila.[5]

Because of certain peculiar features of Tiwi domestic life, to be discussed below, it is difficult to sum up the Tiwi band in any simple formula. People, especially women, changed their band residence frequently in the course of their lives, and being born into a band did not at all require permanent residence with that band, either for males or for females. Thus the district (for example, Tiklaru or Malau) was a firm, fixed, known quantity, but the people who "owned" the district (for example, Tiklauila or Malauila) were a flexible and constantly shifting collection of individuals.

The territorial boundaries between bands were clear and well known to everybody, though they were not the sharp lines on a map such as we regard as essential for a frontier or a land boundary. All pieces of country—clumps of jungle, stretches of grassland, sections of thick woods—had names. One such piece of country, say a thickly wooded area, belonged to one band, whereas the more open country that began where the woods thinned out belonged to another; thus the boundary was not a sharp line but a transitional zone—perhaps of several miles—where the change from trees to open savanna became noticeable, with the band territories thus fusing into one another rather than being separated by sharp lines. The Tiwi, so to speak, thought of the landscape as a sort of spectrum where a man moved gradually out of one district into another as he passed from one type of horizon to the next. Because rivers, and even Apsley Strait, a very narrow arm of the sea separating Melville from Bathurst Island, usually have similar types of vegetation on *both* sides or banks, none of the island rivers nor Apsley Strait was a boundary or frontier between bands. The Mandiimbula, predominantly a Melville Island tribe, owned also the country on the opposite side of Apsley Strait at the southeast corner of Bathurst, whereas the Malauila, the band in the northern half of Bathurst Island, conversely overlapped their ownership across the strait to take in a thin strip of coastline on the northwest corner of Melville.

These details illustrate the fact that the band was the land-owning, workaday, territorially organized group that controlled the hunting, the food supply, and the warfare. Until the white man arrived in force in the coastal waters of North Australia, the average Tiwi regarded the nine bands as the main functional units of his existence, and his loyalty to and identification with his band were given much greater opportunity for exercise than any loyalty to or identification with the whole Tiwi tribe. He did many things as a member

---

[5] In the early 1930s the situation at the Government Hospital in Darwin offered a good illustration of this. The hospital authorities said they gave preference for houseboy jobs to "Melville Islanders because of their greater intelligence and reliability." In point of fact, some of the younger Tiklauila had established a monopoly on hospital jobs and no Tiwi other than a Tiklauila was ever hired there. The whites thought they were hiring Tiwi but the Tiklauila saw to it that they hired only Tiklauila and felt no vestige of obligation to other Tiwi to help them get these desirable jobs. The alleged greater intelligence of the islanders was undoubtedly due to the fact that the Tiklauila, having had a Roman Catholic mission adjacent to their territory since 1911, were more used to white requirements.

of a band, but he did little as a member of a tribe. Only when an outsider turned up did he need to think of himself as a Tiwi, and outsiders were very rare. For the rest of the time he thought of himself as a member of his band, thought of his band as his people, and of his band territory as his country.

THE HOUSEHOLD

Because the band consisted of anywhere from 100 to 300 people, it could not live together in one place, except for very short periods of time. Hunting and gathering in almost any part of the world (except the northwest coast of America in pre-white times) require the human population to disperse itself very thinly over the countryside and live from day to day in small hunting and camping units. Such small primary groups are usually in one sense families and in another sense households, and this is the case among the Tiwi. We propose to call such units "households" rather than "families" for reasons that will soon become apparent. It is true that Tiwi "houses," especially in the long dry season (from March to October), were the flimsiest and most temporary of structures, but the group of people in question was the group who lived together day after day, hunted as a unit, pooled the results of their food getting, and ate and slept together. Functionally this group is identical with an American household, even though the "house" they used was nothing more than a few piled-up tree branches, used as shelter for a night or two and then abandoned. Like the American household also, the Tiwi household usually consisted of a man, his wife (or wives), and their children, though in many would also be included a few leftovers or extras, common to all cultures, such as bachelor uncles, visiting cousins, ancient widowers, and ambiguous "men who came to dinner" and were still there. (Tiwi households did not, however, include maiden aunts, female orphans, or ancient widows, because these could not exist in Tiwi culture.)

Thus the Tiwi household was more or less the same thing as the Tiwi family group, but Tiwi family organization had such a number of unusual twists that we find it desirable to insist upon calling such a group the household rather than the family. There was no ambiguity about its "living together" aspect; there were many ambiguities about its kinship aspects. To some of these unusual domestic usages we now turn.

MARRIAGE BY BETROTHAL

In many nonliterate societies, including most, if not all of the mainland Australian tribes, there is a tendency to believe that the main purpose in life for a female is to get married. The Tiwi subscribed to this idea, but firmly carried it to its logical conclusion; namely, that all females must get married, regardless of age, condition, or inclination. They (and they almost alone among human societies) took the very slight step from saying "All females

Photo 6. "The 'house' they used was nothing more than a few piled-up tree branches." At the left behind the man being painted for a ceremony in the 1928–1929 period is one of the dry season (from March to October) "houses." Note typical "bush" in the distance.

should be married" to saying "All females *must* be married." As a result, in aboriginal times there was no concept of an unmarried female in Tiwi ideology, no word for such a condition in their language, and in fact, no female in the population without at least a nominal husband. Their own explanation of this unique situation was connected with their beliefs about conception and where babies come from. Anthropologists have long been aware that the Australian aborigines generally (and indeed some of the Melanesians, such as the famous case of the Trobriand Islands) ignored the role of the male in human conception and firmly believed that a woman becomes pregnant because a spirit has entered into her body. The Tiwi were no exception, but went a step further than the mainlanders in dealing with the dangerous situation created by the unpredictability of the spirits. Because any female was liable to be impregnated by a spirit at any time, the sensible step was to insist that every female have a husband *all the time* so that if she did become pregnant, the child would always have a father. As a result of this logical thinking, all Tiwi babies were betrothed before or as soon as they were born; females were thus the "wives" of their betrothed husbands from the moment

Photo 7. Remains of the relatively permanent Tiwi wet season camp of Louis, one of the sons of Turimpi, at a Tiklau beach, on the south coast of Bathurst Island, in early June 1953.

of birth onward. For similar reasons, widows were required to remarry at the gravesides of their late husbands, and this rule applied to even feeble great-grandmothers who had already buried several husbands in the course of a long life. It can readily be seen that these rules—prenatal betrothal of female infants and immediate remarriage of all widows—effectively eliminated all possibility of an unmarried female from Tiwi society. They also eliminated any possibility of an unmarried mother of a fatherless child. No matter where the unpredictable spirit chose to create a baby, whether it was in the body of a pretty young woman, a toothless older one, or a youthful teenager, the female would have a husband, and the children when born would have a father. The Tiwi were thus probably the only society in the world with an illegitimacy rate of zero.

The practical application of these two unusual rules had certain unusual consequences. The rule of prenatal betrothal obviously gave a great deal of power to the person with the right to betroth, and in Tiwi this right belonged to the husband of the pregnant woman. We carefully say "the husband of the pregnant woman" rather than "the father of the child" because the right resided in the male head of the household at the time of the birth. Although he was ordinarily both the father of the child and the husband of its mother, there were naturally occasions when a child was born after the death of its father, in which case the right of betrothal unquestionably belonged to the mother's new husband. The clearest statement of this rule is to say that the right of betrothal of all newly born females resided in the husband of the mother at time of the girl's birth. "He who named the child bestowed it."

In most human societies the proportion of males and females in the population is approximately equal, except in the older age-groups where women predominate owing to their tendency to live longer than men. The Tiwi conformed to this norm biologically, but their cultural insistence that all females of every age be married resulted in further unusual features of the domestic situation. No such compulsory marriage was required or expected of males. Hence, the total female population, but only part of the male population, was married. Mathematically this permitted, indeed required, a high degree of plural marriage. The men who held the right to betroth—namely, the fathers of the female babies—could, within certain limits imposed by the kinship system, bestow their about-to-be-born or newly born daughters where they wished, and they certainly did not bestow them on about-to-be-born or newly born males. On the contrary, they bestowed them, generally speaking, where some tangible return was to be anticipated. Put bluntly, in Tiwi culture daughters were an asset to their father, and he invested these assets in his own welfare. He therefore bestowed his newly born daughter on a friend or an ally, or on somebody he wanted as a friend or an ally. Such a person was likely to be a man near his own age or at least an adult man, and hence perhaps 40 years or so older than the newly born baby bestowed upon him as a wife. Or, the father might bestow an infant daughter on a man—or some close relative of such a man—who had already bestowed an infant daughter upon him, thus in effect swapping infant daughters. Obviously, the fathers who did the swapping, even if they were not quite the same age themselves, were bound to be many years older than the infant wives they thus received from each other. Or, third, a father looking for a suitable male upon whom to bestow his infant daughter might decide to use her as old-age insurance—in which case he selected as her future husband not one of the older adult men who would be old when he himself was old, but a likely looking youngster "with promise"; that is, a youth in his late twenties or thirties who showed signs of being a good hunter and a good fighting man, and who was clearly on his way up in tribal power and influence. Such a youth, in his late twenties at the time of betrothal, would, with luck, be in his prime as "a big man" in about 20 years—a time when the father of the infant daughter would be getting old and decrepit and much in need of an influential son-in-law who was obligated to him.

There were other bases upon which infant daughters were betrothed, and indeed the father was seldom an entirely free agent, because he not only had to make his choices for his daughters within the limits imposed by the kinship system, but he was also caught in an intricate network of previous commitments, residual interests, and contingent promises made by other men who had had some prior interest in the baby or the mother of the baby. To mention only the most common limiting situation of this sort, the mother of the baby might have been given to him in the first place on the understanding that when she grew up and had a female baby it was to be bestowed on so-and-so or even returned as a *quid pro quo* to its mother's father, either as wife or as ward.[6]

We have oversimplified the situation, but it should be clear that Tiwi fathers, in an overwhelming number of cases, bestowed their infant daughters on husbands a great deal older than those daughters. It is hard to strike an average, but the overall situation is best expressed by saying that no Tiwi father, except in the most unusual cases, ever thought of bestowing an infant daughter upon any male below the age of at least 25. Taking this lowest limit for illustration, this meant that a youth of 25 had his first wife betrothed or promised to him at that age but had to wait another 14 years or so before she was old enough to leave her father's household and take up residence and marriage duties with him. By this time he was about 40 and she was 14. An age gap between husband and wife at least as great as this, but usually greater, was a necessary and constant result of the Tiwi betrothal system.

No Tiwi young man, then, could expect to obtain his first resident wife through betrothal until he was well into his thirties, at which time this first resident wife would be around 14, having been betrothed to him at her birth or before. But it was likely that his first wife's father, who spotted him in his twenties as a "comer," was not the only older man to want him as a son-in-law. As in our own culture, where the first million is the hardest to make, so in Tiwi the first bestowed wife was the hardest to get. If some shrewd father with a daughter to invest in a 20-year-old decided to invest her in you, his judgment was likely to attract other fathers to make a similar investment. As a result, for *some* Tiwi men, the arrival in residence of the first wife, an event for which they had to wait until their late thirties, was quickly followed by the arrival in residence of a second, third, and fourth (at least), all of them bestowed very shortly after the bestowal of the first. Thus a successful Tiwi, having had no resident wife at all until his late thirties, would accumulate perhaps half a dozen between his late thirties and his late forties as his various betrothed wives reached the age of puberty and joined his household, and from then on he was practically certain to accumulate still more wives as later bestowals grew up and as he was able to invest the daughters borne by his first crop of young wives in transactions that brought in a later crop.

That this is not an exaggerated or overdrawn picture of the number of wives that could be accumulated in the course of a long life by a successful Tiwi household head is shown by the genealogies of the grandfathers of the present generation. Turimpi, who was born in the 1830s and died in the early 1900s, was at his death the most powerful old man among the Tiklauila. Some of his sons were still alive in 1954, and all of them were in the prime of life around 1930.[7] A complete list of Turimpi's wives, not all of them living in his household at the same time or necessarily alive at the same time, contains more than 20 names. But Turimpi was outshone in this regard by several of his contemporaries in other bands. A prominent Turupula of the same gen-

---

[6] In *Tiwi Wives* (Goodale, 1971: 115–116), this variety of marriage contract is designated as Type A.

[7] See Hart, 1954.

eration had a list of 25; the father of Finger of the Wilrangwila had 29; the father of Tamboo and Puti had 22. As late as 1930, men with lists of 10, 11, and 12 wives were still plentiful, and Tu'untalumi, who was aged about 70 in that year and was a man of great influence, had by then accumulated no less than 21.[8]

Such numbers of wives as these per husband are very much higher than usually prevail even among the most polygymous hunting tribes. Obviously, a domestic unit with 12 or more wives in it makes for a very large household. Among the Tiwi, a household even of such men as those just named did not contain all these wives at the same time, mainly because of the very great variation in the ages of a man's wives. As far as bestowed or betrothed wives were concerned, such wives arrived at their husband's household to take up wifely duties therein when they reached the age of about 14. Hence the first of them to arrive (typically when their husband was nearly 40) would be women of nearly 40 by the time the latest of them arrived (typically when the husband was well into his sixties). Even when the husband died, let us say at the ripe old age of 75, there would probably be some of his bestowed wives still under the age of 14 who were as yet too young to join his household. Tu'untalumi, the man of 21 wives, was already about 70 in 1930, yet in his list of 21 wives five were still *ali'inga*—that is, little girls not yet approaching puberty—and two were still babies at their mothers' breast. On the other hand, some of his earliest bestowed wives, who had taken up residence with him when he was in his late thirties, were already dead.

Because of this wide variation in the ages of a man's wives, it is necessary to distinguish between a "list" of a man's wives and those actually in residence in his household at any given time. The resident or active wives—one might almost say the working wives—were always fewer than the listed wives. This would necessarily be so even if marriage by betrothal were the only way by which a Tiwi man could obtain a wife. But although it was the most prestigeful form of marriage and the only respectable way in which a man could obtain a *young* wife, there were other ways of setting up a household. The most important way is one that we have already mentioned—namely, widow re-marriage.

WIDOW REMARRIAGE

To become "a big man" a Tiwi had, among other things, to accumulate a lot of wives. This required time, in addition to everything else. A rising star who accumulated by bestowal seven or eight wives by his middle forties and then died, merely left a lot of widows to be redistributed at his graveside, and by the process of wealth attracting more wealth, or capital creating more

[8] Finger, Tamboo, and Puti were elders prominent in tribal affairs at the time of Hart's fieldwork. Puti was still alive in 1953–54 and well known to Pilling. Tu'untalumi, held in great affection by Hart, but anathema to the Mission Station, died in 1935.

capital, these widows were most likely to be redistributed among his rivals and competitors of his own age group or among men even older than he. Hence, the largest number of wives ultimately accrued to the successful man who lived longest, because he was likely to gather up at least a few of the widows of each of his contemporaries or seniors as they predeceased him.

There was thus a close correlation between increasing age and the number of wives a man had, and the largest households belonging to a few surviving old men in each band. The two conditions, therefore, which were necessary to accumulate a large household were (1) to attract prospective fathers-in-law to invest their infant daughters in you while you were a young man, and then (2) to live long enough to reap the dividends. The longer you lived, the more dividends would accrue to you from one source or another, provided you started off right by attracting betrothals in your twenties and thirties.

But what about the unimpressive young men, the "noncomers," who somehow failed as young men to attract any prospective fathers-in-law to invest an infant daughter in them? As we have seen, even the most highly regarded and well-connected Tiwi young man had to wait until his late thirties or longer before his first bestowed wife was old enough to join him in domestic bliss, but at least while waiting he knew the time was coming. The overlooked or unbetrothed young man had no such prospects. Because the only source of supply of new females was through the birth of female infants whose hands only their fathers could bestow, it would appear as if a young Tiwi male overlooked or ignored by all fathers of bestowable female daughters had no alternative except permanent bachelorhood. Doubtless Tiwi fathers, as a class, would have regarded this as an ideal situation and would have said that permanent bachelorhood was a proper fate for such friendless and hence useless young men, but no social system of such rigidity has ever been discovered by anthropologists. Tiwi fathers were able rigidly to control the marriages of their infant daughters, but they were not able to control with the same rigidity the remarriages of their own widows, and it was widow remarriage that supplied the loophole in the system, or the cultural alternative that took care of young men.

A Tiwi husband was unavoidably and necessarily always much older than a bestowed wife. Therefore he usually died much earlier than she. A girl of 14 who entered into residence with her first husband when he was 50 was likely to be left a widow by him within the next 15 years, and even if she remarried a man of the same age as her first husband, she could easily be widowed for the second time while still herself a comparatively young woman. There were several different patterns, most of them intermingled in the same household, for a female matrimonial career, but the situation may be illustrated by the concrete case of one of Turimpi's widows, an ancient female (in 1930) named Bongdadu. Born about 1865, she was betrothed at birth to a powerful old man named Walitaumi who was at least the same age as her father, if not older. Not unnaturally, he died while she was still a child and well before she was old enough to join his household. Her betrothal was then reassigned, so to speak, to Walitaumi's half-brother, Turimpi, then in his early forties. About seven years later, she joined Turimpi's household as a blushing bride of 14, her husband then being close to 50. In the next 20 years she became Turimpi's most prolific wife and bore numerous children, three of whom, Antonio, Mariano, and Louis, all born between 1883 and 1900, were men of importance in Tiwi politics in 1930, and one of whom, Louis, was still around in 1954.[9] About 1900, when Bongdadu was still only about 35, she passed to M., a middle-aged Tiklauila, and was his wife until his death around 1925. By this date, Bongdadu was over 60 and had borne 10 children, four of whom died young; she was beginning to approach the oldest stage of Tiwi womanhood. Nonetheless, she had to remarry, but by now all of the people who might have claimed any rights of bestowal in her were long since dead, her eldest sons were adult men of some importance and able to protect their mother's interests, and clearly she was unlikely to produce any more children.[10] Her chief value was as a food producer and housekeeper and female politician, roles for which she had been well trained in her long years as wife of Turimpi and M.

Old women in Bongdadu's position had to remarry, but they were in a good position to exercise some choice of their own as to whom they remarried, especially if they had strong influential sons to support them in their wishes. There was a frequent pattern in such cases for the widow, aided and abetted (or perhaps even forced) by her sons, to arrange a marriage of convenience with some obscure nonentity much younger than herself and usually a friend or contemporary of her sons. In 1925, then, Bongdadu, widowed three times already, married as her fourth husband one Dominico, a man of no importance whatever, as was shown by the fact that at this time he was nearly 40 and had not been able to attract even one bestowed wife. He had, however, already married one widow, so that his marriage to Bongdadu gave him a second wife, also, of course, a widow. This marriage is of further interest when we discover that Antonio, Mariano, and Louis, the main sons of Bongdadu by a previous marriage, had some influence in arranging this marriage of their mother to a contemporary and satellite of theirs, and that a year or two before, Antonio had married the ancient mother of Dominico when *she* became a widow. In other words, Antonio and Dominico had married each other's mothers; Antonio while waiting for his oldest bestowed wife to grow up, Dominico with no bestowed wife in sight. The approximate ages of the parties at the time of these marriages were:

Antonio 37	Dominico's mother 55
Dominico 38	Bongdadu (Antonio's mother) 60+

[9] Tiwi personal names are polysyllabic and hard for the reader to remember; hence, wherever possible, we have used "whiteman names" for individuals. The frequency of Spanish names among these "whiteman names," such as Mariano or Dominico, derives from the fact that the original buildings for the Mission Station were built by a number of Filipino workmen whom the priests brought with them.

[10] The Tiwi saw no inconsistency between believing in spirit impregnation and believing at the same time that an old woman was unlikely to bear children. It was to them a matter of probabilities, and of course with them as with us, occasionally an elderly lady did—disconcertingly—have a baby, proving the logic of their position.

Earlier, we mentioned the practice of fathers swapping their daughters within the infant bestowal system; here we find sons swapping their mothers within the widow remarriage system.

This is a relatively simple example of the complexity of Tiwi domestic arrangements, and we hesitate to complicate matters further. But clearly the last remarriage of Bongdadu (to Dominico) and the remarriage around the same time of Dominico's mother to one of Bongdadu's sons, a friend of Dominico, raise some important issues of social structure, particularly the question of whether widow remarriages of this type are to be regarded as a subspecies of bestowal marriages, with the sons having a right of bestowal over their mothers parallel or similar to the right of bestowal possessed by fathers over their infant daughters. Space does not permit any adequate discussion of this fascinating theoretical issue, but we can point out two factors that strongly deter us from regarding Tiwi widow remarriage as a special case of bestowal marriage. One is the self-evident and empirically observed fact that Tiwi widows, who remarried as Bongdadu and Dominico's mother remarried in the quoted case, were usually highly vocal and pretty tough old ladies who were not easily pushed around by anybody, even by their adult and ambitious sons. Whom they remarried in their old age was a matter upon which they had themselves a good deal to say. Second, to any anthropologist familiar with the kinship structures of Southeast Asia and the Pacific countries, there is a great deal of difference, in a society with matrilineal clans such as the Tiwi had, between a father making marriage decisions for his daughters, who do not belong to his clan, and sons making marriage decisions for their widowed mothers, who do belong to the same clan as their sons. We prefer, therefore, to view the overall Tiwi marriage situation and the interrelationship of their two forms of marriage as essentially a system wherein the matrilineal clan had lost its right to make marriage decisions for its female children, that right having been taken over (usurped) by the fathers of those children. The daughters of the clan were disposed of, not where fellow clansmen decided, but where an outsider (the father) decided—thus, bestowal or betrothal marriage. But when the female no longer had a father—that is, when she was old and could only be remarried through widow remarriage—then the right of her clansmen and more specifically her sons (in consultation with her own wishes) to arrange her remarriage became restored as a sort of residual or reanimated right. Moreover, as we will see, it was in line with their own political interests for the sons to insist on exercising such a right.

NAMING RULES

Such a way of integrating the two forms of marriage is supported by the Tiwi rules for naming children, which are very relevant to the issue. We mentioned earlier that the right to bestow a daughter was vested, strictly speaking, not in the actual father, but in the man who named her. Personal names were important in the Tiwi value system[11] and were given to every child a few weeks after its birth by its father or the man currently married to its mother. But whenever a husband died and the widows remarried, all the personal names given to their children by the dead man became strictly taboo, and the new husbands of the widows had the duty (or right) of providing all the children with new names. Because most women were widowed several times in their lives, most children were thus renamed several times in *their* lives, and the names given by the earlier husbands of their mothers dropped completely out of use.[12] Logically, under this system nobody would get a permanent name until his or her mother was dead, because as long as she were alive she would remarry and her new husband would rename all her children, no matter how aged they might be. The Tiwi insisted that logically this was how the naming system was supposed to work, and, in fact, the personal names of even prominent senior men did become taboo whenever their mothers' current husbands died. But convenience proved stronger than logic and the personal names of most men and women became well established in their early adulthood as people became used to them. Although such names did become taboo when the man who had given them died, the taboo in such cases was temporary rather than permanent, and after a decent interval the name would creep back into use, replacing some new and unfamiliar one that had been bestowed by the widow's new husband. In general, the name that thus became permanently or irrevocably attached to a person was the name that a person held when he or she first emerged into tribal prominence or first began to get talked about. For a male, this was usually the name he was bearing in his late twenties and early thirties; for a female, the name she was known by in her early adolescence when she first left her father's household to take up residence with her earliest husband.

That convenience thus overbore logic in the Tiwi naming system by attaching some one semipermanent name to a person despite the rules of name taboo should not cause us to overlook the importance of these rules. In theory, at least, every new husband renamed all his wives' children by all their previous marriages—thus, at least symbolically, canceling out the signs of title of all the previous "fatherhoods" in those children and asserting his own fatherhood right as a new and exclusive one. A widow's new husband was the new household head for all her children, and he took over this position by renaming them all, thus becoming their legal father. If we can stop thinking of "father" as a biological or kin relationship, and think of the word as meaning only "head of the household," the Tiwi concept will become understandable. We will also realize that there is no contradiction or illogic involved in the Tiwi beliefs that male parents were not necessary for conception, but that every child born must be born to a woman with a husband. All they meant was that every child must be born into a household with a

[11] See Hart, 1931.
[12] It can easily be seen what headaches this naming system created for an anthropologist trying to collect genealogies. Individuals would occur in one genealogy under one name and in another under another name, making the task of cross-indexing and cross-checking enormously difficult.

male at its head who belonged to a different clan from its mother—in other words, a "father," in Tiwi context.[13]

The renaming of the children by the new household head was not, of course, sufficient to wipe out the commitments made by previous titleholders. Although the new father could and did change his stepdaughters' names, he could not change their bestowals. The men upon whom the daughters had been bestowed by the previous father made sure of this. The new father was compelled to carry out the marriage arrangements for the daughters made by his predecessors in the fatherhood role, and there was sure to be a terrific row if he tried to alter them. Nevertheless, he acquired some power over the future of the daughters. The man to whom one of them had been promised by the previous father might die, thus making redisposal of the girl possible for him, or some new deal might be arrangeable in which he could use his new assets—for these new stepdaughters were assets, regardless of the fact that their immediate matrimonial future was already settled. The new father could delay his decision as to whether they were old enough to join their betrothed husband or even drop a few hints that he did not think the betrothed husband's right to them was quite as certain as was generally believed. Such actions, of course, were liable to lead to violent reprisals by the betrothed husband, but there was always a chance that he would be open to a deal; for example, by giving an option on one of the women in whom he had an interest, he would seek to hasten the appearance of the girl in his own household or seek to clear whatever shadow upon his title to her the stepfather sought to cast. Even the last husband of an elderly widow who had already passed through the hands of several husbands and all of whose daughters were grown up and married several times already, gained some shadowy rights in the future remarriages of those daughters by marrying their ancient mother. And the validation of these shadowy rights was the fact that as their mother's new husband he had renamed the daughters and he who named them could bestow them. The only catch was, that although he could wipe out all the names bestowed by his predecessors, he could not equally readily wipe out their commitments. All he could do was maneuver within the network created by their commitments so as to try and advantage himself as much as possible by a skillful use of whatever shadowy right in the daughters he had obtained by becoming their current "father."

It is within such a context that the apparent swapping of mothers by Dominico and Antonio must be viewed. By marrying Bongdadu in her dotage, Dominico had acquired some rights in the future remarriages of her daughter, the sister of Antonio, but because his marriage to Bongdadu had been (partly at least) arranged by Antonio and her other sons, Dominico would have to share with them his disposal rights to their sister. Similarly, the marriage of Dominico's ancient mother to Antonio (part, so to speak, of the same "package deal") meant that Antonio as current father had some say in the future

---

[13] Goodale, after review of this passage by Hart, noted that it reflects the women's version of Tiwi marriage as she presented it in *Tiwi Wives* (Goodale, 1971).

disposal of Dominico's sisters when they became widowed, because he had the power of renaming them.

What in effect occurred in this, as in many other cases, was that men of different clans and of about the same age formed a partnership or close alliance wherein "sons" and "husbands" cooperated in arranging the remarriages of their "mothers" and "sisters" by acting as quasi-fathers and treating their mothers and sisters as "quasi-daughters." The partnership or "firm" of Dominico (of the Crane clan) and Antonio, Mariano, and their brothers (of the Red Paint clan) had already arranged the remarriages of Bongdadu (Red Paint clan) and of Dominico's mother (Crane clan), and stood ready to take care of all future remarriages of Bongdadu's daughter (Red Paint) or Dominico's sisters (Crane) whenever any of these women became widowed. Each member of the firm was trying to maximize his own self-interest in this and all the other alliances he had a share in, but operations had to be carried out in this partnership form because the marriage of any woman had to be arranged by her "father," and the father, in the Tiwi rules, had to be a nonclansman of the woman whose marriage he arranged. Hence the Red Paint men needed Dominico, a Crane, as a front man to arrange the remarriages of their sister, and he in turn used Antonio, a Red Paint man, to arrange the remarriages of his sisters. When clansmen made decisions about the remarriages of their sisters, they could only do it by using agreeable nonclansmen as nominal "fathers" and cooperating with them—and the agreeable nonclansmen would of course only come in on the deal if there was something in it for them, as there was for the obscure and unimportant Dominico in the present case. In return for acting as a front for the Red Paint brothers, he got himself a second wife, an excellent food provider though no longer beautiful; he became the ally, even if junior, of some men with assured futures; and he acquired some shadowy residual rights in the future remarriages of a potential widow. Dominico did himself a lot of good by marrying Bongdadu; if he hadn't married her, he would never have attracted much tribal notice and hence would not have warranted mention in these pages.

We find that the whole complex situation makes most theoretical sense if we see it as essentially an institutional struggle between clan rights and the father's rights in women. Tiwi fathers, as suggested above, had taken away from the clan the right to make marriage decisions for newly born female members of the clan. As mechanisms validating this success of father's rights against clan rights there existed two rules: He who bestowed the name had the right to dispose in marriage; and all names given by a woman's previous husband were canceled by his death and a new set of names given to all her children by her new husband. Strictly and universally enforced, such rules would put *all* control over the marriages of *all* women, of every age, in the hands of their mother's husbands—that is, men from outside the clan of the women being disposed of, in other words, fathers in the Tiwi sense. But the Tiwi system failed to achieve such a result though their rules are pointed toward it. They achieved something close to it as far as infant or even young girls were concerned, because the fellow clansmen of such girls were either (as brothers) too young and unimportant to have any power to resist this alien control over their sisters' hands, or (as mothers' brothers and hence older men) too involved and absorbed in their own activities *as fathers* to take any position asserting clan rights as against fathers' rights. To be successful in tribal life, an ambitious young Tiwi male was best advised to forget his mother and his sisters' daughters (all members of his clan) and concentrate on getting wives for himself. Only by getting wives could he have daughters, and only by having daughters could he build alliances and obtain influence, power, and more wives. To get wives for himself, he could not use his mother or his sisters or his sisters' daughters, because their disposal was in the hands of the men who had named them—that is, their fathers. But there came a time in the life of an older man when his mother was old, and *her* mother was dead, and therefore the rights of the last man to name his mother had lapsed. And a similar situation would arise in the case of his sisters when their mother's last husband died. By this age, a man so situated was likely to be powerful enough and skilled enough in the rules of the game to exert some control over the late remarriages of his elderly sisters and even of his mother, were she still alive. Whenever this occurred, although the resulting situation might have the superficial appearance of clan solidarity—with sons, mothers, brothers, and sisters all acting and planning together as a partnership—such a surface appearance was illusory. The motivations involved in it were scarcely altruistic desires on the part of the brothers to look after their mothers and elderly sisters, but rather efforts by the brothers to use to advantage, in their intricate political schemes, some women of their own clan (their mothers and elderly sisters). Earlier in life these men had been prevented from such manipulation by the control over those women exercised by nonclansmen (their husbands or fathers) through the naming rules. Put another way, we might say that Tiwi men as a group had acquiesced to the system wherein "the father" had control over all marriages of his "daughters," because every Tiwi man hoped to be a "father" himself; but having acquiesced, every Tiwi male tried to beat the system, especially as he became older and more influential, by intriguing in the remarriages of his mother and elderly sisters—matters in which, according to the strict letter of the law, he had no right to interfere, because bestowal rights resided with the "father" or "fathers" of these women. One factor that greatly contributed to the setting aside of the rights involved in the naming system was the fact that because, on the whole, old men married young women and young men married old women, in many cases the nominal "father" of an elderly woman was very much younger and less influential than were her brothers, or her sons by an earlier husband. The brothers and/or sons, therefore, were able to override the wishes of their sisters' nominal father because the seniority system was on their side in such contests, even though the renaming rules were not.

Although it was very rare indeed for any Tiwi male to have a resident young wife until he was nearly 40, long before that age he was likely to acquire an ancient widow or two. In at least 90 out of every 100 cases a man's first resident wife was a widow very much older than himself. According to a complete genealogical census carried out in 1928–1929, nearly every man in the tribe in the age group from 32 to 37 was married to an elderly widow. Many of them had two elderly widows and a few had three. But very few of them, and certainly not more than one out of five of them, had a resident *young* wife. About half of them had bestowed wives, but these were mostly toddling infants who would not come into residence with them for another ten years or more. Even for the most promising and rapidly rising young man, the first young bestowed wife was not likely to arrive until several years after his marriage to a widow.

To get a start in life as a household head and thus to get his foot on the first rung of the prestige ladder, a Tiwi man in his thirties had first of all to get himself married to an elderly widow, preferably one with married daughters. This was the beginning of his career as a responsible adult. The widow did several things for him. She became his food provider and housekeeper. She served as a link to ally him with her sons. As her husband, he acquired some rights in the future remarriages of her daughters when they became widowed. And she, as the first resident wife in his household, stood ready to be the teacher, trainer, and guardian of his young bestowed wives when they began to join him after they reached puberty.

LEVIRATE, SORORAL POLYGYNY, AND CROSS-COUSIN MARRIAGE

We have emphasized infant bestowal and widow remarriage because it was the elaborate development of these two matrimonial mechanisms that brought about the unusual, perhaps unique, character of the Tiwi household. Other matrimonial mechanisms, more usual in preliterate societies, were also used by the Tiwi but always in combination with or as minor adjuncts to the two basic mechanisms. Thus, a man often remarried his dead brother's wives, or at least some of them, within the institution of widow remarriage. Such a practice is known to anthropologists as the levirate, and tribes are said "to have" the levirate or "not to have" it. The Tiwi, with their pluralistic approach to the whole area of marriage relationships, can hardly be said to fall into either category. To them, every widow had to remarry and among the many possible candidates for her, the brothers of the dead husband were recognized as having a reasonable, but far from automatic, claim. Whether the brothers jointly, or any one of them singly, were able to translate that claim into marriage depended on the other claims. Brotherhood in itself gave no exclusive right to widows, but of course a brother, being necessarily of the same clan and frequently of the same band as the deceased husband, was well in line to assert a claim to the widow if he could make the claim good. Cursory inspection of the genealogies reveals, however, a surprisingly small number of cases of men taking over the widows of their deceased brothers. At best it was a very minor factor in Tiwi marriage customs.

Another Tiwi pattern, that is, sororal polygyny—sisters being married to the same husband at the same time—was more common. It occurred both in connection with infant bestowal, by a father promising *all* his daughters by a particular wife to the same husband, or in connection with widow remarriage, whereby two or more full sisters, previously married to the same husband, passed together on his death to the same new husband. Sororal polygyny occurred more frequently in the first form than in the second, largely because, as already mentioned, widows had more say in their own marriages than baby girls had, but there was nothing obligatory nor required about it, as is shown by the frequent cases in which a father bestowed all his daughters by one wife on the same man but on the early death of that man rebestowed them *seriatim* on several different husbands. One got the impression, though no Tiwi ever made the point explicit, that within the Tiwi bestowal system the prevailing high rate of infantile and child mortality was an important factor in sustaining sororal polygyny to the extent that it did exist. A father who bestowed upon a man the first daughter borne by a certain wife was almost obliged to bestow upon the same man the second daughter of the same wife if the first one died in infancy. Moreover, because most fathers bestowed their daughters with an eye to their own advantage, it was clearly desirable if he wanted to cement the goodwill of a prospective son-in-law, to promise him *all* the daughters produced by a certain wife, so that even though most of them died in infancy, at least one or two would be delivered in good condition at the age of puberty. The aim of bestowal was to win friends and influence people, and a bestowal of a child who died before she reached the son-in-law did a father little good. A shrewd father could avoid this risk by following the sororal principle; a stupid or feckless father who scattered his daughters widely could well end up with as many disappointed sons-in-law as friendly ones, as the infantile and child mortality took its heavy toll of his young daughters. In the genealogies, sororal polygyny in some form occurs much more frequently than levirate marriages, but nonetheless its incidence is such as to indicate that it was a relatively minor feature in Tiwi marriages and that its occurrence was most frequently due to careful fathers trying to insure sons-in-law against disappointment, and themselves against charges of nondelivery.

No account of marriage in any Australian tribe can go very far without raising the difficult matter of the kinship system, because all the accounts we have of mainland Australian tribes tell us that all marriages there took place within a rigid kinship framework, which required everybody to marry somebody who was automatically his or her cross-cousin (for example, a man and a daughter of his mother's brother).[14] Enough has been said already to indicate that in Tiwi marriage nothing was automatic. Females were given in marriage by their fathers, or (to a lesser extent) by their brothers, or (to a still lesser extent) by their sons. But fathers died and were succeeded by the men their widows remarried, and these men renamed all the widow's children,

---

[14] The classic work on Australian kinship systems is Radcliffe-Brown, 1930–1931, and there is a large technical literature on the subject. See also Elkin, Berndt, and Berndt, 1951; R. Berndt, 1955 and 1957; Murdock, 1949.

and by renaming them established some rights to make marriage decisions for the females. Therefore, cross-cousin marriage in Tiwi was merely part of the total system of marriage and had to adjust itself to the rest of the system. In theory, fathers could only bestow their infant daughters on men who stood to them in the relation of sisters' sons. Conversely, every man who received a bestowed wife received her from a man who was technically his mother's brother and of course the girl's father. To this extent the Tiwi were a tribe who practiced cross-cousin marriage and their kinship system belonged to one of the commonest Australian types, that which Radcliffe-Brown called Type I, having investigated it among the mainland tribe called the Kariera.[15] But a kinship system of the Kariera type could not accommodate all the complexities that had been introduced into Tiwi life by the emphasis on infant bestowal and widow remarriage. In particular, the generations kept getting badly mixed up, as for instance in the very common case of old men bestowing their infant daughters on other old men of their own age group, and in return receiving as infant wives (or wards) daughters of those old men. With this happening constantly, it was difficult to maintain the kinship principle that recipients of wives were always sons of the donor's sister and donors were always brothers of the recipient's mother. Which was mother's brother and which was sister's son in the case of two old men busily swapping daughters was a problem that put a severe strain on a Kariera-type kinship system. And widow remarriage introduced further complexities. We have already mentioned the case of two young men, Antonio and Dominico, who through a judicious use of widow-remarriage had ended up married to each other's elderly mothers. This was no isolated case; many pairs of men of like age were married to each other's mothers. Who called whom "father" and who called whom "son" became an insoluble riddle in such cases.

To avoid further involvement in the labyrinthine complexities of Australian kinship organization, all that we need say here is that the Tiwi had unscrambled the potential confusion introduced into their kinship categories by inventing a few new terms which, superimposed upon their Kariera-type system, kept everything straight. In Kariera, and generally among all the mainland tribes, no kinship distinction was made between potential "in-laws" and actual "in-laws." A Kariera male called all the girls who were eligible for marriage to him by the same term (*Nuba*, usually translated mother's brother's daughter); all the fathers of such girls by the same term (*Kaga*, usually translated as mother's brother); and all the mothers of such girls by the same term (*Toa*, usually translated father's sister or mother's brother's wife). When he married one of these girls he still called her *Nuba*, he still called his wife's father *Kaga*, and still called his wife's mother *Toa*. But not in Tiwi. For them, all potential wives were, in theory, mothers' brothers' daughters and all potential wives' fathers were mothers' brothers. But when a man married any such girl, he immediately called her by a new and different kinship term that can only be translated as "wife," and corresponding new and separate terms were used

[15] See Brown, 1913.

for the actual wife's father, actual wife's mother, and even for the actual wife's father's sister. Thus marriage introduced for a Tiwi a new set of relatives with new kinship terms different from those he used toward his general run of cross-cousins, mother's brothers, father's sisters, and so on, and these "relatives by actual marriage" terms, being based on actual marriages rather than kinship categories, were capable of handling in a fairly orderly manner all the complexities introduced into Tiwi domestic life by such customs as old men exchanging infant daughters or young men marrying each other's mothers. We may sum it up briefly by saying that Tiwi marriages operated within a general framework of cross-cousin marriage kinship categories identical with the categories of the Kariera, but that females had become such important assets in power and prestige relationships among the senior men—marriage had become, so to speak, such a political affair—that a new set of kinship terms based on actual marriages had to be superimposed on the terms geared to cross-cousin marriage; in cases of conflict or anomaly or confusion in the cross-cousin terms, the terms based on actual marriages were controlling or took precedence. This is only another way of saying that in theory all Tiwi marriages were rather idealistically approximated to marriages between cross-cousins, but in practice they departed quite far from such an ideal; so far, in fact, that extra kinship terms had been introduced to take care of the relationships created by such departures.

"DISPUTED" WIVES

There is still one more category of wives to be mentioned, a category for which the Tiwi had no name in their own language but which in pidgin English they referred to as "stolen" wives. A few women so labeled were likely to turn up in the "list" of the wives of most big men, but analysis of the circumstances in each case makes it clear that "stolen" was an unsuitable label and that wives so designated were most often in a status that should be called either "disputed" or "shared." In legal terms they were wives in which there was or had been a divided interest. To explain fully the nature of these cases would carry us over into both the Tiwi legal and sexual systems, and here we are trying to confine our analysis to those aspects of marriage that have consequences for household organization. Because these disputed or shared wives had to at least reside in some household and had at least a nominal current husband at any given moment of time, all we need to note about them is that in any listing of a man's wives we have to include "disputed" wives in addition to all the other categories of wives mentioned previously.

THE HOUSEHOLD: AN OVERVIEW

In the discussion so far we have selected only those aspects of the Tiwi family complex that had close bearing on the nature of the household. These aspects can be briefly summarized in the following list.

1. The high number of wives per husband that a successful man was likely to acquire if he lived long enough.

2. The two distinct mechanisms by which wives were acquired—infant bestowal and widow remarriage.

3. The operation of the bestowal system in such a way as to prevent even the most promising young man from achieving coresidence with a bestowed wife until he was at least nearly 40 years old.

4. The tendency for success to lead to more success, whereby *some* astute men received into their households a number of young wives in rapid succession after the age of 40.

5. The tendency of younger men and of nonbetrothed younger men in particular to marry elderly widows while waiting for betrothed wives to grow up or, in the case of those with no bestowals in sight, to enable them to start a household of their own.

6. As a result of the integrated operation of all these customs, the strong tendency in Tiwi households for husbands to be very much older than their wives (as a result of infant bestowal) or very much younger than their wives (as a result of widow remarriage) or—what was commonest of all in the bigger households—some combination of both. Hence many a Tiwi husband had some wives much older than himself, including some already dead (but still counted), and some very much younger than himself, including some who were still babies in their mothers' wombs (with their sex still undetermined). All these dead wives, current wives, and not-yet-born wives were still counted in an husband's list, and the length of his list was a measure of his influence, power, and importance as a household head.

It is now perhaps clear why we chose to begin our account of Tiwi culture with some discussion of Tiwi marriage. Compulsory marriage for all females, carried out through the twin mechanisms of infant bestowal and widow remarriage, resulted in a very unusual type of household, in which old successful men had 20 wives each, while men under 30 had no wives at all and men under 40 were married mostly to elderly women. This unusual household structure was the focal point of Tiwi culture. It linked together in an explicable unity the kinship system, the food-gathering system, the political and prestige system, the totemic system, the seniority system, the sexual system, and the legal-moral-religious system of the tribe. Or perhaps all these should be labeled as subsystems under the household structure, the master system that unified them. We turn therefore to consider the Tiwi household as it affected the food gathering and leisure-time activities of the people.

2/Life in the Bush

ORGANIZATION: BAND AND HOUSEHOLD

The preceding chapter should convey something of what a Tiwi band really was. The casual way in which people left one band and joined another shows that the band was in no sense a tight political or legal group. Old men preferred, on the whole, to bestow their daughters on men in other bands,[1] but far from this indicating any tendency toward patrilocality there was at the same time a strong tendency on the part of such selected sons-in-law, especially if they were young and mobile, to move into the band of the father-in-law, partly, at least, to ensure that the donor did not change his mind. Even the faint prospect of a wife was sufficient to cause young men to change bands, and change of band residence by senior men was not at all rare.

The emphasis on widow remarriage was another factor that influenced band residence and made the whole matter of band affiliation extremely fluid and arbitrary. For widow remarriage not only caused elderly women to move perhaps several times in their lifetimes, but also caused their younger sons to move with them. Such unmarried sons preferred home cooking and followed their elderly mothers outside the band if remarriage required the widows to move. Almost invariably the question "Why is So and So (a youth of 15–25) living in Turupi if he is really a Malauila?" evoked the response (obvious to a Tiwi) "Because his mother is there." Conversely, mothers often followed their sons, especially when the son began to acquire young wives who needed senior female supervision. Such mothers divided their time between the household of the son (or even several sons) and the household of the nominal husband, and if such part-time residence in two (or more) households involved part-time residence in two (or more) bands, the arrangement did not provoke any comment, nor was it thought to be in any way odd.

The fluidity of band affiliation was so constant a feature of Tiwi life that almost the only firm generalization that can be made about it is that when "a big man" with a large household had lived most of his adult life in the territory of a band, and had been up to the time of his death one of the

---

[1] Goodale, after reviewing this passage, noted that her data indicate that local endogamy was the ideal pattern in traditional Tiwi society; but that big men preferred to bestow their daughters on men from other bands, thereby enlarging their social network.

dominating elders of that band, his children, both male and female, would be regarded as "really" members of that band during *their* lifetimes, regardless of where marriage took the girls, or where their own life careers or the remarriages of their mothers took the boys. Thus in 1928 the three oldest men of Malau—Ki-in-kumi, Enquirio, and Merapanui—were regarded as core members of the Malauila band. Reference to their family trees reveals that the latter two had been born in Malau to a big man of that band in the previous generation and had resided in Malau all their lives. Ki-in-kumi, however, always thought of as equally a Malauila, in fact had been born in Rangu to a Rangwila father and had moved to Malau as a youth when his marriage prospects had seemed to him best in that district. This move had happened so long ago that only old people remembered it, and as a result all three old men were generally regarded as "real" Malauila and the children of all three would be so be regarded all their lives. Such identification would hardly carry over for more than one, or at best, two generations. In explaining the matter, we have had to use the English word "really" in quotation marks because the Tiwi themselves had no corresponding concept. If one asked "Why is he a Malauila when he never seems to live there?" the answer would be "Because his father was, and he grew up there." It was only in pidgin English that one could talk of a "real Malauila" or a "real Rangwila." In Tiwi language and thought, Malau or Rangu was a firm, fixed, unchanging piece of country; the Malauila or Rangwila were the households, of constantly changing personnel, who hunted there, and a man had to belong to one of those households practically all his life and have his father before him also a permanent resident of the same district before his identification with that district was sufficiently close to approximate the degree of identification that is implied in the European concept of a "real" Malauila or "really" a Rangwila.

The crux, then, of Tiwi territorial organization was not the band but the household.[2] A band was merely the temporary concentration in one district of semiautonomous households, which were the food-collecting, living-to-gether, and sleeping-together units of Tiwi life. People were not members of bands as part of any political or legal system; they were members of households as part of a domestic system. What held the unit together was the central position and dominance of the father or husband, and hence the life of a household was only as long as his lifetime. When he died, the household broke up and the surviving members joined other households, perhaps in the

---

[2] There has been a prolonged argument in the anthropological journals about the Australian territorial unit, especially as to whether it was patrilineal or matrilineal. For the Tiwi, such a problem could not arise. A father bestowed his daughters where he wished and at puberty they joined their husbands. Where his sons found wives was no concern of the father, and hence where they established their households was of no interest to him either. The father would wish, however, that they would establish their households as far away from his as possible because then he would not have to worry about them interfering with his young wives. On the other hand, it was thought to be "unfatherly" actually to throw sons out. See Murdock, 1949; Elkin, Berndt, and Berndt, 1951; Radcliffe-Brown, 1956; R. Berndt, 1955 and 1957 for the main contributions to the mainland argument, which we think becomes pointless when dominance of the household ties over band ties existed, as it did among the Tiwi.

same district, perhaps in some other band territory. Such change of household was carried out by the individuals concerned, not quite at will, but certainly not with sufficient uniformity for any political or legal label to be put upon it.

Uniformity was derived from the fact that every Tiwi had to live in a household. The universal prohibition on unmarried females was obviously one expression of that requirement. For men, the requirement was less firm, and if a young man wanted to live entirely alone he was free to try—although there is no record of any man having tried it for more than a few weeks at a time. Even if his mother were dead and his father or stepfather did not welcome him, he attached himself to some household because, apart from any question of loneliness, this was the only way by which he could eat regularly. For Tiwi households were primarily autonomous food-producing and food-consumption units. A household made its own decisions, camped where it saw fit to camp, moved on when the food quest made it advantageous or necessary to move on. A large household, such as that of Ki-in-kumi or any other big man, was a complete community in itself, with the old man as executive director. He laid down the daily, weekly, and monthly work and travel schedules for the women, the young men, and the children. Most of the time the work went automatically because all the adults and the older children knew their jobs.

DAILY ACTIVITIES

By shortly after dawn each day, the household was up, and after a light breakfast, usually of leftovers from the previous night, everybody left camp to go to work. The women and children (except perhaps the 5- to 10-year-old boys, who were rather useless at that age) scattered in every direction from the camp with baskets and/or babies on their backs, to spend the day gathering food, chiefly vegetable foods, grubs, worms, and anything else edible. Because they had spent their lives doing it, the old women knew all about gathering and preparing vegetable foods, and they supervised the younger women. This was one important reason for men marrying widows, and even a man with many young wives was quite likely to remarry an elderly widow or two nonetheless. A husband with only young wives might have a satisfactory sex life, but he still needed a household manager if he wished to eat well. The supervision of the female members of the household was left to the old women and, provided the returns were good, the husband did not attempt to interfere nor to give orders concerning the details of women's work.

After the women had scattered out in a wide circuit from the camp, the husband might hunt, but only if he were not too old. In hunting kangaroos,[3] wildfowl, and other game, keen eyesight is essential, hence Tiwi men did very

---

[3] Actually there are no kangaroos on Melville and Bathurst Islands; the chief meat animal is a slightly smaller species of marsupial technically called the wallaby. Because the distinction is important only to zoologists, and as many of the so-called kangaroos in American zoos are in fact wallabies, we prefer to use the more familiar word.

little hunting once they were past about 45, though they hated to admit their hunting days were over. The meat, fish, and game provided for the large household of an old man was obtained by the young men, and this was about the only thing an old man thought his sons or his stepsons were good for. Typically the young man, when he returned at nightfall with a kangaroo, which he had spent most of the day tracking down and spearing, would ignore the old man and dump the carcass at the feet of his mother as if to say, "I brought this back for you, not for that old So and So."

As the women straggled back to camp toward sundown with the results of their day's gathering and the young hunters brought in their bags, cooking began and the main meal of the day (usually the only hot meal) was eaten. The Tiwi themselves had no doubt about the close relationship between plural marriage and good eating. "If I had only one or two wives I would starve," the head of a large household once told the missionary who was preaching against plural marriage, "but with my present 10 or 12 wives I can send them out in all directions in the morning and at least two or three of them are likely to bring something back with them at the end of the day, and then we can all eat." This was a realistic appraisal of the economic situation and it is to be noted that he put the emphasis on the food obtained by the women gatherers rather than that supplied by the male hunters. Based on the observations of 1928–29, it would appear that the Tiwi ate pretty well, especially in the larger households. Kangaroo and other marsupials, and some of the larger lizards (for example, the goanna) were very plentiful in the bush, as were fish and turtles and dugong on the coasts and wild geese in many districts. But all these were extras or dividends; the staple everyday foods were the vegetable foods gathered day after day in apparently unending quantities by the women. For most months of the year there was always plenty of kwoka,[4] a porridgelike dish prepared by soaking and mashing the small nuts of a native palm. These nuts grew in such quantity that in every large camp baskets or dishes of kwoka, at various stages of preparation, were always available, even for midnight snacks if anybody woke up hungry. Kwoka was about as dull and tasteless as Scotch porridge, but equally filling, and naked small boys full of kwoka had stomachs distended like balloons. In the wet season the place of kwoka was taken by kulama, a yam whose ripening and growing season was much shorter than that of the nuts from which kwoka was made. It was on the abundance of the kulama yams during January and February that the Tiwi supported the more elaborate of their collective ceremonials.[5]

---

[4] Goodale, after reviewing this passage, noted that her data state kwoka to be ripe and eaten during a somewhat more limited period, including only the late part of the wet season and the early part of the dry season.

[5] Pilling's and Goodale's 1954 observations and her 1980 information are not consistent with Hart's report that during January and February the availability of kulama supported collective life. The period of collective life continued several months later. An informant of Pilling who had lived in the traditional period stated that the ceremonial season throughout its entire length was a time when kwoka was the mainstay of diet. Goodale's and Pilling's informants stated that kulama yams were too toxic to be eaten regularly; they were rather scarce and were, in fact, rarely, if ever, consumed in a nonceremonial context.

The abundance of these and other vegetable foods, plus the ample supply of game and fish in many places, meant that under aboriginal conditions the Tiwi lived at a food-consumption level much further above the near-starvation level than was the case with many of the mainland tribes.[6] Even to talk about the Tiwi in near-starvation terms seems quite incongruous, for there was an abundance of native food available the whole year around and their only problem was to collect or catch it. We regard the development of their large multiple-wife household as essentially their own evolutionary solution to the problem of finding the most efficient unit of food production. Abundant food was there in the bush in its raw state; the most efficient way to extract it was by a work unit represented by such households as those of Ki-in-kumi, or Tu'untalumi, with the old remarried widows directing the young women and the hunting and fish spearing being done by the younger males.

Even the smallest households nearly always contained at least one old female veteran of the food quest who knew the bush like the palm of her hand and could wrestle some food out of the most inhospitable district. The only households that ever went hungry—and they only overnight or at worst for 24 hours or so—were the small households of only one or two wives, especially if both wives were young and inexperienced or young and flighty or both. Such households were uneconomic and were rare. On the other hand, the apparently absurd households such as those in which two young men shared their respective elderly mothers as wives, made good economic sense. Any attempt by two such young men to substitute two young wives or even four young wives for the two old ladies would have drastically reduced the standard of living of the household. When young wives arrived in Tiwi households they were not regarded as replacements for old wives, but joined as reinforcements and apprentices to the skilled workers—the veterans. The sexual aspects of marriage were necessarily subordinated to the housekeeping or food-production aspects, which is why in the previous section we spoke of every young man laying the foundation of his household by marrying an elderly widow usually long before there was any young wife in sight.

Because the bigger the household the more food it produced for its own consumption, there was a tendency for the smaller and therefore hungrier households to hang around the fringes of the bigger ones. Though every household was autonomous and could camp and collect food anywhere in the band territory in which it roamed, it was rare to find all the households in a band distributed evenly over the available territory. In Malau, Enquirio's household and that of Merapanui were usually to be found camped together, because the two men were full brothers and not in competition with each other. Also camped with or near them on any given occasion would be a few other small households. Such a combined group as this would, all told, amount

---

[6] As was pointed out earlier, the best-watered and most fertile areas of the mainland were the areas attractive to white settlement, and the tribes who inhabited such areas (for example, Victoria or coastal Queensland) were wiped out quickly. Most of the mainland tribes who survived long enough to be studied by modern anthropologists were tribes whose habitats were unfavorable both for native and for white occupation.

to between 40 and 50 people camping at the same spot and remaining together for weeks at a time. Under mainland conditions in most areas, a gathering of 40 people for 10 days at a time in the same locality was unheard of, except on special rare ceremonial occasions, because of the poverty of the food supply. The prevalence of such large camps among the Tiwi supports our general thesis that their native food supply was, for Australia, unusually plentiful, and that, in this sense, the Tiwi were a "rich" Australian tribe.

When camped together thus, the various households kept their distance, with the main fires and shelters of each separated by some 20 or 30 yards from the others, and during the day when everybody (except the old men) was out food collecting, the camps were almost deserted. When the food gatherers returned in twos and threes in the late afternoon, each household would cook and eat at its own fires as a unit, but if they wished, members of the smaller households, in which food returns for the day were probably smaller per capita than those of the bigger households, would "drop in during supper" upon the latter and supplement their own slender meal. Such hospitality was always extended on an individual basis; some member of the bigger household, usually a senior wife, would offer to one of the visitors a piece of meat or a dish of *kwoka* and if rebuked by her husband she would justify her act by mentioning her own kin relationship to the visitor, as if to stress that the kindness was her own individual gesture and did not commit the whole household to friendliness. Heads of large households were, however, generally very permissive if such handouts were made by senior females of their household to women or children of other households; it was handouts to adult male outsiders, especially young male outsiders, that were likely to provoke snarls or reprimands from the old man. This was in line with the general hostility of all old men to all young unmarried men that ran through all aspects of Tiwi culture.

After darkness fell, such a camp, with three or four households all resting within easy hearing distance of each other, became highly animated with men visiting from fire to fire as the women, who were not encouraged to walk about after dark, gossiped around their own fires. Little productive work could be done after dark, though a few cooking chores and food-preparation activities were performed, and most people went to sleep early unless the shouted conversations from fire to fire earlier in the evening had started an argument. If an argument did arise, the participants might go on abusing each other at long range for hours, with many of the listeners becoming involved and the rest remaining awake to enjoy the row.

Such rows were almost invariably outgrowths of the constant suspicion with which older men regarded younger men. This suspicion was in turn part of the price the Tiwi had to pay for the efficient type of food-production unit that they had evolved. This production unit, to reach maximum economic efficiency, required the vast majority of all females to be concentrated in the households of a very small number of husbands; namely, the very oldest men. As a necessary correlate, men under 28 had no wives at all and very few men under 40 had any wife except elderly and physically very unattractive widows.

The efficient economic organization thus obviously created a moral and social problem—the problem of how to keep the unmarried young men away from the young women. The old head of the household had a double role: he was at the same time the executive director of a work unit that he expected to work for him, and the husband of many of its members whom he expected to be faithful to him. The young wives were willing, under supervision, to meet his first expectation, but found it difficult, even under the strictest supervision, to meet the second. Successful supervision of the morals of young wives was easy to achieve at night because each camp was then gathered together and it was relatively easy for the husband and his senior wives to guard the young wives closely. But during the daytime matters were different. Then the young women of the household were widely scattered through the fairly dense bush and it was impossible for the old wives to watch them every minute of the day. And the young men of other households, or even of their own household, were hunting game in the same neighborhood. Encounters, whether by chance or by previous arrangement, were likely to occur and probably occurred with a high degree of frequency. We say "probably" because no anthropologist working with a tribe which has neither courts nor written records can ever know how often casual extramarital offenses take place. (There is even some difficulty in obtaining reliable statistics on such matters in our own society, as the attacks on the late Dr. Kinsey's statistics indicate.) We therefore make no statement about how common the act of adultery was in Tiwi culture, but we can say that, judging by the public accusations of adultery, its practice must have been widespread indeed. In any Tiwi camp comprising more than two households, few weeks went by without an outraged and angry old husband shouting accusations at one of the younger men sitting by another camp fire a few yards away. The young man accused would (usually) deny it; the old women of both households would enter the argument, the young man's mother protesting his innocence, the old man's elderly wives (who had of course been the informers) giving details of time and place and circumstance; the young man would produce, or try to produce, an alibi and appeal to a friend to bear him out; the old man would call the friend a liar and the youth's mother an old witch; the youth's mother would retaliate by shouting things she knew (but had never before revealed) about the private lives of everybody in the old man's household, including the old man himself when he was a young bachelor. A good time would be had by all, including the listening anthropologist, but nobody would get much sleep. Such nocturnal uproars, always starting with accusations hurled by an older husband against a younger man and always involving incidents that had allegedly occurred while the young wife was somehow left unchaperoned for a short period during her daytime wandering in search of food, were a commonplace of nightlife among the Tiwi; but no case was ever reported, observed, or hinted at in which even the most adventurous and enterprising bachelor had succeeded in seducing, or had even attempted to seduce, a young wife when she was back in camp after nightfall. The deeds were always done in the secrecy of the bush during the daytime; it was the recriminations and accusations that occurred in the public glare of the camp-fires at nighttime.

Sometimes these disputes or accusations went no further than the nocturnal shouting of charges. Often the young man accused the previous night quietly slipped away to some other camp and was not seen the following morning. The matter might then die, depending largely on whether the old husband wanted to carry it further or was content to drop it. If the young man was still in camp the following day, the old man might insist on a duel then and there, but it would take place only if the camp were large, because Tiwi duels were essentially legal actions and as such needed a sizable audience for their correct staging. Disputes between men, of which old men accusing young men of seduction were by far the most common type, usually remained at the verbal level until a large body of spectators was available. Because such large concentrations of many households were necessary for the performance of the main collective ceremonials, it was at the time of these ceremonials that most verbal arguments were pushed by the aggrieved party to the action level.

During the dry season (April to November) when travel was easy, the only collective ceremonials sufficiently important to draw together a large number of households were those held for the funerals of big men. In the wet season (November to March) when the grass and bush were high and travel was difficult, the main collective phases of the male initiation ceremonies were held (see Chapter 4), and these brought together for a few weeks at a time large numbers of households. The funeral ceremonies for adults were always held some considerable time after the death and burial of the deceased. How long a period elapsed between the death and the funeral ceremonies depended on the expected size of the gathering, and this figure correlated, at least roughly, with the importance of the deceased. Here again the overriding consideration was food supply, because the chief mourners (that is, the deceased's closer relatives) had to feed everybody who came to the funeral while the ceremonies lasted, which might be almost a week. The more important the dead person the bigger the crowd at his funeral, and hence the greater the amount of time needed by the mourners to arrange the catering. As much as a year might elapse between the death and the time when the mourners felt that the funeral arrangements—especially the food supply, but also the ceremonial preparation—were sufficiently well in hand to permit them to set a date and send out invitations for the funeral ceremonies. Funerals, therefore, were not held at regular times but were individually scheduled at times fixed by the chief mourners. They were always held in the dry season, however (except those of young children, to which nobody came in any case), and therefore an old man who had a dispute to settle or a case to try publicly could always depend on a few big funerals being held in the not very distant future, which would provide the large audience necessary to make the settlement of the dispute legal. During the wet season the *kulama* phases of the initiation ceremony always drew a large attendance; the annual time of these was pretty definitely fixed by the ripening of the *kulama* yams.

Photo 8. Kulama *ceremony participant doing his inherited Shark Dance, in* *February 1954 in the bush near Paru.*

Hence the verbal wrangles in the small scattered encampments at night, about seduction during the day, could have any one of three outcomes, depending largely upon the determination of the old man-accuser and the demeanor of the young man-accused. If by the following morning the young man had disappeared and showed no further interest in the old man's menage, the matter might end there. Or the old man might let matters rest until the time of the next big gathering of people at a funeral or at the *kulama* rituals, and then revive the issue under such public circumstances that the accused young man could not slip away unpunished. If he followed this second course, the old man went to the gathering covered from head to foot in white paint, the Tiwi uniform for anybody who came in anger and intended to pick a fight with somebody. The decision between these two lines of action lay, of course, with the old man, and although that decision was to some extent determined by how vindictive and revengeful he felt, nonetheless it was also influenced by how this dispute was related to all the other feuds, disputes, deals, marriage exchanges, and so forth, in which both parties were already involved. Like a good lawyer in our own culture, the old man had to consider, before he took the matter to court, who the young man was and who his friends and relatives were, and had to ask himself whether in seeking vengeance for the blow to his pride he might not be doing himself more political harm than the injury was worth.

spectators who came for the excitement, even though not personally involved, provided of course they were camped somewhere in the vicinity.

This second type of collective gathering, of which the smaller funerals and the single duels were the main occasions, might then require the attendance of a household head, accompanied by some or all of his household members, perhaps five or six times a year. These gatherings would each last less than 48 hours, and because the people the household head met at them would mostly be people of his own band or of closely adjoining bands, the excitement of seeing unfamiliar faces—people not seen for over a year perhaps—would be absent. We may reckon that attendance at these smaller, more localized gatherings, and the participation in group activity that they entailed, took up two more weeks, all told, out of the yearly round. When these two weeks are added to the six or seven already estimated for the time spent by a busy public man at the large gatherings, we find that even the busiest and most gregarious senior elders spent less than 10 weeks out of the 52 in collective activity outside their immediate households.

To complete the list of occasions that called for joint activity by the members of several households, we must include the joint kangaroo hunt. This activity was very localized and very spasmodic, occurring only when and where conditions were right and somebody felt sufficiently energetic to organize it. Much of the Tiwi country is a mixture of dense scrub and relatively open savanna; kangaroo are relatively easy to hunt in the latter but very hard to get near in the denser types of vegetation. The native method of hunting was based on getting as close as possible to the animal before it saw or heard the hunter. If it detected the hunter, it fled, and no Tiwi in his senses ever threw a spear or a throwing stick at a moving kangaroo.[8] Only when the animal was standing still and the hunter was close enough to aim carefully at a vital part was the spear thrown. At certain seasons of the year, particularly after the end of the wet and early in the dry season, many sections of good kangaroo country gave very poor hunting returns because the grass had become so high and rank that the hunters were unable to get near the kangaroo. In this event, a senior man of the district might decide to convene a grass-burning posse. To it he invited more or less whom he pleased, so long as he included other household heads of the same band and other senior men from outside it whose ancestry gave them some claim to be invited. At the appointed time the hunters assembled, perhaps 10 or 15 adult men, with younger ones doing the actual hunting and the older ones supervising. The women and children acted as beaters; the grass was set on fire over a big area, and the kangaroos rounded up and killed while dazed by the smoke and the noise. The bag of animals killed in such a concerted hunt sometimes ran higher than one kangaroo per participant, so that every man, woman, and child present was able to gorge himself on kangaroo meat for a day or two. This sudden glut of meat was not, however, the main object of the burning, but a dividend. Even though

---

[8] The up-and-down movement of a hopping kangaroo in flight makes it an extraordinarily difficult target even for skilled white hunters armed with shotguns or rifles.

few kangaroos were caught in the smoke and confusion, the burned-over area would provide good visibility for kangaroo hunting during the rest of the dry season, because the new tender shoots that sprang from the burned-over grass were a favorite food of the kangaroo and served to lure them out of the denser scrub areas and the mangrove swamps where hunting them was always difficult.

These occasional joint hunts, like the occasional small fights and the funerals of unimportant people, usually brought together only the members of households who lived relatively close to one another, so that although they are included in the list of events that interrupted household isolation, they did not, as a rule, involve any interaction between members of any wider group than the neighboring households. Perhaps the whole matter of activity beyond the household and the band can be illustrated best by an actual case. We have already mentioned the venerable Tu'untalumi, an old man resident among the Tiklauila, who as late as 1929, and despite the fact that by then the Tiklauila were the band most subject to mission influence, nonetheless had a list of 21 wives. In other ways besides his record of polygamy, Tu'untalumi was a pillar of the old culture. Though past 70 and much too old to hunt, he was a most enthusiastic and indefatigable song and dance composer, and in his zest for the ceremonial he made a point of attending every big festival and as many smaller ones as he could get to. The whole tribe respected Tu'untalumi as a big man, liked him as a person, admired him for his steadfast support of Tiwi traditions, and most of all accepted him as a sort of leading authority on ritual matters. When dubious or disputed points of ceremonial were submitted to him, his decision, given clearly and firmly and with much citation of precedent and the distant past, was accepted without demur. His presence at a gathering located outside his own district was always a source of gratification to the household that had convened the gathering. The fact that Tu'untalumi had seen fit to attend not only made that household feel important but also provided its members with a technical guide and arbiter for unofficial help in running the rituals. The old man loved going to parties— and he was always a welcome guest—and years of such activity had given him such a sturdy, wiry constitution that despite his near-75 years he could outdance and out-sing and out-party most of the men 50 years younger than himself.[9]

Because Tu'untalumi was a senior Tiwi household head who spent more of his time attending festivals, funerals, fights, and other collective occasions than did most of his contemporaries, it is instructive to examine his movements over a full year. If he had kept an engagement book during 1928–1929, it would have looked something like this:

---

[9] There is no suggestion that Tu'untalumi was in any way an official ritual leader. All old men, by virtue of their years, were to some extent ritual leaders; he had merely worked harder and longer at it than most of them. His tirelessly joyful personality had a good deal to do with his success in the self-established role. In a culture that might be thought likely to make all its men gloomy, anxiety-ridden introverts, he was a warm, happy, dignified old extrovert and he was widely admired.

Early April (end of wet season): Leaves his home base in Tangio where he has spent most of the wet season and visits the Mission station to attend a few small funerals (children who have died at the Mission in the preceding months). During these funerals a series of fights and duels also takes place. Total people present: perhaps 50 or 60. Time thus spent in helping to wind up public business: five days. Returns home to Tangio and remains there for rest of April.

End of April: Goes to Rangu with a big party of other Tiklauila for a funeral (junior elder). Fairly big funeral, lots of people, lots of disputes. Time away, including leisurely journey to and from Rangu, about two weeks. Gets back home about middle of May.

Middle of May—end of June: Lives quietly at home with his household in Tangio.

About July 1st: Goes to Mission for a few days, "visits" with whoever is there. Tries out a new composition of his own (song and dance) on group camped at Mission. Returns home for rest of July.

Last week of July: Taking his younger wives and their children with two senior wives in charge of them, sets out for Malau for a big funeral with lots of people and fights. There he performs his new dance; is much consulted on ceremonial matters by the Malauila; gets into a few fights himself but handles them with dignity and honor; remains in Malau two weeks; stops off to visit and attend a small funeral with the Munupula on his way back; has a fight with a Munupula while there; returns to the Mission; stays there a day or two dispensing all the news from Malau and Munupi to those camped there; issues invitations for a grass burning in some sections of Tangio which were not burned in April or May. Goes on home to Tangio where some of his older wives have remained during his absence. Total time away: about three weeks.

End of August: Is joined in Tangio by several other Tiklauila and Rangwila households whom he has invited. Grass burning and joint kangaroo hunting goes on for four or five days. Dancing and partying at night. After five days most of visiting group leave and he and his household remain alone in Tangio until well into October.

Middle of October: Rains about to commence. Last chance for travel before the wet season. Goes to another district for the naming ceremony of a new baby (he is its mother's father, having bestowed the mother on the man now naming the child). Goes on from there to the Mission. Finds a large party there about to visit the Mandiimbula on Melville Island, ostensibly for a funeral but really for a big argument since Tiklauila–Mandiimbula relations were badly strained at this time.[10] Joins this party. They go in force to the Mandiimbula country. Big fight. He is not much involved in the fighting, concentrates on the dancing.

End of October: Returns to Mission. War party disbands. He returns home to Tangio and remains there until the initiation ceremonies begin in

---

[10] We have tried to keep out of the text those factors in the 1928–1930 situation which were clearly due to post-white influences, and this friction was of that order. Briefly, Mandiimbula fathers with daughters bestowed on Tiklauila husbands were failing to deliver the girls at puberty to those husbands, hoping instead to hire them out as prostitutes to the Japanese pearling boats, which periodically visited the Mandiimbula and Yeimpi beaches in search of women. See pp. 111–112 and p. 149 for a full discussion of this outside influence as well as that of the Mission, which (for different reasons and motives) was also in the girl-buying business at this time.

late January. During this period (November–January) makes occasional very short visits to neighboring households and is occasionally visited by neighbors who drop in on him from no great distance away.

End of January: *Kulama* phase of initiation begins. As guardian of ritual, he is in much demand by the various groups with boys of suitable age. All the Tiklauila and Rangwila households gather together (about 300 people) for nearly four weeks to conduct these ceremonies. Much feasting, much dancing, he in the center of everything. Very few fights or disputes, which is the way he likes it.

End of February: Finish of *kulama* season. Finish of ceremonies. Households disperse. He and his household return to Tangio and remain there for the balance of the wet season, which usually ends toward the end of March.

During the year for which we have listed the details, Tu'untalumi attended three big funerals, one big *kulama* ritual, several small funerals, and made a few other miscellaneous visits to other districts. In addition, he was the host at a joint kangaroo hunt in his own district and attended the naming ceremony of one of his daughters' children. He also was a member of one war party. Although this hectic social whirl totals up to about 13 weeks spent away from home or with a large party of guests in the home, even the busy and popular Tu'untalumi spent about 39 weeks out of the year living alone with his household and seeing nobody except members of that household. Because there were few other Tiwi as gregarious as he, we may take this figure as an outside limit and conclude that the great majority of "big men" spent at least four-fifths of their time in the isolated environment of the single household, engaged largely in the daily routine of getting a living and supervising their wives and children in their unending food quest.

The mobility of people other than household heads was much less. Women and children could move only with the permission, and usually in the company, of their lord and master. Occasionally old and trusted wives might be sent, unsupervised, on a journey by their husbands or their brothers, usually to carry messages and bring back gossip, but young wives were never trusted to be out of sight either of the husband or of elderly female supervisors. Young men were less subject to their fathers' orders and hence were fairly free to come and go as they pleased, but the universal suspicion that all husbands bore toward wandering young men put severe restrictions on their mobility and prevented them from attaching themselves to any household or camp in which they did not have some close relative.

The fact, then, that a man like Tu'untalumi was (in Tiwi terms) very mobile did not necessarily mean that members of his household shared his degree of mobility. When he took most of his large household with him on his journeys away from home, as he often did, it was always because he was going a considerable distance and was traveling slowly, living off the country as he went. In such cases he liked to have a large retinue to feed him on the way and also to permit him to entertain in fitting style when he arrived. For although it was true that at a funeral or at an initiation the relatives of the deceased or of the novices were supposed to take care of the feeding of all the visitors, nonetheless, wealthy and generous men like Tu'untalumi believed in taking along with them a bevy of young wives, with a couple of efficient elderly widow-wives in charge of them, to contribute to the food-getting and food-preparing activities. Of course the supervision of the young wives' morals in the strange environment was often difficult, especially in the hectic atmosphere of a big ceremonial, but this worry was compensated for by the fact that the visitor who came so attended was contributing a number of extra food providers to the labor force of the harassed hosts and thus making a generous gesture, and also by the fact that such a visitor was not dependent upon the hospitality provided by the hosts. Having his own food-producing unit with him, he could live better and stay longer than if he had come alone or only as one of a party of men. In this respect, as in so many others, a Tiwi household head's decision had to be reached by balancing against one another the two competing motives of, on the one hand, the desire to eat well and, on the other, the desire to keep his young wives safe from prowling bachelors. Ki-in-kumi, the wealthiest man of the Malauila band, usually decided not only to leave his wives at home but also not even to go himself. But Ki-in-kumi was a gloomy, pessimistic old man. Tu'untalumi usually decided to do the thing in style, travel with a large retinue, have all the comforts of home while in strange districts, and take his chances on the strange bachelors. He clearly believed that a good booming ceremony with lots to eat and himself in the center directing the dancing was well worth the risk of a few of his young wives being seduced offstage. Men like Ki-in-kumi thought Tu'untalumi an old fool for not leaving his young wives at home, and Tu'untalumi probably thought that old Ki-in-kumi might as well be dead, especially since his death would be the occasion for a really magnificent funeral.

The matter of men traveling to distant camps for ceremonials illuminates again, and from a new angle, the great value of elderly widows in the household. Tu'untalumi, during his visit to Malau in August, was able to split his household efficiently by taking a couple of old wives with him to supervise his young wives on the journey and leaving other old wives at home in Tangio to begin storing up food for the grass-burning project, which he intended to stage on his return. It will be noticed in the account of his movements that he began issuing invitations to the grass burning on his way home from Malau, showing his confidence that the elderly wives he had left at home would have the preparations well in hand during his absence. A big man with a big household really needed three or four elderly widows because these enabled him to split his work force in various ways as his various political and social obligations required and to be sure of trustworthy supervision of each of the segments. A man without widows in his household, or with only one, could not do this; in fact, it was hard for a man without widows to attend ceremonials at all, or even to receive a large party of visitors to his household. And, as we have already pointed out, since such a man would probably go hungry very often because he would not dare to send his unsupervised young wives into the bush to gather food, there were practically no such men nor such households. Widows were indispensable to a senior Tiwi, both in his public and in his private life.

MAKING THINGS

Throughout this chapter we have been stressing the contrast between the dull routine of life in an isolated Tiwi household during the greater part of the year and the sort of life typical on those relatively rare occasions when something special—a festival, a funeral, a fight, a grass burning, a naming ceremony, some collective phase of men's initiation—required the assembling together of several households for joint activity. Before leaving the daily life of the isolated camp, we should mention one other area of activity—namely, the manufacturing activities of the tribe. The Tiwi did not manufacture much, but spears, throwing sticks, canoes, digging sticks, baskets, bodily ornaments, graveposts, and all the miscellaneous paraphernalia used in ceremonials had to be made in whatever leisure time people could find during the long weeks and months when each of the households lived more or less in isolation from the others. Crude and simple as these artifacts were, their construction required time, and only the older men had the time and the skill based on experience to make the more important of them.

Largely because of their failing eyesight, the older men hunted very little and hence tended to remain in camp all day while the young men were hunting and the women were gathering. There were, of course, some old men who took advantage of this time to do little except doze in the shade, but most of the household heads spent a fairly active day in camp engaged in making things. Here we find another aspect of Tiwi culture that results from the relatively favorable food supply. Some of the Tiwi artifacts, particularly the highly decorative graveposts and ceremonial spears, are unique among Australian tribes, and the carving and painting of these graveposts and spears were skills possessed only by the senior men. They were provided with the leisure time necessary to develop and use these skills by the efficiency in food production of the large household, which all old men were expected to accumulate with age, and which many old men did succeed in accumulating. We said earlier that the bigger the household, the better its members ate. We now add the further correlation that the bigger the household, the more leisure time was provided for its head to engage in manufacturing and artistic production. Tu'untalumi has been cited as an example of a large household head (12 resident wives and 13 children at home in 1928–1929) who loved ceremonial affairs. It would be wrong to infer from this that Tu'untalumi only loved going to parties. He also loved preparing for them, and this preparation (for him as for all other senior men) included the manufacture of ceremonial spears, the preparation of graveposts, and the composition of songs and dances. In the long dull periods between trips outside his home district, he spent most of the days and many of the nights in the creation of these ceremonial necessities. He was not a full-time specialist in the sense that he

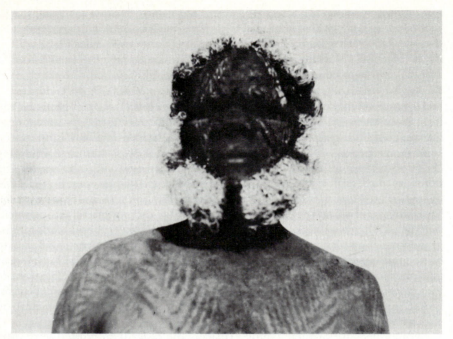

Photo 9. Timalarua, the canoe maker.

made spears or posts to exchange with other men who had neither the time nor the skill—the rules of kinship required that every senior man make his own ceremonial spears and contract for his own posts. Tu'untalumi manufactured his graveposts to meet his own ritual obligations, but he took a more magnanimous view of those obligations than did most men. Put in our terms, we might say that he was wealthy enough (in the size of his household) to be generous with his own productions. One example of this attitude was his attendance at funerals that other men of equal kinship to the deceased did not find it necessary to attend; his frequent contribution of an extra gravepost to those provided by the chief mourners of the deceased was a similar gesture. "Tu'untalumi not only came to our mother's funeral, he also made a gravepost for it" was a very gratifying reflection for an obscure group of mourners to cherish among their memories, and of course it was acts of this sort that made the old man so well liked and admired. The economic point of the matter, however, is that only a man with as large a household as his could afford the gesture of giving away, in a situation where kinship obligations did not demand it, a gravepost that required about a week's full-time work.

It was, however, sad to observe that as an artistic producer Tu'untalumi, like many intellectuals in other cultures, tended to operate in too many media. His work as a composer of songs and dances was universally admired, but his graveposts, although appreciated, were not regarded as being as outstanding, technically speaking, as those of another old man, his crony Timalarua.

In personality, Timalarua, a successful household head (11 living wives, 10 children at home), was quiet spoken, placid, and only mildly gregarious, and he is mainly of interest because in his leisure-time activity he paid but routine attention to song and dance compositions and concentrated rather single-mindedly on making canoes, ceremonial spears, and graveposts. Frequently, on the banks of some creek or river in Tiklauila territory, a party wanting to cross would scout around and find a canoe hidden in the weeds. Everybody would use it to cross, and the question "Whose canoe is it?" would elicit the reply, "Oh, it's always there and everybody uses it who wishes to cross." But if the question were "Who made it in the first place and put it there?" the answer would be, "Probably Timalarua. He likes making canoes; he makes them all the time." He also liked making spears and posts, though he was not as generous with them as Tu'untalumi. When one of his posts appeared at a funeral, people would point it out admiringly saying, "Timalarua made that one" and the speaker would trace the lines and designs on it with his finger, using much the same gestures as an art critic in a modern gallery. When a post by Tu'untalumi was identified and admired, however, the admiration was for Tu'untalumi the generous person rather than Tu'untalumi the artist. One was a wonderful craftsman, the other was a wonderful man. But acclaim given to the song and dance performances of the two men was just the reverse: The dances of Timalarua were adequate but not outstanding, those of Tu'untalumi were in a class by themselves.

Comparison of the activities of these two old men illustrates the impossibility of drawing any line, in the simpler cultures at least, between artistic production and technological production. The canoes and the posts manufactured by Timalarua and the posts manufactured and the new dances created by Tu'untalumi were all, so to speak, in the same category, as far as the Tiwi were concerned. The distinction we might make between the canoes as "useful" products and the posts and dances as ceremonial or artistic products never occurred to them. All were objects or products that only successful old men had the required skill and leisure to make. The fact that one old man liked to make canoes and leave them around for other people to use, and another old man liked to compose dances and perform his compositions widely for other people to enjoy, to them merely indicated individual taste and choice; it did not make the first a craftsman and the second an artist. This point has been overlooked in most of the theorizing about primitive art; perhaps a necessary first step in the development of primitive artists is for a society to be able to provide a few men with enough leisure time to be able to cultivate what might perhaps best be called hobbies, because a hobby can equally well be something "useful" to society, like canoe making, or something personally satisfying, like dancing or decorating graveposts.

The huge, heavy, painted spears made by these old Tiwi men were mainly used only for display, and even the oldest men were positive that this had always been the tradition. In fact, they seemed a little shocked at the implication that such beautiful and valuable objects could ever have been used for such mundane purposes as hunting or warfare. The cutting and painting of such spears took time and skill—more time than a gravepost—and no important man went to the smallest gathering without bearing on his shoulder at least half a dozen of these symbols of his importance. If on his way through the bush he sighted a kangaroo, he dropped his painted spears and stalked the animal with an ordinary spear, or more probably left it to the young men in the party who carried only ordinary ones. The painted spears were symbols of wealth and status and roughly corresponded to white tie and tails in our culture. No important man could afford not to have them, even though for most of the year they were unused. Before leaving home on a journey, it was often necessary for a man to renew the paint on his spears, for it rubbed off easily. Because paint was an aspect of ritual, its use, even the renewal of old paint, was senior men's prerogative; women were not supposed to touch it.[11] The analogy with formal dress even extended to the borrowing of ceremonial spears. An important man, caught short of them, might borrow some from a contemporary who had plenty, and though everybody would know that his spears were borrowed, he at least was properly dressed for the occasion, though stark naked otherwise.

Baskets made of bark with gummed sides were made by the women, but the painted designs upon these baskets were applied by the men, in line with their monopoly on all work that required paint. These baskets of various sizes but little variation in shape were used for all domestic tasks involving the collection, storing, transporting, and preparing of vegetable foods, and were sufficiently watertight to enable water also to be carried in them. Ordinary wooden spears (without barbs or painted designs) and a great variety of throwing sticks were made by all men, young or old, but important old men bothered with them very little, considering such routine manufacture beneath them. These workaday spears and throwing sticks lay around every camp in abundance, and a man who needed spears or sticks in a hurry could always gather up a bundle in a few minutes. Small boys picked up the techniques of making spears and throwing sticks by spending time with older boys who in turn improved their skill both in making and using hunting weapons by spending time with the local young men.

Although much of this learning was fairly random, other instruction was not. During his initiation period a youth spent long intervals isolated in the bush with a couple of older teachers from whom he received training in religious and ritual matters. At the same time, of course, it was inevitable that the novice absorb some of the older men's experience in bushcraft. There was no corresponding initiation period for girls. What they learned, they learned first from the older women of their childhood household and later from the older women of the husband's household into which they moved as

---

[11] Hart reported: "Female mourners were required to daub their bodies with white clay as a sign of mourning, but this paint was smeared haphazardly over their bodies and faces without any attempt at regularity or design, in contrast to the careful paint designs on men's bodies."

Goodale notes that in 1954 at Milikapiti both men and *women* painted elaborately. By 1980, such painting was rarely worn by either sex.

child-brides after puberty. In all households the supervision by the elderly women of all younger women included the training of both female children and young wives in the things all females should know—things that were mostly concerned with collecting and preparing vegetable foods and the making of baskets.

In pre-white times Tiwi males wore no clothing whatever. The Mission insisted on calico loincloths, but, at least in the 1928–1929 period, one could observe the spontaneous gesture with which men, on leaving the Mission, automatically threw off their loincloths at the Mission fence and headed for the bush as naked as the day they were born. Women, in pre-white days, habitually carried a piece of bark that they held in front of themselves whenever they met a male. As soon as string or rope was introduced by the early white contacts, the women found it more convenient to tie some sort of band around their waists and double the piece of bark over this waistband. This was much handier because it left the hands free, but the bark, being stiff and unsecured, was at best a very capricious covering, and old women in the midst of public arguments often tore off their aprons and threw them at their opponents as a gesture of contempt.

Young women were more decorous and fussed modestly with their bark aprons when young men were present. Theoretically, young women were supposed never to meet either young men or men outside their own household, and so the bark apron, carried in the hand, was in aboriginal times merely something to have in case of emergency. It was noticeable in Tiwi ceremonies that when the women danced, they did nothing with their hands. We think this was because, in pre-white days, their right hands, at least, were needed to hold their bark aprons in front of their pubic regions, because at dances they were in the presence of strange men.

This brief account of the daily and yearly life of the Tiwi households enables us to draw a few important conclusions about their economic life:

1. Compared with many of the mainland tribes, the Tiwi were economically rather well-off, in that the bigger household units were usually able to produce a food surplus.
2. This food surplus varied directly with the number of working wives that a household head possessed.
3. A household head with many wives was therefore, in Tiwi terms, a wealthy man who could retire entirely from the food quest and devote his time to other activities.
4. Such men were able to devote full time to activities such as manufacturing useful and ceremonial objects and participation in ceremonial affairs and public life.
5. Wealthy men, active in one or all of these pursuits, were the "big men" of the tribe. In each band there were two or three such men, and in the whole tribe perhaps less than 20 had attained full success or were ranked by public opinion as being the most admired and influential. The next chapter examines the career patterns by which every male Tiwi sought to become, and a few succeeded in becoming, a big man.

3/The Prestige and Influence System

To become a really big man, or even a minor figure among the elders, a Tiwi had to devote all his adult life to that goal. Careers were built up and influential positions gained not by executing spectacular coups at any one time, but by slow, devious maneuvering and dealing in influence throughout adulthood. Men in their early thirties invested their very small assets in the hope of large returns 20 years later, and if the anthropologist witnessed the initial investment, he was not around to witness the final return; or if he witnessed the return, he found it difficult to reconstruct all the relevant details of the initial investment. A man in 1928 bestowed his daughter in a certain direction because of some deal back in 1900, arranged by men many of whom were now dead. And the bestowal in 1928 was done in such a way as to bind the hands of men negotiating in 1960, some of whom were infants in 1928.[1]

The Tiwi influence and career patterns can best be compared to a sort of nonstop bridge game wherein the scores were never totaled up nor a new game ever started on a clean slate.[2] Whenever an observer came in, he always entered in the middle of the game and found the current hands being played with all the old scores back for at least two generations influencing the play of the present hands. The game never had a beginning or an end; every new player had to start in the middle and make the best of whatever assets he had by way of kinship, clanship, household membership, and help from older players. Similarly, any attempt to describe the operations involved or the "rules" of the game must perforce start in the middle.

The "game" was one of trying to win friends and increase prestige and influence over others. The "assets," in a tribe with such minimal material

---

[1] A typical illustration of this situation arose during the writing of this book. In 1928–1929 Hart had observed Padimo beginning to acquire a number of bestowed wives. Being interested in the status of Padimo 25 years later, he included Padimo in a list of inquiries to Pilling. Pilling's reply: "Re Padimo. I am almost certain that he was the 'Paddy' who died leaving several widows, in February 1953, about three months before I got to the Islands. The natives did not like to talk much about him while I was there (because of the taboo on dead men's names) and his widows were still being fought over. The fights over his widows did not end until the week I left (if they really did then)." Thus the deals that Hart saw in 1928–1929 were having delayed repercussions when Pilling was there in 1953–1954.

[2] We use bridge rather than poker as our analogy because nobody ever "went broke" in Tiwi influence competition and nobody ever "won the pot," because there was no pot to win. The scoring was always, so to speak, on a comparative basis and everybody, even the most unsuccessful man, had some score relative to his competitors.

57

possessions as the Tiwi, were mostly intangible ones such as friendship, "help," goodwill, respect of others, control over others, importance, and influence. Even in our culture such things are difficult to express in concrete or tangible symbols. The most concrete symbol of Tiwi success was the possession of surplus food, for this not only permitted its possessor to make gifts to others and throw large parties for which he picked up the check, but also gave him lots of leisure time to devote to social and political life. Because a man required a large number of women in his work force if he was to build up a surplus of food, in the final analysis it was control of women that was the most tangible index of power and influence. Women were the main currency of the influence struggle, the main "trumps" in the endless bridge game.

It should be noticed that we stress the value of women as women rather than as wives or bestowable daughters. To a smart Tiwi politician, wives or daughters were assets but so was his mother—if submissive to her son's wishes. So were his sisters—if amenable. A bachelor at the age of 30 who had several sisters was a lucky young man, especially if those sisters already had daughters to their current husbands. As successful old men used their infant daughters to gain influence and buy satellites, so young men used their mothers and their sisters—if they could.

Thus the psychological line between the attitude of a man toward a wife and his attitude toward a sister or a daughter was a very thin one. A Tiwi elder had many women related to him in some way—as wives, as daughters, as stepdaughters, as sisters, as sisters' daughters, as wards, and as mother— and all of these were part of his assets or capital. The fact that he had sexual rights to the wives and not to the daughters or the sisters was only of minor relevance. What was of major relevance was that they were all women whom he could use—or try to use—as investment funds in his own career of influence seeking. The devious details of Tiwi prestige and influence operations are much easier to follow if one keeps in mind the crucial fact that the Tiwi men valued women as political capital available for investment in gaining the goodwill of other men more than they were interested in them as sexual partners. Some of the more senile elders were quite vague about the young girls in their household; such an old man was sure only of the fact that a girl, by being in his household, was part of his capital. Which were his daughters and which were recently joined young wives was a question that had to be referred to the old wives who kept track of such academic details.

Women were, however, a form of capital that possessed the power of talking back to the investors. As daughters or as wives they were quite thoroughly subordinate to the wishes of their fathers or husbands, and Tiwi wives were as frequently and as brutally beaten by their husbands as wives in any other savage society. But as mothers and as sisters the women were not coerced by their sons and their brothers. On the contrary, sons or brothers wishing to use their mothers or their sisters in their political schemes (typically when those mothers or sisters became or were about to become widows) could only do so with the active collaboration of the women concerned. Tough-minded young widows could drive a hard bargain with their brothers as to where they remarried, because each needed the other to make the remarriage acceptable to the tribe at large and to beat down the other competitors (the dead husbands' brothers, for example) who wished to control the remarriage of the widows. Young girls thus had no bargaining power but young widows had a good deal. Old mothers with influential senior sons were extremely powerful. Any affront to an old woman was an affront to her sons, and some of the strongest influence networks were alliances of several senior brothers, in which their old mother seemed to be the mastermind and the senior sons largely the enforcers of what the old mother and her middle-aged daughters (their sisters) had decided among themselves.

Thus, for women, as for men, age and political skill were the crucial factors in determining their position. Young girls were chattels and as such were passed on from husband to husband. But with increasing age, smart young women, especially in alliance with their smart young brothers, could control their own fate with some firmness, and if they and their brothers had a shrewd old mother (also with powerful senior brothers still alive) to advise them and support them, then the decisions of such a group as to where the girls remarried were very difficult decisions for anybody else to combat or oppose. Not as independent operators, but as behind-the-scenes allies of their sons and brothers, Tiwi mothers and sisters enjoyed much more essential freedom in their own careers as often-remarried widows than would appear at first sight in a culture that ostensibly treated all women as currency in the political careers of the men. No matter how males, both old and young, might connive, they were constantly aware that no remarriage of a widow could ever be arranged and made to stick unless the widow herself was agreeable.

In the limited space available, all we can offer are a few samples of how the influence game was played by a few selected individuals of various ages. Age was of great importance in Tiwi careers and therefore we select our samples from all the adult male age-groups. We have selected them all from the same band—the Malauila—so as to show as clearly as possible the interplay between one career and another for men of the same band. And finally we select men of the Malauila band for our examples because in 1928–1929 it was a band little affected as yet by the outside influences—Catholic missionaries and Japanese pearl divers—which were beginning to modify Tiwi marriage customs among some of the other bands.

THE BEGINNING OF TIWI CAREERS

The Malauila in 1928–1929 consisted of 49 males and 60 females of all ages. The males were divided into the following age groups:

20 years and below	28
between 21 and 30	7
between 31 and 42	7
between 43 and 55	4
over 55	3
Total	49

Of the 28 males aged 20 or below, none had a wife of any kind, and none of them expected or were expected to have one. This group comprised the male children—boys and youths—and such males were of no importance whatever in the Tiwi scheme of things. They lived in the households of older men and were ignored by the male elders.

The next group, the seven men between 21 and 30, was the group of young men whom the elders were just beginning to take seriously. The younger of them were almost indistinguishable from the "youths," whereas the older of them were beginning to be watched by the seniors with some interest. Of the seven, six were neither married to a wife of any sort nor promised a wife. One, called Banana by the whites, was a man of about 28 and married to a middle-aged woman who was childless by three previous husbands, but she was in the category of "disputed" wife since her young husband had only been able to acquire and hold her because of abnormal circumstances arising from the presence of white buffalo-hunters on Melville Island some years previously. Under pre-white conditions, none of the seven men under 30 would have had a wife of any kind.

The years between 30 and 40 were the crucial years for Tiwi men in their establishment of households and careers. It was during this period that men normally married their first ancient widows and the "likely to be successful" became sorted out from the less-likely. As they passed into their thirties, men were allowed to enter for the first time into the influence game and, as the most junior players, they entered it by becoming subordinates and satellites of the bigger and more senior players, or by making alliances among themselves so as to pool their small individual assets.

In this age group in 1928–1929, there were seven Malauila men ranging in age from around 31 to 42. One (Tiberun) was still unmarried and unpromised. He was thus (at age about 33) the oldest bachelor in the band. Not unnaturally he spent a good deal of time with other bands or at the Mission in the hope that his failure to get started in Malau might be remedied by elders of other bands or even by the priests. Tiberun was an older full brother of Banana, the 28-year-old married irregularly to a woman whom he had "stolen." A glance at their family tree revealed one potent reason why Tiberun was still a bachelor and why Banana had acted so impulsively and thereby gotten himself in the bad graces of the elders. The two men were the eldest of four brothers without any full sisters and as such they were necessarily handicapped in their career struggle. Elders seeking satellites or contemporaries seeking allies looked askance at men without sisters, for such men could have no sisters' daughters to use in the marriage-arrangements struggle. The mother of Tiberun and Banana was dead, but even were she still alive, few men would have been interested in marrying a widow whose only living children were sons. Widows without daughters and bachelors without sisters rated very low in the scale of desirable assets sought either by elders or by contemporaries.

Tiberun was thus the only bachelor in the 30–42 age group. Of the remainder we select Teapot as an example of another man who failed to get started.

Teapot was at least 35, and about seven years previously he had "stolen" a wife from an elder. This wife was no ancient and shopworn widow like the wife Banana had "stolen," but a young girl who had been betrothed in due form to an elder by her father. How Teapot had managed to get away with her is too complicated an incident to unravel here, and in any case it hadn't done Teapot much good. After presenting Teapot with a baby boy the young woman died, and Teapot, with a now 6-year-old son, was more or less an outcast among the Malauila. No elder wanted him as a satellite and none of his contemporaries wanted him as an ally. His mother was dead and his only sister was married to a Munupula elder. This sister in Munupi was his only asset and one that a different man might have used as a means to better himself. But Teapot, instead of using this small asset to get started on a career, had chosen to defy the rules and "steal" an elder's bestowed wife. "Stealing" an old widow was reprehensible conduct in the eyes of the elders; stealing a young bestowed wife was unforgivable. Hence Teapot, since his crime, had received no bestowal, had been able to marry no widow, and was wanted by no one as an ally.

A complete contrast to these two unsuccessful men in their thirties was provided by the case of Gitjara, who was about the same age as Tiberun. Gitjara, it is true, had sisters, and that was always a help. Using his sisters (already married and bearing children to an elder) as bait, Gitjara when he was about 28 proposed an alliance to L.F.B., a rather feeble man about five years older than himself, who was not doing very well in the influence race. The gist of the proposal was that, because both their mothers were still alive and each married to an old man who could not last much longer, Gitjara should marry the ancient mother of L.F.B. when she became a widow, and L.F.B. should marry Gitjara's mother when that old lady became a widow. Perhaps the idea originated with the two old women rather than with either of the young men. Because such arrangements were essentially plots or schemes, it is impossible to determine who conceived them in the first place—old women ambitious to aid their sons or young men ready to use their mothers as long-term gambits ultimately to provide themselves with young wives. Mother-exchange operations were probably first conceived at high-level strategy conferences in which smart mothers and dull mothers, smart sons and dull sons were all present, and the final plan emerged from consensus.

In this case the former husbands of the two old women both died conveniently soon and within about three years of each other and, according to plan, there came into existence a household of two men in their thirties each married to the elderly mother of the other. Gitjara and L.F.B. thus set up jointly the foundations of their households and began their careers as a joint enterprise.

Gitjara had two sisters, both married to White Man, an elder, and already the mothers of daughters to him. By marrying Gitjara's mother, L.F.B. automatically became the nominal father of these women, and in the event of White Man's death would have, as such, some say in where they remarried.

But the right of the stepfather to redispose widowed stepdaughters was always disputed by the brothers (or even sons) of the stepdaughters, provided those brothers (or sons) were old enough or influential enough for their wishes to be taken seriously. Thus we may say that in putting L.F.B. into position as his own stepfather, Gitjara's main object had been to get a satellite or henchman of his own into the position of stepfather of his sisters (the wives of White Man) so that when they became widows there would be no conflict between the wishes of their brother and the wishes of their stepfather as to whom they should remarry. L.F.B. as stepfather was, so to speak, a stooge for Gitjara the brother.

Conversely, L.F.B. had two sisters both married to Ki-in-kumi, the most powerful elder in Malau. By marrying the mother of L.F.B., Gitjara became the stepfather of two of Ki-in-kumi's wives, thus immediately (despite his youth) becoming technically the father-in-law of that powerful old man, and a man with some say in where those two wives of Ki-in-kumi would remarry on Ki-in-kumi's death. As stepfather of such widows, Gitjara would have to make his wishes prevail as against the wishes of their brothers, but the only brother was L.F.B. and his vote was obviously in Gitjara's pocket.

By engineering this double shuffle of two elderly widows, each with daughters, Gitjara had launched his career as a marriage manipulator. Almost before it was concluded he became involved in another widow operation. We will omit the intricate details, but can say that he emerged from this with a second wife for himself, this one (naturally) also a widow but quite a young widow. This woman had already borne four sons and one daughter to her previous husband but was still young enough when Gitjara took her over in 1926 to bear him a son (her last) in 1927. In Tiwi terms the acquisition of this widow by Gitjara was a real achievement for the young man, not because of her comparative youth nor because of the son she bore him but because among the children by her previous marriage was a daughter aged about 9 at the time she remarried Gitjara. To become the stepfather of such a young girl was a real asset for the young operator. Her dead father had bestowed this child on Summit, another of the same Malauila age group of 30-year-olds and hence one of Gitjara's rivals and competitors in the influence struggle. This created an intriguing situation because Summit, having had this child bestowed on him at her birth some nine years previously, had thus acquired a bestowed wife at about age 27; Gitjara now 33 or so still had not received a bestowal. By remarrying the mother of Summit's young bestowed wife, Gitjara had turned the tables on one of his chief competitors among his age group. He could not, of course, alter the bestowal; in five or six years' time the girl would take up residence with Summit. But as the stepfather who renamed the girl and the head of the household in which she would live for the next five years, Gitjara was in an excellent position to make Summit enter into a deal or two with him. He could drag his feet as to the time of the delivery of the girl to Summit; he could drop hints that there was something irregular about the bestowal to Summit in the first place, and so on; but whatever form of pressure he chose to exert on Summit, the latter well knew that all Gitjara wanted was to be cut in on some of Summit's deals and to be included in the network of Summit's alliances. The next move was now clearly up to Summit.

If Summit wished the 9-year-old girl now in Gitjara's household to be transferred promptly and without argument, he would be well advised to give some consideration to Gitjara, perhaps even the promise of one of his still-to-be-born daughters either as a wife or as a ward. Although not necessary, it would be a politically wise gesture. If he did so, both men would be gambling in futures. Because Summit's young wife was now 9 years old, it would be at least six or seven years before she could produce a daughter (if at all) and another 14 or 15 years before any such daughter (if she lived) would be old enough to join Gitjara's household either as a wife or ward. Hence, under any such arrangement between the two young men, Summit would be giving something to Gitjara but in such a way that the latter could not collect for at least 20 years and might never collect.

Anthropologists will note that such arrangements still conformed to the patterns of cross-cousin marriage. Gitjara as *de jure* father delivers his "daughter" to Summit and thus becomes technically Summit's mother's brother or wife's father. Twenty years later (if all goes well) Summit delivers his daughter (by Gitjara's daughter) to Gitjara, thus becoming technically the mother's brother or wife's father of Gitjara. Gitjara himself might marry this daughter of Summit by his own stepdaughter or treat her as a ward given to him by Summit and bestow her on some other man selected by himself; in the latter case he would be acting as father to his stepdaughter's daughter. There were no clan barriers to such an arrangement, because fathers had to belong to clans different from those of their wives and of their daughters, stepdaughters, and daughters' daughters.

There were, of course, alternative actions or "deals" open to Summit and also to Gitjara, depending upon their plans in other directions. The pattern described previously, however, was extremely common in Tiwi marriage arrangements, and often it was the reason why some very old man would receive some female infant as a wife: an agreement of this type had been made 20 or 30 years before, when the now senile old man was in his thirties and when the mother of the baby he was now receiving was married to some man long since dead. The circumstances were certainly right for such an arrangement in the Gitjara-Summit case of 1928.

If we now pause and look at the marriage career of Gitjara at the point it had reached by the time he was 33, we can separate out three distinct types of operation in which this admirable young man had engaged. His first marriage, with L.F.B.'s elderly mother, had brought into existence a joint household of young men and elderly widows, which not only was a very satisfactory housekeeping arrangement but also put Gitjara and his ally, L.F.B., in a position to exert some influence on all the subsequent remarriages of their respective sisters.

Gitjara's marriage a few years later to a second widow put him in a position to enter into marriage arrangements even more directly, because the second widow had a daughter promised to Summit but still too young to take up residence with him. By dragging his feet on the fulfillment of this promise, Gitjara could put pressure on Summit and extract from the latter some sort of consideration to facilitate the delivery of the girl. Gitjara was thus well in the marriage-broker business before he had any children of his own and indeed before he had received any bestowal. This was the second type of operation for an up-and-coming young man, and it was one wherein a shrewd and aggressive operator would use the daughters of other men (that is, of a widow's previous husbands) in such a way as to attach all sorts of codicils and contingent interests and second mortgages to the original bestowal of those daughters, many of these collectable in full only in the far distant future, after all prior interests had been satisfied or had lapsed.

The third type of operation engaged in by Gitjara was, of course, to try and attract bestowed wives of his own. His vigorous operations, by age 33, in the widow remarriage field, were not only ends in themselves but also were the type of operation that attracted the approval of older men with daughters to bestow. Hence it is not surprising to find that by 1929 Gitjara, married to the two widows already mentioned, had received two bestowals. The older of these was a girl of 10 rebestowed on Gitjara in 1927 when the man died upon whom she had been bestowed at birth. The second was a baby born in 1927 whose father was Tomitari of the Rangwila. (The choice of Gitjara as a son-in-law by Tomitari was so interesting that we will discuss it later in this chapter.) Both these bestowals were made *after* Gitjara had engineered his remarriage of the two widows and as far as kinship was concerned had no connection whatever with these widows or their close relatives. We conclude, therefore, that widow remarriage could be used by alert and aggressive men in their early thirties for three purposes: (1) to establish households and obtain elderly housekeepers; (2) to establish low-priority rights in the daughters of the widows' previous husbands; and (3) to attract attention to themselves as smart operators and gain the attention and approval of older men. As an outgrowth of the third purpose, they were likely to attract bestowals. Hence we may say that among the Tiwi the best road to obtaining a young wife or several young wives was for a young man to be first successful in the manipulation of the remarriages of elderly widows, who were always in large supply. If a man showed skill and know-how in his early thirties among the widows, then in his late thirties and early forties young wives would be bestowed upon him in abundance. Such a lesson could not have a better exemplar than Gitjara. By age 33 he had done so well among the widows that his first *young wife* would be joining his household by the time he was 38 or 39, and another was already a year old. Clearly he was a young man of promise and one to be watched—and cultivated.

Summit, a man slightly older than Gitjara, must be dealt with very briefly, because the reasons for his success would take us too far afield. In 1929 he had a list of six wives, the only resident one being an elderly widow. The other five were bestowals and the eldest of these was the girl of 10 whom we have already mentioned as being in the household of her stepfather, Gitjara.

Two more, younger than the 10-year-old, were in the household of Padimo (see below) and the remaining two were in the household of one of the elders of the Rangwila band. Summit, in Tiwi reckoning, was a Rangwila himself and had only moved to Malau a few years before. Some four years previously he had been a young Rangwila with no less than five bestowed child-wives. Three of these had been given him by an elder in Malau, two by an elder of his own band. The Malauila girls were older than the two Rangwila girls and his Malauila father-in-law was older than his Rangwila father-in-law. Summit therefore moved north to supervise personally his interests in Malau. He had, however, been outmaneuvered when the Malauila father-in-law died, because Gitjara had then been able to remarry the mother of Summit's eldest child-wife and Padimo had been able to remarry the mother of the other two little girls. Having thus moved to Malau to be near to and a satellite of his elderly Malauila father-in-law, Summit now found himself the technical son-in-law of two young men of his own age group who were among his keen competitors in the influence struggle. To ensure that his three promised Malauila child-wives joined his household when old enough, he now needed to make some arrangements with Gitjara and Padimo. Summit had gotten his bestowals rather early and rather easily but he still had the problem of nailing them down.

While thus engaged in acquiring five bestowed young wives and trying to promote their safe delivery when ready, Summit had married a widow not much more than 40 years old but childless by her two previous husbands.[3] Such a widow at least provided him with a food-getter and housekeeper and enabled him to establish a household into which his five bestowed wives would enter as they successively reached the proper age. Thus Summit's household in 1929 consisted only of himself and his *palimaringa* wife. Within the next 15 years it would be increased by the addition of at least five young wives, plus any new bestowals, plus any further widows Summit might find it to his interest (and power) to remarry.

Padimo, who thus enters our story as one of Summit's rivals and one of his nominal fathers-in-law, was also a Rangwila who had moved to Malau at the call of an elderly father-in-law. He presents another pattern of Tiwi upward mobility and one that was statistically more frequent than the rather tortuous road followed by men like Gitjara. Padimo had been chosen as a nephew worth supporting by old Ki-in-kumi, the wealthiest of the Malauila. The earliest proof of Ki-in-kumi's patronage of Padimo had come in 1925–1926 when an old man died, leaving eight widows of very diverse ages. Three of these "widows," aged respectively 17, 13, and 9 at the time of the death of their first husband, were daughters of Ki-in-kumi. Being so young and their brothers being equally young, their father's right to arrange their re-

---

[3] Such women who had reached middle age without surviving children were called by a special term, *palimaringa*, in Tiwi and the term referred to childlessness rather than barrenness. Summit's widow, for example, had borne two children, both of whom had died in infancy, and she was classified as a *palimaringa*. When a *palimaringa* became very, very old indeed, the word changed to *timaringa*.

marriage was unchallenged and Ki-in-kumi reassigned[4] them as wives to young Padimo, then aged about 33. The eldest of the three girls had already borne two female children to the dead man, these being the two girl babies mentioned earlier as having been promised to Summit.

As well as the three young widows, Padimo had also obtained at the same redistribution the oldest of the dead man's eight wives. It was at the same redistribution that Gitjara had obtained his second widow (the mother of the girl promised to Summit). Thus through Ki-in-kumi's influence, Padimo had obtained four "widows" of the eight left by the man who died in 1925–1926; Gitjara, working without a powerful patron, had been lucky to obtain one.

Ki-in-kumi had subsequently followed up this initial selection of Padimo as a favored sister's son by giving further daughters to him as they were born. Consequently, by 1929 Padimo's wife list consisted of the following:

A. One extremely ancient widow.
B. One wife aged about 20, daughter of Ki-in-kumi, mother already of two daughters by a previous husband who, before his death, bestowed these daughters on Summit.
C. One wife aged about 17, daughter of Ki-in-kumi; had just had her first child (who lived only a week); had previously been bestowed on the dead husband of wife B, but was too young to join his household before he died.
D. Three more girls, daughters of Ki-in-kumi, the eldest about 12 and hence old enough to have been bestowed on the same previous husband as wives B and C; the other two aged 2 and 1 and hence born since his death. All three of these were still resident in their father's household.

With a lineup such as this by the time he was 36, Padimo was clearly in process of going places in Tiwi society. The only weakness one could see in his position was that it all derived from the favor of one patron, and no old man with daughters, other than Ki-in-kumi, had seen fit to bestow a girl upon him. It should be noted that in 1929, though Padimo had two young wives resident in his household, he still had no children of his own. His first child, born that year, lived only a few days. The only children in residence were the two girls promised to Summit by the previous husband of their mother. Their bestowal on Summit was a matter beyond Padimo's control though he could use them to force some concessions from Summit just as Gitjara could with the girl in his household. But as Padimo's young wives began to bear daughters of his own, his bestowal of them would be less encumbered by the commitments of any predecessor. While Ki-in-kumi lived, Padimo would have to consider

---

[4] It is difficult to decide whether such reassignments of female children by their father, on the death of the man to whom he had first betrothed them, should be called "rebestowals" or "remarriages." We prefer the first word because such "child-widows" were usually reassigned by their fathers (if still alive) without any challenge to his rights to do so. They therefore do not differ from original bestowals at birth except for the awkward semantic fact that the man to whom such a "child-wife" was reassigned was technically her second husband.

his obligations to that old man and at least consult with Ki-in-kumi as to how he should bestow his female children, because any such children would be the daughters' daughters of the old man. Nor would the death of Ki-in-kumi leave Padimo entirely free to bestow his own daughters anywhere he wished. Many of the girls already given to him as wives by Ki-in-kumi had mothers who possibly, and brothers who certainly, would outlive Ki-in-kumi. On the old man's death, all of his numerous wives would remarry—some of the older ones probably to ambitious younger men—and these new husbands of the widows of Ki-in-kumi would begin interfering with and trying to alter the arrangements made for his daughters by the old man during his lifetime. Thus Padimo would find himself stuck with a group of new and antagonistic fathers-in-law in place of the old, indulgent father-in-law who had been responsible for his success so far. Padimo's problem was basically how to hold, after Ki-in-kumi's death, the favored position he had gained during the old man's lifetime through the old man's favor.

In the meantime, with Ki-in-kumi still alive and powerful, Padimo had the biggest and fastest expanding household among the Malauila men in their thirties. The only remaining man in this age group was Boya who was the oldest of them all, being at least 42 years old in 1928. As might be expected, his career illustrates some new facets of the Tiwi influence struggle.

Structurally the position of Boya was simple, but politically it was complex. His father had been a henchman and satellite of Ki-in-kumi in the early career of that old operator and roughly had had somewhat the same relationship to the young Ki-in-kumi as L.F.B. had to Gitjara. Boya's father, the satellite, left only two widows (an indication of his mediocrity) and these two widows had been remarried by Ki-in-kumi, the patron. One of these widows was Boya's mother, and Boya was too young at the time to have any say in where his mother remarried. Ki-in-kumi's interest in marrying Boya's mother was not of course because he thus acquired Boya as a stepson, but because he acquired Boya's sisters as stepdaughters. Stepsons were liabilities that new husbands had to take over in order to get rights in the real assets—the step-daughters.

Some years later, when Boya had reached a reasonable age like 30, Ki-in-kumi had arranged for him to marry a very ancient and childless widow (*palimaringa*) more than 20 years older than himself. This was all that Ki-in-kumi considered he needed to do for his stepson, and in Tiwi terms it was almost a gesture of contempt and an open indication that Ki-in-kumi, by providing him with an old woman who was childless but could cook, was not interested in helping Boya toward a career. Since the joining up of Boya to the old woman took place shortly after the death of Boya's mother, who had lived with her sons in Ki-in-kumi's household, Ki-in-kumi by producing the old widow for Boya was telling him in effect to get out and start his own household now that his mother was dead.

In 1928 we found Boya aged about 42 married to a female of 65. But he, she, and Boya's younger brother of 24 were still living in Ki-in-kumi's household. Ki-in-kumi's detestation of him was notorious and yet Boya had by now no less than four young bestowed child-wives growing up elsewhere. No one of these bestowals had come from Malau but were bestowals from different fathers of baby girls in other bands. At first sight this presented a curious situation. Within his own band Boya appeared a complete failure, suffering so severely from Ki-in-kumi's hostility that he had received no bestowals and at age 42 did not even have a separate household of his own. But how could this judgment be squared with the four bestowals from elders of other bands? Clearly none of the causes of success so far analyzed fitted the case of Boya.

Further research into who lived with whom as distinct from who was married to whom revealed that not only was "the household" of Boya, his elderly wife, and his younger brother an integral part of the Ki-in-kumi "establishment," but also that Padimo with his "household" was part of that establishment. Padimo, like Boya, had one elderly wife but he also had five bestowed wives, all daughters of Ki-in-kumi. We said earlier that the two eldest of these five girls being now aged 20 and 17 respectively were in residence with their husband, whereas the three youngest, not having reached puberty, were still "with their father." Actual observation showed that this was an academic distinction because the households of Padimo, the son-in-law, and Ki-in-kumi, the father-in-law, were parts of the same establishment. When one of Ki-in-kumi's daughters bestowed on Padimo became old enough to "leave her father and join her husband," she did not have to move her residence or even change her daily work routines. She merely sat at night around the campfire of her older sisters (Padimo's wives) instead of around the campfire of her younger sisters (Ki-in-kumi's daughters). She remained part of the same establishment.

Padimo, it will be remembered, was the young man whom Ki-in-kumi had attracted from Rangu to Malau by liberally bestowing him with child-wives. Padimo had thus moved into the northern band and by 1928 had moved right into Ki-in-kumi's camp, where he functioned as a sort of executive officer and heir apparent to the old man. In the same camp, though in a very different capacity, was Boya, the 42-year-old despised stepson. Many roads thus led to Ki-in-kumi's household, but before discussing the large establishment of that wealthy elder, we will first summarize, in Table 1, the marital conditions of the eight young men we have been discussing.

This table presents a summary of many of our earlier attempts at generalization. The only Malauila under the age of 43 who had a bestowed young wife old enough to live with him was Padimo, who was thus exceptionally lucky. Leaving out young Banana, five of the seven men between the ages of 30 and 42 had young females promised to them, but these were mostly babies or children who would not come into residence for several years. Six of the seven had married widows, mostly elderly widows, well in advance of the arrival of young wives and before any father had bestowed a daughter on them. Finally, and a point not made before, men of this age group rarely had any children of their own. The only entries in the last column of Table 1 are the irregularly born son of Teapot; Padimo's first daughter who died virtually at birth; and the 1-year-old son of Gitjara who was the last child born to his second ex-widow. Tiwi men rarely had young wives until they

TABLE 1   THE MALAUILA YOUNG MEN IN 1928–1929

Name	Age	Resident Old Wives (Ex-widows)	Resident Young Wives (Bestowals)	Promised Wives (Under 14)	Own Children
Tiberun	33	0	0	0	0
Banana	28	1	0	0	0
Teapot	35	0[a]	0	0	1
Gitjara	33	2	0	2	1
L.F.B.	38	1	0	1	0
Summit	36	1	0	5	0
Padimo	36	1	2	3	0[b]
Boya	42	1	0	4	0

[a] Teapot's "stolen" wife was dead.
[b] Padimo's first child, born in 1929, lived only a few days.

were around 40; they even more rarely had any children of their own before that age. Padimo's dead baby and Gitjara's 1-year-old son were exceptional; the zeros in the last column against the names of Boya (42), L.F.B. (38), and Summit (36) represent the normal situation for Tiwi men of such ages.

In terms of success (as measured by bestowals) Padimo and Summit (largely through the patronage of elders) and Boya and Gitjara (largely through their own operations) were the coming young men among the Malauila. Of the others, L.F.B. was approaching 40 with few assets and no influence, and the other three, Tiberun, Banana, and Teapot, had not even got started in the influence race.

A VERY SUCCESSFUL ELDER: KI-IN-KUMI

The most influential man in Malau and the head of the biggest household was Ki-in-kumi. Because he had been born around 1863–1864 and had been a "young operator" somewhat before 1900, the deals by which he got his career launched were difficult to reconstruct. The results of them, plus the fact that he lived long enough to draw full dividends from them, gave him by 1928–1929 a wife-list of 21. These had been accumulated as follows:

When around 30 years old he remarried two elderly widows and a year or two later received his first bestowal. Thus by age 33 he had three wives. On that foundation he went ahead thus:

		Total
At age 33		
Had two widows and one bestowed wife		3
Between age 33 and age 43		
Remarried two more widows and had three more bestowed wives join him	+5	8
Between age 43 and age 53		
Three more bestowed wives came into residence	+3	11
(During these 20 years at least five bestowed wives died in infancy or childhood)	+5	16

Between age 53 and age 65

Two more bestowed wives joined him and he married two more widows (one the mother of Boya)	+4	20
Now at age 66 there is still one more bestowed wife, aged about 9, in her father's household	+1	21

Thus his list of 21 wives was made up of 6 elderly widows and 15 bestowed or rebestowed young wives.

By 1928–29 five of his bestowed wives had died before puberty and one was still with her father. Three of his six widows were dead. Subtracting these nine women, we find that his current household contained 12 resident and active wives: the oldest about 60, two in their fifties, four in their forties or thirties, three in their twenties, and the two youngest around 17 or 18 years of age. Almost all of them had borne children since joining his household, but the death rate had been high among Ki-in-kumi's children and from all of his wives he had only eight living children of whom six were girls. Five of these six daughters he had bestowed or rebestowed on Padimo (see above) and the sixth on a middle-aged Rangwila. His oldest living daughter was the girl of 20 married to Padimo. His oldest living son was a boy of 18, despite the fact that Ki-in-kumi had been "a married man" for over 35 years. This was a situation which many Tiwi elders found themselves in at the close of long and successful lives. With numerous wives, numerous stepsons, large households to be managed, and large estates to be liquidated after their deaths, their oldest real sons (as distinct from stepsons) were still boys or youths and as such quite unsuitable as executive assistants while the old man lived or as heirs or executors after the old man died. Quite apart from kinship considerations, the Tiwi emphasis on age and seniority made it impossible for Ki-in-kumi to utilize in any capacity his 18-year-old son. A youth of that age was a nonentity, whoever his father.

Confronted by this situation, Ki-in-kumi in his advancing years had summoned Padimo, a sister's son in his early thirties, to come from Rangu and become his chief lieutenant. The youth of his own son had been a factor in his selection of Padimo. The presence in his camp of an older stepson, Boya, had been another factor. Boya, the stepson, was more than 20 years older than the son, and at least six years older than Padimo, the chosen instrument. Padimo, as we have seen, moved right in, fused his own small household with Ki-in-kumi's large one, and became Ki-in-kumi's Man Friday. Boya, the stepson, though married to a widow, refused to move out. Thus, among other things, we have to distinguish between Ki-in-kumi's household of 12 resident wives enumerated previously, and Ki-in-kumi's establishment, which contained Padimo, Boya, and the various people attached to them by marriage or kinship. Padimo had an old wife and two young wives (daughters of Ki-in-kumi). Boya had an old wife and a younger brother. There were a number of younger stepchildren of both sexes also resident with Ki-in-kumi. The full size and makeup of his establishment is given in Table 2.

TABLE 2   KI-IN-KUMI'S ESTABLISHMENT

(Ages in parentheses)

	Males	Females
Head (Ki-in-kumi 66)	1	0
Oldest stepson (Boya 42)	1	0
Sister's son (Padimo 36)	1	0
Old wives (of all three adult men)	0	5
Young wives (including Padimo's 2)	0	11
Young males (sons and stepsons)	8	0
Young females (daughters and stepdaughters)	0	5
Totals	11	21

THE ESTABLISHMENTS OF MALAU

There were, besides Ki-in-kumi, six other elders of the Malauila band. Two of these, the brothers Enquirio and Merapanui, were well over 60 and deserve, both by age and by success, to be labeled senior elders. The remaining four ranged in age from about 45 to nearly 60 and because none of them were particularly successful we call them the junior elders. In Table 3 we have listed the seven "establishments" in which lived all the members of the band. We mean by an establishment a food-production and food-consumption unit. Ki-in-kumi's establishment contained three married men—himself, Boya, and Padimo—and therefore contained three households. Economically it was one establishment, because the 16 wives it contained worked as a team and the food they produced was consumed by the 32 total members of the establishment. For comparative purposes in Table 3 we list Ki-in-kumi's establishment

TABLE 3   THE FOOD PRODUCTION UNITS OF MALAU

Unit	Married Males	Unmarried Males[a]	Old Wives[b]	Young Wives	Girls Under 14	Total Persons
I	3	8	5	11	5	32
II	3	9	1	7	11	31
III	3	2	2	3	5	15
IV	1	5	0	1	1	8
V	1	2	0	1	2	6
VI	2	5	3	0	1	11
VII	1?	4	1	0	0	6
Total	14?	35	12	23	25	109

[a] Unmarried males include all males from male infants to men around 30, or more.
[b] The division between old wives and young wives is arbitrary. Several of the young wives were 40, others only 14 or 15.
? The question mark in Unit VII refers to the difficulty of deciding whether Banana should be classified as married.

as Unit I and give the personnel breakdown of the other six establishments that made up the total population of Malau. Unit II is the joint enterprise maintained by the other two senior elders, the brothers Enquirio and Merapanui. To this we have added the pathetic and ostracized Teapot and his motherless son, because when they ate at all they ate as hangers-on of the Enquirio-Merapanui menage. Unit III is the establishment jointly maintained by the brothers White Man and Ku-nai-u-ua. Because the oldest wife of Ku-nai-u-ua was Summit's mother, that young man, together with the elderly ex-widow who was so far his only resident wife, lived in this establishment. Units IV and V present no difficulty; they are the small households of the other two junior elders Pingirimini and Tipiperna-gerai respectively. Unit VI is the joint enterprise of Gitjara and L.F.B., containing largely old ladies and young men. Unit VII is the remarkable menage that had gathered round the elderly widow whom young Banana had illegally "married." To this couple had attached themselves Tiberun (Banana's unmarried older brother), two younger brothers, and another male orphan who had apparently moved in for want of some better place to eat. The Banana menage thus had somewhat the appearance of a case of economic polyandry and somewhat the look of a fraternity house with an elderly housemother in residence. We include it as Unit VII because by so doing we are able to include in Table 3 all the 109 people who made up the Malauila band in 1928–1929 and allocate all of them to the economic units in which they functioned as food producers and food consumers.

The data in Table 3 merit close study. These seven establishments illustrate in capsule form several of the more significant emphases in Tiwi career patterns; indeed each might be said to illustrate some time point in the life careers of adult men and/or some degree of success or lack of success in becoming an influential man.

THE POLITICS OF WIDOW REMARRIAGE

Ki-in-kumi's large establishment was the sort of setup that every Tiwi sought to achieve but few accomplished. An establishment such as his meant wealth, power, prestige, and influence for its head, and, in Malau, Ki-in-kumi was the only man with such a household. With 11 males, many of them food producing; 16 women, all of them food producing; and several of the girls under 14 able to assist the older women, the amount of food this unit could collect in a day provided an ample food surplus for the establishment. A man whose household was a surplus food producer was a successful man. Moreover, because the large work force that produced the food surplus contained numerous young wives who (usually) could be relied upon also to produce numerous female babies, he was doubly blessed with both the requisites—surplus food and surplus daughters—necessary to increase his influence and make more people beholden to him or dependent on him. Of the 35 married women in Malau, 16, or over 45 percent, were in this one establishment.

By comparison, the other old men of Malau were less successful.[5] Through pooling their work forces, Enquirio and Merapanui had achieved an establishment (Unit II) almost as big as that of Ki-in-kumi, and probably its members ate almost as well as the members of his, but their effort was a shared effort and their influence and prestige had to be divided between them. They had been lucky with daughters but, divided between the two fathers, the 11 daughters in their establishment were less impressive than Ki-in-kumi's 8, and the total of 7 young wives between them was quite overshadowed by Ki-in-kumi's 9. The two old brothers were successful men and headed a successful operation, but their prestige and success must be rated at least one whole degree below that of Ki-in-kumi.

Another pair of elderly brothers, White Man and Ku-nai-u-ua, had also joined forces (Unit III), but the results can be judged as only fair. They were at least the best off of their age group, the 45- to 55-year olds, but the competition in that age group was weak, as can be seen by comparison of their establishment with Units IV and V, the households of Pingirimini and Tipiperna-gerai. Perhaps the best indication of the respective success in life of the seven oldest men is that given in the column of Table 3 headed "young wives." Of the 23 such women in the band, 18 were in the establishments[6] of the three oldest men (Units I and II); the next five men in age shared the remaining five (Units III, IV, and V).

It might be thought that the small establishments of the unsuccessful junior elders like White Man, Ku-nai-u-ua, Pingirimini, and Tipiperna-gerai could be expected to increase sharply in size and these men to grow in relative prestige and influence when death removed the three old men at the heads of Units I and II and made their wives available for redistribution. The working of the Tiwi system made this possibility unlikely. Unsuccessful junior elders could not expect to step into the shoes of successful senior elders merely by outliving them; nor could one rise to power in the gerontocratic system merely by living past 55. What was necessary was age *plus* ability, and the time to demonstrate the ability was in one's thirties. If it was not demonstrated and recognized by then, a man could not forge ahead in his middle forties and early fifties, for by then it was too late. This fact gave a certain cyclical quality to the transfer of influence in Tiwi. The influence of successful senior elders, to the extent that such an intangible thing was transferable at all, tended to skip a decade and bypass the men currently in the junior elder category in favor of the men in the current "young operator" category. Because Ki-in-kumi was already quite old, there was in 1929 a great deal of political maneuvering going on in Malau and elsewhere in anticipation of his death, and it was clear that the people most likely to profit by his death and the redistribution of his 12 resident wives (one-third of all resident wives in the band) were the men aged from 32 to 42 such as Padimo, Boya, Summit,

---

[5] It will be noticed that as we move into the older group of men we have to use their native names, because most of them had no "whiteman" names.

[6] Two of these 18 were of course actually married to Padimo, but still part of the establishment of their father, Ki-in-Kumi, because Padimo's wives all lived with Ki-in-kumi's wives.

and Gitjara, all of whom were jockeying for position to take advantage of the death of any old man, especially such a wealthy elder as Ki-in-kumi. Some of the widows would undoubtedly remarry into other bands, but these younger Malauila, living with or near the old man's establishment, were already taking advantage of their strategic location to make some preliminary deals and marriage arrangements for the old man's widows even before his death. Neither Padimo, as Ki-in-kumi's son-in-law, nor Boya, as his nominal "son," could themselves marry any of the widows, but as resident members of his establishment and the only two men so situated, each was in an excellent spot to act as an honest broker in the disposal of Ki-in-kumi's large estate. Anybody interested in obtaining a widow or two at the death of Ki-in-kumi was well advised to have a few quiet words with either Padimo or Boya well ahead of time. Both of them had wives who lived and worked every day alongside Ki-in-kumi's womenfolk and thus they each had ideal communication systems to the women's side of the band. This was why they had held off setting up their own separate establishments though they were both married men. Neither were "heirs" of Ki-in-kumi in any strict Western use of that word, but it was obvious that it was their careers that would be promoted and their spheres of influence that would be enhanced by the death of Ki-in-kumi. The junior elders, all approaching or past the age of 50 with only small establishments and small spheres of influence, were being bypassed in the transfer of the old man's assets.

Every Tiwi anxious to obtain a Ki-in-kumi widow recognized the strategic positions of Padimo and Boya; the problem was to decide which broker to retain, because the positions of the two men in relation to Ki-in-kumi were so different. For the past four or five years Padimo had been the right-hand man and trusted lieutenant and undoubtedly it was he upon whom Ki-in-kumi was relying to carry out his own wishes about the distribution of his widows. We said earlier that old men found it difficult to control the remarriage of their widows with the same unchallenged authority with which they bestowed their daughters. Nevertheless they tried hard in many cases to do so. Ki-in-kumi was one who tried hard to make the decisions for his widows, by selecting Padimo as his trusted executor. If Padimo faithfully carried out the old man's wishes after he died, then the widows were not likely to come on the open market; they would be redistributed in accordance with the terms of Ki-in-kumi's will (in both senses of the word "will").

Though, of course, Padimo might prove to be a dishonest executor of the estate, there was a safeguard provided in that the new husbands whom Ki-in-kumi had selected for his wives were all aware of his wishes and hence if Padimo tried to depart from those wishes the cheated heirs would bring charges of double dealing and broken promises against him. But regardless of Padimo's honesty after the death, his position as Ki-in-kumi's trusted lieutenant clearly made him an unsuitable agent before the death for those numerous men who wanted some of Ki-in-kumi's future widows and who had not seen any indication that Ki-in-kumi had included them among his beneficiaries. The obvious young man for such men to use as their go-between and agent was Boya. Ki-in-kumi was hostile to him and had given him nothing willingly. Boya's presence in the old man's establishment was based on the nominal tie of Ki-in-kumi being the last husband of his mother to rename him before she died. Viewed thus, the two young men in Ki-in-kumi's household can be said to have become agents for two different networks of intrigue. Padimo was the manager and agent for all the men, including Ki-in-kumi himself, who wanted to perpetuate and continue the existing alliances and arrangements that Ki-in-kumi had built or helped to build during his long and successful career; Boya was the natural agent for all the men who, being outside that set of alliances, had nothing to gain from Ki-in-kumi's death unless his death dissolved the network of alliances and arrangements of which Ki-in-kumi had been the main architect. Padimo's responsibility was necessarily a sort of holding-together and preserving operation as the executor of an existing estate; Boya's clients were men hoping for fragmentation and subdivision not only of Ki-in-kumi's widows but also of the alliances and deals of which the widows were a part.

It is incidentally amusing, and also indicative of how the ever-present kinship ties affected all such deals and redeals, to note that if some of Boya's clients succeeded in grabbing off some of Ki-in-kumi's widows—despite the opposition, before his death, of Ki-in-kumi and the presumed opposition, after the death, of Padimo the executor—they were very liable thus to become automatically fathers-in-law of Padimo, because several of Ki-in-kumi's wives already had daughters who were bestowed on Padimo.

The question then of which agent was employed by the numerous men yearning to acquire one or more of Ki-in-kumi's widows was fairly well settled by the respective roles that the two young men occupied in the household. Men already well inside the Ki-in-kumi-centered alliances were relying on Padimo; men outside those alliances were relying on Boya to engineer a fluid situation and a more open market. In choosing an agent in this as in any other "deal," there was also the question of fee. Neither Padimo nor Boya would become involved or make any soundings among the widows unless there was something in it for them. Hence the client had to find out whether a promise of general goodwill and friendship was all that Boya (or Padimo) would ask in return for his services or whether the price would be much higher—perhaps as high as the bestowal of the client's next baby daughter. It was in such ways that widow-remarriage arrangements and infant bestowals were intertwined; a much-delayed bestowal to an apparently unrelated individual would be the ultimate payoff to the broker or agent who had engineered a widow remarriage for the bestower years before.

This role of agent in the disposal of a dead man's widows was a type of operation best suited to men in the first stages of their own married lives— that is, to men in their middle thirties or very early forties who had perhaps married their first or second widows and who had as yet no young wives of their own in residence. Having no young wives to guard, they were able to get around easily on diplomatic missions and they had their own listening posts inside the world of women in the person of their own mothers (if still alive) and in the elderly widows whom they themselves had married. The ambitious young brokers were tipped off by their mothers and elderly wives as to how the young wives wished to be distributed and what the competing young brokers were trying to arrange. Thus when a wealthy old man like Ki-in-kumi died, the redistribution of his wives through remarriage was a matter that had been decided beforehand by an extraordinarily complex tangle of semisecret arrangements and deals and promises, but the people most influential in arranging the redistribution were the young brokers who usually got few, if any, of the young widows for themselves but who collected their rewards in reputation, influence, alliances, and future bestowals from the men for whom they had acted as agents.

Thus the death of Ki-in-kumi or of any other old man with many wives tended to disperse the wives all over the tribe, with only one or two, or at most three, going to any one new husband. A large estate was almost always fragmented by the death of the old man who had built it up, and any one of his contemporaries was able to take over only a very small fraction of it at best. The levirate and sororal polygyny, though present, worked very feebly. The men who benefited most—not immediately, but eventually—were the young operators.[7] In such a manner Padimo and Boya were sure to be the long-term beneficiaries of Ki-in-kumi's death though neither of them could remarry any of his widows. The real heirs of the wealthy old men of 60 and over were the young men who happened to be between 32 and 42 when those old men got near to death. The men between 45 and 55 whose brokerage business 10 years earlier had not been very skillfully handled, or who happened to be at the brokering age when no big households were being liquidated, found themselves in the position that Pingirimini and Tipiperna-gerai occupied in 1928–1929. We know they had not been successful dealers in their thirties because we found them around the age of 50 with only one resident wife each and relatively few bestowals in prospect. Their earlier dealings in widows had not laid the right foundations for successful careers as elders. Even before he was 40, Padimo had five or six bestowed wives either in residence or in prospect, and Boya, not much over 40, had several already promised. The death of Ki-in-kumi in the near future would bring both of them more reputation and ultimately more bestowals in return for their skill (if they showed it) in the disposition of the estate. The inferiority of Pingirimini and Tipiperna-gerai to these younger men in the marriage and influence struggle was already apparent and would be even more accentuated by Ki-in-kumi's death.

---

[7] At least some of the so-called "stolen" or disputed wives were widows who had insisted on marrying the younger agent instead of the older client, which put the young broker in the embarrassing position of saying to his client, "I cannot make delivery of the widow I acquired on your account; she insists on marrying me instead." Such an incident did not do his agency business much good but tended rather to frighten off clients.

THE POLITICS OF BESTOWAL

The previous discussion of how younger men were indirectly benefited by the deaths or impending deaths of wealthy older men does not pretend to give an exhaustive list of all the considerations that went into the reallocation of a dead man's widows. We built our analysis around those factors that were paramount in the case of Ki-in-kumi's household. Other cases were different to the extent that there were real adult sons involved in them rather than a nominal "son" like Boya, or because in them the old man had not chosen a clear-cut executor as Ki-in-kumi had chosen Padimo, or because an old man had surviving brothers close to him in age and alliance who would emphasize the levirate principle and seek to have it followed in the relocation of their dead brother's widows. The few points we were seeking to emphasize among the many that might be emphasized in any exhaustive treatment of Tiwi widow remarriage are: (1) that widow remarriage was a very flexible area in which the ultimate disposition of the widows was decided by the manipulations and wishes of a wide range of individuals, including both relatives and nonrelatives. The dead man himself; the fathers of the wives, if still alive; the brothers of the widows, if adults; the widows themselves, if strong minded; the executors of the dead man, if clearly nominated; and the numerous dealers and brokers on behalf of remote clients or even on their own account—all tried to make their own wishes prevail. The result was that no two cases were ever alike, but on balance (2) it was younger men rather than older men who were most likely to enhance their reputations and increase their assets in the long run as the results of these widow redeals, even though in the short run it was the older men who remarried most of the widows, especially the younger widows.

We have briefly discussed what we have labeled the politics of widow remarriage before discussing the politics of infant bestowal, although logically it might appear that infant bestowal should be taken up first. We have followed this order because, in Tiwi life, infant bestowal was reserved for fathers, and a Tiwi was at least a middle-aged man before he became a father at all. Before he could have a daughter to bestow, he had to be the father of one; and before he could become a father, he had to have a baby girl bestowed upon him and wait for her to grow up to child-bearing age. The much-married Ki-in-kumi did not have his first actual daughter (as distinct from wives' daughters begotten by previous husbands) until he was 45, and Enquirio was closer to 50 than to 40 when his first real daughter was born. We are inclined to call such daughters free or unencumbered daughters because the stepdaughters brought into a man's household by widows, even young widows, were already bestowed by act of the widows' previous husbands and the new husband's control over their marriage was therefore encumbered by the dispositions made by his predecessors.

Thus most men did not have and could not expect to have any free or unencumbered daughters to bestow until they were well into their forties. By that time a man was a prisoner of his past. When at last he had free daughters he was no longer a free man but a junior elder with a mass of obligations both to older men and to younger men, which he had contracted in the previous 20 or 30 years. Even his initiation, which had started when he was only about 15, left him under obligation to the older men who had initiated him. Any bestowals he had received had almost necessarily come to him from older men. In his thirties, it is true, he had operated in the widow remarriage area and put some older men under obligation to him by acting as their agent. But in his agency activities he had also contracted debts, usually in fee-splitting or log-rolling agreements with other agents of about his own age. Thus all his past activities, from his initiation at 15 until the arrival of his first free daughter at (let us say) age 45, were on balance a story of obligations contracted and debts of gratitude assumed in his career of upward mobility. The more successful he had been up to now, the stronger the pressure on him to begin paying off those who had helped him, because it was assumed that his very success was a clear indication of how much obligation he must have to other men, especially older men and contemporaries.

If this line of reasoning had been the only relevant one, a Tiwi of age 45 just presented with his first free daughter would have had problem enough deciding which of his many obligations to liquidate first by his bestowal decision for that daughter. Unfortunately he was at the age when he had to consider the future as well as the past. Some of his old obligations were to men who were very old and unlikely to live much longer. Others were to men of his own age with whom he had been partners 10 years before, but by now it was clear that some of these would never amount to much and paying them off would reap no dividends for the future. Failure to meet the obligation might incur their enmity, but in view of their lack of success, perhaps their hostility was a lesser evil. In 1929, Gitjara, who had needed L.F.B. to get his own career launched, was ready to drop him as a partner now that Gitjara had attracted favorable notice in the form of two bestowals. The junior elders, though obligated to older men like Ki-in-kumi, were not bestowing their scanty free daughters on the older men but upon each other while waiting for the power alignment in Malau to change with Ki-in-kumi's death. Perhaps the clearest case of the pull between the obligations of the past and the planning for the future in the bestowal of free daughters was provided by Merapanui. He was a man who owed or thought he owed very little to his elders. None of them had ever bestowed a girl on him, and he reached 50 with nothing but an ancient widow. The fortunate death of an elder brother had suddenly provided him with bestowable daughters rather later in life than the average. By 1929 he had been able to bestow no less than four, and every one of them went to men much younger than himself and in other bands. Merapanui, being relatively free of old debts, was investing his daughters in young men with a future, but unlike Ki-in-kumi who had invested most of his daughters in one younger man, Padimo, old Merapanui believed in diversifying his investments.

Thus the politics of bestowal marriage were just as complicated as the politics of widow remarriage but, because a man was 10 or more years older when he became involved in the former than when he became involved in the latter, a rather different set of motivations prevailed. At 35 as a mobile operator in the widow field, a man was trying to launch a career, and if he had no obvious assets—no living sisters or mother or important mother's brothers—he was often trying to launch it on a shoestring. By 45 the same man was well along in his career and was a junior elder—the head of a household with at least one young wife in residence and a man beginning to have bestowable daughters of his very own. He now saw tribal politics and reputation building in different perspective from the way they had looked to him 10 years earlier. Then he had put his services and his wits and his diplomatic skills at the disposal of older men in order to gain favorable notice from the elders. But now that he was an elder himself, albeit still low in the pecking order of elders, he was no longer their satellite but rather one of them and therefore in competition with them. Now he no longer wanted to build up his client's business; he wanted to build up his own household and his own influence. With the arrival of his first free daughters he was no longer content to work for and accept the leadership of older clients; he was in business as an elder for himself. His free daughters were therefore bestowed not as acknowledgments of his obligations to older men but as inducements to younger men to accept him as their patron. With his first free daughters a man was in position to become emancipated from the dominance of the elders because with the arrival of those daughters he could start bidding against them for the allegiance of men younger than himself.

One of the neatest examples of the switch in life career was provided in 1928 by the case of Tomitari. All Tiwi life careers and marriage arrangements were so tangled that one was delighted to find a relatively open and shut case. Some of the principals involved were relatives of Padimo, who was originally a Rangwila before Ki-in-kumi, his patron, lured him to Malau. Padimo and three sisters were the children of a Rangwila man and woman whom for simplicity's sake we will call Padimo's real father and real mother. The father bestowed the three girls on another Rangwila named Inglis who was about the same age as himself. (If we tried to answer *why* he did, the case would no longer be simple.) Padimo's father died while the four children were still young, and their mother remarried a relatively young man named Tomitari. This occurred in about 1914 and the situation then was as follows:

GENEALOGY I
THE INGLIS-TOMITARI RELATIONSHIP 1914
(Males are in italics; ages are in parentheses)

Padimo's Father (just dead)	1. =		*Padimo's* Mother (40)	=	2. *Tomitari* (30)
Inglis = (44)	Sister I (21)	*Padimo* (20)	Sister II (13)	Sister III (10)	

Fifteen years or so later, all parties were still alive; the two youngest sisters had joined Inglis as wives and all three sisters had borne children to him, including girls. Thus the situation in 1928–1929 was:

GENEALOGY II
(1928–1929)

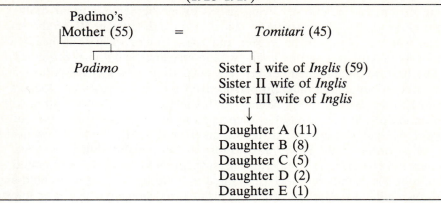

The three sisters of Padimo had borne five daughters to Inglis and as they were successively born Inglis had bestowed the first three on Tomitari. Inglis, however, did not bestow the fourth or fifth nor any of his daughters by other wives on Tomitari.

The master clue to the whole matter was the marriage in 1914 of Padimo's widowed mother to Tomitari, then little more than 30. His function had been to act as trustee or stand-in for Inglis' interest, not in the widow but in her daughters who had been bestowed on Inglis by their dead father. The young Tomitari as stepfather of the girls had to ensure their safe delivery to Inglis' household. (One was there already but the other two were not.) Tomitari accomplished his mission, acquiring the widow, of course, as a wife in the process; the girls arrived safely in Inglis' household and Inglis paid off handsomely by bestowing their daughters on his honest agent who had held off the competitors.

But by 1923 or thereabouts Inglis had stopped paying off. Tomitari by then had received three bestowals from Inglis. (Actually he had received about six, but three died in infancy.) Moreover, he was no longer a young man but was entering the junior elder class and, having received wives from other sources than Inglis, was getting to the point where he would soon have free daughters of his own. He had no intention of performing any more services for Inglis who was now nearly 60. Hence Inglis had not bestowed any daughters on Tomitari since 1923; those of his daughters who had been born since that year were bestowed on men other than Tomitari and men who were younger and less successful than he.

As we see it, the deals involving widows, particularly the payoffs to young agents for acting to promote the interests of older men, had distorted what might be called the pure theory of Tiwi bestowal. According to the pure theory, mothers' brothers bestowed their daughters on selected sisters' sons, and the older man who gave a young man a wife and became his wife's father was performing a kindness toward a favorite nephew for which the nephew should be grateful. But the Inglis-Tomitari operation shows how the theory had become distorted in practice. In order that Inglis might have some young daughters whom he would be free to bestow on his favored young nephew, Tomitari, in 1914 he had had to arrange the young man's marriage with an elderly widow to ensure safe delivery to him (Inglis) of some young wives who would bear him those daughters. Everything went smoothly and no slipup occurred, yet by the time Inglis was in a position to give a wife to his favored young nephew, he found that the latter was no longer a dependent young man but a successful junior elder, competing with him in his own field of identifying and using talent among the younger men. Tomitari's first daughter, born in 1927—not to any daughter of Inglis but to an older wife—was bestowed by its father on the distant but very promising Gitjara, a man of 32. Gitjara was thus selected by Tomitari as a promising satellite at about the same age as Tomitari in 1914 had been selected by Inglis. Moreover, Tomitari by this time, far from being the grateful nephew of old Inglis (as the theory stipulated), was looking forward with anticipation to the old man's death, because when that occurred, among the widows of Inglis would be the three sisters of Padimo of whom he was still the nominal father. It was by acting as their stepfather when they were children that he had got his own career started. They were indeed the foundation stone of his own career and, having profited so much from them as children, he was keenly interested in their redisposition whenever Inglis' death should put them on the market again. Thus he was simultaneously the husband of some of Inglis' daughters and nominal father of some of Inglis' wives. In the first status, he was expected by the theory to be a grateful son-in-law of Inglis; in the second status, the facts of Tiwi life required him to see Inglis' death as providing him with an opportunity to derive some new benefits for himself from his position as nominal father of the three wives of Inglis whose delivery to Inglis' household he had himself engineered.

Thus the politics of bestowal cannot be separated from the politics of widow remarriage. Every case of one had endless repercussions in the other. Sisters' sons who were promised young wives by their mothers' brothers were always too old to be grateful by the time the bestowal occurred or by the even later time when the bestowed child was old enough to come into residence. Mothers' brothers, in turn, were unable to endow their nephews any earlier because they as younger men had been caught in the same trap. The only way out was by deals in which older men and younger men collaborated. Ideally such collaborative efforts should always have been between mothers' brothers and sisters' sons, but amid such fierce competition and endless log rolling this was not possible, and in many cases the mother's-brother—sister's-son relationship was a *result* of collaboration between older man and younger man rather than a cause. The bond arose from the deal rather than from their original kinship, particularly when the two men involved were very close in age.

The collaborative deals between older men and younger men were essentially designed to compensate for the older man's inability to bestow a young wife upon the younger man at a reasonable age. As was stated before, not until he was about 45 would the older man have a free or unencumbered daughter. By then his younger collaborator and satellite had attracted the attention of older and wealthier men with many unencumbered daughters. After performing all his services to Inglis, young Tomitari had not had to depend on him for his first bestowal. A wealthier man than Inglis had reached over Inglis' head, so to speak, and bought Tomitari's allegiance by the bestowal of a young wife who provided Tomitari with a free daughter several years earlier than any child the daughters of Inglis could provide. With this first unencumbered daughter, Tomitari promptly bid for the allegiance of Gitjara. Put in terms of allegiances, Tomitari had from 1914 until about 1923 been the henchman of Inglis. During those years he passed from about age 30 to age 40, and his main patron was Inglis, who passed from about 44 and on the fringes of the elder group to about 54 and accepted among the elder group. Then—and this was typical of the shift of allegiance that occurred in most life careers—a senior elder more wealthy in wives and daughters than Inglis bid for Tomitari's allegiance, and Tomitari became his henchman. Five years later, in 1928, Tomitari was a coming junior elder in Rangu and a man of influence in his own right. His oldest bestowed wife had already borne him a daughter whom he used to make Gitjara *his* henchman. The three wives (daughters A, B, and C) of Inglis were nearing the stage when they would join his household and he had other bestowals from other quarters. His relation to Inglis was no longer that of henchman but of rival, because they were now both successful elders in the same band and competitors in the struggle to make younger men dependent on them. Far from bestowing any more daughters on Tomitari, Inglis was bestowing his daughters (now plentiful) on men of Gitjara's generation (though not on Gitjara). Having more free daughters than Tomitari, he had more men of that generation to patronize, but because Inglis was 60 and Tomitari only 45, time was obviously on the side of the latter.

Thus the crux of the Tiwi system of influence-satelliteship-marriage arrangement-wealth centered around what happened to a man in his thirties. This is what we meant when we said earlier that old men with many daughters bestowed them on young men who looked to them like "comers." Old men with many free daughters were usually well over 50. "Comers" were men in their thirties. In so choosing the "comers," the old and wealthy men reached right over the junior elders and the 40-year-old group down to the ranks of the young operators. In this way we may say that the real power group, the successful old gerontocrats, chose their own successors. They chose young men 20 or more years younger than themselves (as Ki-in-kumi chose Padimo) because men at such an age were not rivals or competitors. A man so chosen in his thirties could be already powerful and fairly wealthy by his middle forties (like Tomitari in 1928) and very wealthy in his fifties. Such men went up fast because of their selection by the group in power. Those not so chosen had to go up the hard way by accumulating what position and influence they could by manipulations of the few available females not controlled by the wealthy old men. The "haves" left a small minority of women available to the "have-not" men to keep them quiet, but the great majority of females were concentrated in the hands of a few old men and these old men chose their own successors. Thus the Tiwi system actually deserves to be called a primitive oligarchy as much as it deserves to be called a gerontocracy. It was run by a few old men who ruled it not so much because they were old but because as young men they had been clever and then had lived long enough to reap the rewards of their cleverness. These rewards made up Tiwi wealth—many wives, much leisure, many daughters to bestow, many satellites and henchmen, and much power and influence over other people and tribal affairs.

of the system were soon forced back into conformity by outraged public opinion and its punitive sanctions. Unless he fled to the mainland with his girl, the young bachelor who stole an old man's young wife had to restore her sooner or later to her rightful husband. Under pre-white conditions they could not flee to the mainland; if they tried, they both probably drowned on the way or at least were never heard of again.

Thus the isolation of the Tiwi made the rule of the gerontocracy much more absolute, and the enforcement of it much more effective than was possible for any of the mainland tribes where violators of the rules could skip across the border. Tiwi bachelors had to be satisfied, by and large, with casual and temporary liaisons and even in these, because of the constant suspicion of the old husbands and the constant spying and scandalmongering of the old wives, they had to be prepared to be often caught and, when caught, to be punished. Thus we come to another of the main emphases in Tiwi culture—the enormous frequency of disputes, fights, duels, and war parties arising directly or indirectly out of cases of seduction. If we may call this area of life the legal area, then over 90 percent of legal affairs were matters in which women were in some way involved.

The Duel   The Tiwi formula for handling seduction was very straightforward and clear-cut in its formal outline. Because senior men had young wives and young men had not, seduction was necessarily viewed as an offense by a young man against a senior man. Hence the charge was always laid by the senior and the younger man was always the defendant.[1] At night in camp the accuser hurled his charges at the offender. We described earlier the alternatives available at this stage to both parties. Two of those alternatives were for the old man to press the matter to a public "trial," either the next day, if the camp was already a large one, or else on the next occasion when both men were present in a big gathering.

The basic shape of all Tiwi trials was standardized in the form that we have been calling the duel. Everybody present—men, women, chldren, and dogs—formed a rough circle in an open space, sitting or standing according to their degree of excitement at the moment. At one end stood the accuser, the old man, covered from head to foot in white paint, with his ceremonial spears in one hand and a bundle of the more useful hunting spears in the other. At the opposite end stood the defendant, with little or no paint on him, perhaps holding a hunting spear or two in his hand (a sign of insolence), perhaps holding only throwing sticks (less defiant, because the stick was an inferior weapon more appropriate to young men), or perhaps entirely weaponless (a sign of proper humility and the deference to his seniors that all bachelors ought to show in such situations). The accuser, with many gestures, partic-

---

[1] Under pre-white conditions this had to be so. After the arrival of the Catholic missionaries, some young men through Mission manipulation got a young wife at an age that would have been impossible earlier. This resulted in an occasional case around the Mission where a *young* husband charged a man older than himself with seducing his wife. The resulting duel, with an older man as defendant, was regarded by the Tiwi as both embarrassing and ludicrous, perhaps analogous to the average American's attitude toward female professional wrestlers. (See Hart, 1954 for a case of this sort, the duel of Bob v. Louis.)

ularly with much stamping of the feet and chewing of the beard, told the young man in detail precisely what he and all right-minded members of the community thought of him. This angry, loud harangue went into minute detail, not only about the actual offense, but the whole life career of the defendant, and paid particular attention to occasions in the past when the old man even remotely, or some of his relatives, even more remotely, had performed kindnesses toward either the young man or some of his relatives. It is difficult to summarize briefly one of these harangues, but the general formula, subject to much variation by each individual accuser, appeared to be the building up of as much contrast as possible between the criminal or antisocial character of the young man's actions and the fact that he was a member of a network of interpersonal relationships in which mutual aid and reciprocal obligations were essential. The Tiwi orators, of course, did not put the matter in such abstract terms. They listed the long catalogue of people who had done things for the young man since his birth, and for his ancestors and relatives, until the catalogue took in practically the whole tribe—past, present, and future. And what had he done to repay his obligations to all these people? "Why, the miserable, ungrateful wretch spends his time hanging around my camp, etc., etc. And not only my camp, but last year it was widely believed that he was indulging in similar actions around the camp of my esteemed fellow-elder, So and So." We do not think that we are overintellectualizing the content of these harangues if we say that they involved the old man's reminding the young man of his debt to society, and his attempting to convey the idea that social life needed mutual aid and trust between all its members.

After 20 minutes or so of this sociological abuse and blame pinning, the old man threw aside his ceremonial spears and began to throw his hunting spears at the defendant. This active phase of the duel conformed to a stereotyped pattern, which in some respects resembled baseball. The old man stood about 10 feet farther away from the young man than the pitcher stands from the plate. The young man had to avoid being hit by the spears. To do this he was permitted to jump from side to side or into the air, or to duck, but he was expected always to land on approximately the same spot as he had been standing on when the first spear was thrown. Thus there was no marked strike zone, but an implied one. If the accused jumped well away from the strike zone, he was jeered by the crowd. If the old man was wild, he was jeered too, but more respectfully. Under such rules a modern baseball hitter, having no bat in his hand to worry about, would almost never be hit by an old man's spears. The main danger was the spear that pitched in the dirt. Although clearly outside the strike zone and hence an indication that the old man was really wild, such a spear was likely to carom off the ground at an unexpected angle and inflict a severe wound before the spectators (as collective umpires) had time to call it—in which case the duel was over and the accused was punished.[2]

---

[2] Two cases of broken legs below the knee within 6 weeks of each other in 1928 give some indication of the force with which such badly aimed spears would bounce off the ground.

Apart from those that unpredictably deflected off the ground, or even off a neighboring tree, the young man could dodge the old man's spears indefinitely if he wanted to. He was much younger and hence almost invariably in much better shape than the older man. But if he did this, the old man soon began to look a little ridiculous, and Tiwi society thoroughly disapproved of young men who made old men look ridiculous in public. Continued dodging and jumping and weaving of the body, no matter how gracefully they were done, were not prolonged by any man who hoped in time to become a respected elder himself. The elders in the last analysis controlled bestowals, and holding one of them up to public ridicule was sure to antagonize all of them. So the young man, having for 5 or 10 minutes demonstrated his physical ability to avoid being hit, then showed a proper moral attitude by allowing himself to be hit. This took even greater skill in bodily movement. Trying to lose a fight without making it too obvious to the crowd and without getting hurt too much oneself is a problem that confronts some professional athletes in our own culture, and few of them do it with as much skill as the younger Tiwi in the same situation. A fairly deep cut on the arm or thigh that bled a lot but healed quickly was the most desirable wound to help the old man inflict, and when the blood gushed from such a wound the crowd yelled approval and the duel was over. The young man had behaved admirably, the old man had vindicated his honor, the sanctity of marriage and the Tiwi constitution had been upheld, and everybody went home satisfied and full of moral rectitude. Seduction did not pay.

This was the Tiwi duel as it ideally should be conducted, and in perhaps as many as two-thirds of all such disputes it was so conducted. Divergences from this form clearly arose from the unpredictability of human beings and their fondness for trying to exercise choice instead of following a set pattern. Though the dice were heavily loaded against them, some Tiwi young men chose defiance instead of repentance. There were various avenues of defiance open to them. The mildest was to refuse to allow the old man's spears to hit the target. Slightly more brazen were the young men who turned up at the beginning of the duel with throwing sticks or hunting spears in their hands, even though they used these not to throw but to knock aside contemptuously the spears of the old man. More brazen still was the young man, rare but not unknown, who went so far as to throw missiles back at the older accuser. All such attempts to defy the traditional pattern of the duel met with the same response, and that very quickly. The duel began as usual with the two antagonists facing one another inside the circle of spectators. As soon as it became apparent that the young man was not conforming to the normal pattern of meekness and nonretaliation, there would be immediate activity on the sidelines. Two or three or four senior men would leave the spectators and range themselves alongside the accuser, spears in hand. Other senior men would quietly leave their seats and sit down in the audience alongside close relatives of the young defendant, particularly his full brothers or his father, if they were present, and gently lay restraining hands upon them. Within a few minutes there was no longer an old man facing a young man but as many as four or five old men facing one young man, and no sign of support for him. His close male relatives would keep their seats or (more often) allow themselves to be led away as if they did not want to witness what was coming next. Never, in any of these cases, did any supporter of the young man step into the ring and line up with him. He remained an isolate, faced by several older men, and of course he had no chance. It was easy to dodge the spears of one opponent, because they had to be thrown one at a time; it was impossible to dodge the spears of more than one, because they could be thrown more or less simultaneously.

Usually this baring of its teeth by society-at-large was enough. The group of elders did not need to throw many spears simultaneously. The accused capitulated by throwing aside his spears or throwing sticks, or if the defiance had been only of the mildest form—namely, an undue prolongation of the dodging—he allowed his accuser to score a direct hit and the duel ended in the normal way. In the rare cases of the accused refusing to give up, even when confronted by a menacing line of several elders, a concerted volley or two from them quickly knocked him out, and in pre-white days, usually killed him.[3] Crime thus paid even less for the accused who chose defiance than it did for the accused who allowed himself to be wounded in a duel by a doddering ancient three times his age. The greater the amount of defiance, the more clear it became that the doddering ancient, acting ostensibly as an outraged husband, was the responsible agent of society dispensing public justice. If he needed help, all responsible elders went to his aid, and the kinsmen of the accused stood aside and let justice take its course.

Warfare   Apart from the occasional castaways and the very occasional other visitors such as "Malays," the Tiwi in pre-white times had nobody to fight with except each other. Duels of the type we have just described were their only formula for settling disputes, and these occasionally became sufficiently broadened to warrant being called warfare. The expedition of Tiklauila and Rangwila to the country of the Mandiimbula, which was listed in Chapter 2 among the travels of Tu'untalumi in 1928, was an example of this sort of activity. At least half a dozen senior members of the two first-named bands had disputes with various individuals among the Mandiimbula. Some of these were seduction cases but some of them involved charges by elder against elder, of nondelivery of bestowed daughters, or other types of broken promises. Some of these cases had been going on for years, and settlement of them at the level of the individual duel had failed. The aggrieved individuals in the two Bathurst Island bands therefore pooled their grievances, persuaded many of their relatives and friends who were not aggrieved to join them, and a large party of men of all ages set off for the Mandiimbula territory.

---

[3] Since the coming of white administration, the Tiwi have found that when a man is killed in a native duel, there is a strong likelihood that white policemen will appear and will drag some of them off to Darwin where incomprehensible proceedings called murder trials then take place. To avoid such nonsense, since about 1925 they have tended to use throwing sticks rather than spears in their fighting. Throwing sticks, although dangerous, seldom kill people outright and as long as nobody is killed, the police in Darwin show no interest in native fights on the islands.

This party, comprising about 30 fighting men all heavily armed and all wearing the white paint indicative of anger and hostile intent, was a "war" party, and its coming to their territory was recognized as such by the Mandiimbula. On arrival at the place where the latter, duly warned of its approach, had gathered, the war party announced its presence. Both sides then exchanged a few insults and agreed to meet formally the next day in an open space where there was plenty of room. After a night mostly spent by both sides in individual visiting and renewing old acquaintances, the two armies met next morning in battle array, with the 30 Tiklauila-Rangwila warriors drawn up at one end of the clearing, and about 60 local warriors at the other end. Immediately the familiar patterns of the duel imposed themselves. A senior individual on one side began a harangue directed at an individual on the other. When he ran out of breath, another individual began his complaint. Because each accused Mandiimbula replied individually to the charges made against him, the whole proceeding remained at the level of mutual charges and replies between pairs of individuals. Angry old men on both sides often seemed to be trying to find a basis that would justify or provoke a general attack by one group upon the other, but always failed to find it because of the particularity of the charges. The rules of Tiwi procedure compelled the accuser to specify the sources of his charges and his anger, and these always turned out to be directed not at the Mandiimbula band, but at one, or at most two or three, individual members of that band. And when another old man took the center of attention, his anger would be directed at quite different individuals. Hence when spears began to be thrown, they were thrown by individuals at individuals for reasons based on individual disputes. Unlike the seduction duels, however, these duels occurred mostly between two senior men, and the danger of a direct hit was much reduced because of the poor marksmanship of both parties. On the other hand, the danger of somebody getting hurt was increased because a fight between two old men was likely to spread as other older men were drawn into it to support one on the other side—in which case, a wild melee occurred with badly thrown spears flying in all directions. This was probably a good thing, because soon somebody was bound to be hit, thus ending the fight. Not infrequently the person hit was some innocent noncombatant or one of the screaming old women who weaved through the fighting men, yelling obscenities at everybody, and whose reflexes for dodging spears were not as fast as those of the men.

As soon as somebody was wounded, even a seemingly irrelevant old woman, fighting stopped immediately until the implications of this new incident could be assessed by both sides. For such an old one was never really irrelevant; she was somebody's mother and somebody else's wife and somebody else's sister and therefore the question of who threw the spear that wounded her gave rise to a new series of wrangles, which had to be integrated into all the old ones. A man who had been quietly sitting, minding his own business and having no quarrels with anybody, would suddenly leap into the center of the stage and announce that the damaged old lady was his mother and therefore he wanted the hide of the rat that had damaged her, and a whole new argument was in progress.

If the person wounded in the first flurry of spear throwing was a senior male, that similarly led the arguments off in some new direction because his kinsmen in *both* war parties felt compelled to support him or revenge his wound or inflict a wound on his wounder. Frequently it appeared that the original matters of dispute, which had brought the two war parties together in the first place, were forgotten and lost in the new disputes and fights that originated on the field of battle. Such a view was supported by the frequency with which one found at the end of the day that the main casualties and the main headline performers had been people who had gone to the field of battle in the morning with no quarrel with anybody, and not even wearing white paint. Even the most peaceful spectator in the most remote corner of the gallery was likely to find himself in the center of the ring before the day was over at a Tiwi "battle."

Despite this apparent confusion and near anarchy of procedure, however, the main outlines were quite clear. The bands were not firm political entities and therefore could not do battle, as bands, with each other. Everybody, on both sides, was interrelated in the same kinship system. An angry old Tiklauila, abusing and throwing spears at an angry old Mandiimbula, might have as the basis of his complaint the fact that the Mandiimbula father had promised but not delivered one of his daughters. Because Tiwi bestowals were from mother's brother to sister's son, the spear throwing was patently a case of sister's son abusing his mother's brother, and the fact that the two men belonged to different bands was not germane to their dispute. The angry Tiklauila elder could not demand support from other Tiklauila *as Tiklauila* in the case at issue for it involved a dispute between kinsmen whose band affiliations were irrelevant to the subject matter. Mainly for this reason the so-called war party of one band against another band turned out to be only a loose collection of individuals, each with his own case to argue, who found it convenient, and safer, to travel together into the territory of another band and argue all their individual cases on the same day at the same place. Tiwi interpersonal relations were primarily kin relations between members of all bands, territorial loyalties were shifting ones, temporary and necessarily quite subordinate to kin loyalties. Hence warfare, in the sense of pitched battles between groups aligned through territorial loyalties, did not occur and could not occur among the Tiwi.

The confusion of the so-called battle itself was also due to the primacy of kinship and friendship ties. When a man with a grievance started his harangue on a battlefield, he was never quite sure of what support he would get or where it would come from. He was pretty much on his own, even though he had arrived there as a member of a large war party. This situation stemmed from the coexistence, on the one hand, of the intricate web of kinship that united everybody present and made the problem of who would support whom unpredictable enough, and, on the other, the intricate network of deals and promises and personal alliances and obligations that every senior Tiwi man had woven inside the kinship system. A Tiwi elder did not, for example, have one category of relatives called his mother's brothers; he had at least three different categories of mother's brothers. There were those mother's brothers who had given him nothing, those who had given him wives, and those who had promised him a wife but were dragging their feet on delivery, or even trying to renege on their promise. In pressing a case against one of this third category, an elder might quite conceivably alienate some of his mother's brothers of the second category. Nor could he be sure of the support of even his own brothers, because they were certainly cultivating, and possibly undercutting him with, the same donors of daughters as he was involved with. Perhaps the nondelivery, which was the whole basis of his case against the mother's brother, had been instigated by his own brother trying to engineer a rebestowal of the girl to him. Because of the two networks, that of formal kinship obligations and that of marriage deals, two Tiwi seniors engaged in a dispute had no impartial body to whom they could submit their arguments about breach of contract. Disputes between a young man and an elder could be submitted to the publicly witnessed duel, because these were not breaches of contract but cases of trespass by the young men, and as such were crimes. Impartial public opinion upheld the old men and punished the young men every time. The old men's arguments with each other, however, could not be so adjusted, because they involved marriage deals (as distinct from seduction) and in marriage deals everybody was involved and nobody was impartial. Where any senior stood on any marriage deal in dispute depended on how that deal fitted into his own conniving. In that area of life, every adult man had his own axes to grind and a disinterested group of umpires was impossible to find.

Thus Tiwi battles had to be the confused, disorderly, inconclusive things they always were. They usually lasted all day, during which about two-thirds of the elapsed time was consumed in violent talk and mutual abuse between constantly changing central characters and satellites. The remaining third of the time was divided between duels involving a pair of men who threw spears at each other until one was wounded, and brief flurries of more general weapon throwing involving perhaps a dozen men at a time, which ended whenever somebody, even a spectator, was hit. As a result of this full day of violence, perhaps a few of the cases would be settled that night—by a father handing over his delayed daughter, or a man with a disputed wife relinquishing her to her rightful husband—but when the war party left next day to return home, the number of cases settled was likely to be less than the number of new feuds, grievances, and injuries that had originated during the day of battle. For not only did the participants carry away from the battlefield a vivid memory of all the physical wounds, intended or accidental, inflicted by whom on whom, but they also brooded long and suspiciously upon who had supported whom and why, either verbally or with spear in hand. In addition, all the incidents of the battle, in minute detail, were relayed to the rest of the tribe who had not been present, and many of these absentees would discover, among the proceedings, things they did not like or suspicious-looking actions on the part of some of their competitors or putative friends. These they would weave into their own strategies and store up for future use. An elder frequently found some basis for a new grievance against somebody in the events of a battle at which he had not even been present.

Finally, through all these disputes and hostile actions between senior men ran their united suspicion of bachelors. The only "battle" in two years between large groups drawn from distinct bands that had a clear-cut and definite final act was one fought in Rangu in late 1928. On that occasion, after disputing and fighting among themselves from early morning until mid-afternoon, all the old men present from both war parties gradually channeled all their anger toward one unfortunate young Mandiimbula bachelor whom they finally accused of going around from band to band creating misunderstandings between various elders. Several elders on both sides testified publicly that their mistrust of each other had started shortly after the bachelor in question had begun hanging around their households; whereupon the senior warriors of the two opposing armies had no difficulty in deciding that most of their suspicions of each other "were all his fault," and with great unanimity ganged up on the bachelor and quickly clubbed him into unconsciousness for being a trouble-maker and a suspicion spreader. In the midst of battle the gerontocracy had reasserted its solidarity by finding a bachelor scapegoat upon whom to unload all their mutual suspicions and aggressions.

SNEAK ATTACKS
by Arnold R. Pilling

In the years since 1959, when the first edition of *The Tiwi* was written, Pilling occasionally reviewed those features of Tiwi society that by reason of culture change or seeming nonsignificance had been omitted from the original 1960 monograph. Of these characteristics, it has now become obvious that at least one is of such theoretical significance that its continued omission is inappropriate. It is to be noted that this area was never explicitly discussed between Hart and Pilling during their few conversations before the death of Hart; nor has Pilling had the opportunity to review Hart's surviving fieldnotes in relation to these topics.

This feature of Tiwi society—the sneak attack—occurred in the area of legal behavior and completely disappeared from Tiwi practice as a by-product of Cooper's mainlanders' gun using in 1911, about the time that Bathurst Island Mission was founded and well before Hart's visit of the late 1920s.

The term *kwampi* designates those Tiwi males who formerly attempted to kill or injure during sneak attacks. Such raids used secrecy and deception as techniques. Pilling recorded 19 pre-Cooper trouble cases involving *kwampi*; four such episodes took place in the Cooper period; none after the Mission was founded. Pilling's cases listed 54 deaths at the hands of *kwampi* and 19 injuries. Of the deaths, only four of the killed were women; killings of females were considered improper. *Kwampi* attacks could occur at night, just before dawn, or in the daytime. Tiwi took special precautions when they expected a *kwampi* raid; a watch was kept at night while the camp slept. When the danger was considered especially great, the active adult males slept in hiding on islets in the mangroves. *Kwampi* employed the giant, finely carved, highly

Photo 10. The five objects on the left are kwampi *spears, the highly carved and painted spears formerly used by Tiwi during their sneak attacks.*

painted, double-barbed spears as their weapons. It was such spears that pincushioned the body of the British doctor killed by Tiwi in the 1820s.

In the ideal *kwampi* pattern, the brother of a man unjustly killed sneaked up and killed his brother's murderer. As Cabbagee said to Pilling of such a counter-killing: "That proper. Clear."

The following *kwampi* case as told to Pilling by Rita and Pawpaw occurred about 1891: Five Malauila youths, including Puti of the Crocodile clan and Paparanirilamani, went visiting the Tiklauila homeland. While they were there, Paparanirilamani seduced a wife of Parlipamarangata, a local Crocodile clansman; and the latter learned of it. When the five visitors were traveling homeward, Parlipamarangata and three of his "brothers" in the Crocodile clan ambushed the group, spearing Paparanirilamani. The latter ran off and was never seen again; the avenging husband had overracted. When the four Crocodile clansmen returned home, Pungamurnuwa, the Tiklauila leader of the clan of Paparanirilamani's father, demanded that the death be avenged; and Parlipamarangata and one of his clan "brothers" in the *kwampi* party were speared before they swam away to safety. Malauila and Rangwila men also decided to avenge the death of Paparanirilamani; they came as *kwampi* and speared, but did not kill, Parlipamarangata and Pungamurnuwa, the latter injury being appropriate. The injured men ran away, shouting, as Pawpaw put it: "Fair go"; and that ended the matter.

In nineteenth-century Tiwi society, injury, and sometimes death, at the hands of *kwampi* was an accepted form of dealing with a wrongdoer without any duel having to be prearranged. It allowed punishment of a nonlocal hostile party to occur. Without such an alternative available after 1911, only the sanctions of the imposed Australian national legal system acted as a brake on continued hostilities between antagonistic groups.

The novice anthropologist is warned by this instance not to overlook social control patterns that have recently been forced out of use by a controlling power. The surviving tribal culture may be thought of as only a part-culture, for it has significantly altered its ways; patterns imposed by the dominant culture now, in fact, having to be included to understand the society as it is working in what might be called "the colonial period." It is noteworthy that the luminary, early twentieth-century anthropologist Malinowski, well known for his study of the Trobriand Islanders near New Guinea, reported a society controlled primarily by public opinion, when, in fact, it was one in which the British, with their own resident armed force, had recently barred local leaders from meting out capital punishment.

RELIGIOUS ACTIVITIES

If by religious activities we mean those beliefs and practices that pertain to unseen or supernatural forces, including rituals whose performance somehow affects those forces, then Tiwi religion readily crystallized around three focal points. These were: (1) their elaborate system of day-to-day taboos; (2) the elaborate set of beliefs and rituals pertaining to death; and (3) their complicated initiation ceremonies for young men. Add to these their myths and folklore about creation and their tribal past, and the whole of Tiwi religion has been covered. Space permits only brief mention of these three focal points.

Taboo   In earlier chapters we have pointed out several aspects of life in which Tiwi culture diverged sharply from what anthropologists have come to regard as Australian mainland norms, and we have suggested that these differences from the mainland are most reasonably to be attributed to either Tiwi isolation or favorable food supply, or some combination of both factors. In their religious life this same line of explanation continues to have validity. To those familiar with the cultures of Australian tribes, perhaps nothing is so startling as to be told that the Tiwi almost completely lacked what we must call "negative" magic or sorcery. Such familiar mainland practices as bone pointing or "singing" a man to injury or death were completely unknown on the islands, and though references to people dying through supernatural agency were often made, it was very hard to learn of magical techniques or known practitioners. Briefly, the Tiwi may be said to have believed that magical acts were possible but to have lacked any knowledge of how to perform them. If, as anthropology is wont to teach, magic is used in the simpler societies to handle and control the unpredictable or mysterious areas of life, then this absence of magic among the Tiwi needs an explanation. Our hypothesis is that the Tiwi did not use magic in human relations because they had never invented magic for use in other unpredictable areas of life—for example, to control the natural world. And they had never invented magic to control their natural world because their physical environment was on the whole a satisfactory and not a hostile universe.

If we run through the areas of life that many of the simpler peoples use magical means to control, we find that many of them were not problems for the Tiwi. The rainfall and water supply were more than adequate; the food supply was good, needing only people to come and gather it; wild animals (except snakes and crocodiles) were unknown; tropical diseases (except yaws) scarcely existed; cyclones, tornados, and earthquakes were very rare, and thunder and lightning were no more frightening there than in, say, Chicago. Death, of course, is mysterious and unpredictable everywhere, but to handle that they had most elaborate burial and mourning customs that were not magical but collective rituals. Perhaps the most favorable feature in the whole friendly Tiwi universe was the absence of any neighboring tribe. Their cultural isolation removed all fear or suspicion of what the foreigners next door might be up to, and one gets the impression from the literature, though it has not been systematically explored, that the hotbeds of magic making and sorcery were areas of the primitive world, like Melanesia or Central Australia, where people were acutely conscious of their neighbors and always expecting magic and sorcery to be directed by them across the village or tribal boundaries. The Tiwi, having no neighbors, had nobody to be suspicious of except each other, and their suspicions of each other were mostly rational suspicions, of men motivated like themselves and using the same political tricks against each other.

The strongest support for the hypothesis that the Tiwi found their environment a friendly and reassuring universe to live in comes from their wide elaboration and reliance upon the forms of magic called taboo. As a tribe they were magic free, but they were taboo ridden. Their generic word for anything sacred or forbidden or untouchable was *pukimani*, a word that in its most common form referred to a state of special being in which a person or thing temporarily was. Thus mourners were *pukimani* for the period of their mourning, youths undergoing initiation were *pukimani* during the ceremonies, a woman who had just given birth was *pukimani* for a week or two afterward. Dead bodies were *pukimani* until buried; graveposts were *pukimani* once erected on the grave; the names of dead people immediately became *pukimani* on their deaths and could not be used, and the same was true of all the names bestowed by a dead man on the children of his household and all the other words in the language that sounded similar to the name of the dead man.[4] All ceremonials and rituals were *pukimani* as were the main

[4] When a man named Tibuki died in 1928, a crisis occurred at the Mission where the natives were supposed to make their requests in pidgin English. How could they now ask for tobacco, since that word was now *pukimani*?

performers and the armlets, neck ornaments, and other ceremonial objects. People in a *pukimani* state had to observe all sorts of avoidances of and abstentions from everyday actions, particularly with regard to food and sex. Close relatives of dead people could not touch food but had to be fed by nonmourners. That pillar of rigid orthodoxy, Tu'untalumi, was virtually never able to feed himself but was in a *pukimani* state almost the whole year round and needed one of his wives to feed him. (Another advantage of a large household.) Certain spots in the bush or on the banks of streams were *pukimani* places; the dimly seen outline of the Australian coast was *pukimani* as was the ocean near Cape Keith where the Tiwi ancestors had first created the Tiwi world; and finally, the violation of a *pukimani* restriction rendered the violator *pukimani*.

Pukimani as thus applied to people, places, things, names, words, restrictions, and avoidances, meant both sacred and taboo, and was clearly one of that widespread class of words and concepts that is almost standard among the simpler societies. The only noteworthy thing about its Tiwi form is that *pukimani* was a state that people did not actively seek to enter but that happened to people regardless of their wishes. Furthermore, when a man found himself in a state of *pukimani*, his behavior was automatically prescribed for him and for the duration of his *pukimani* condition he observed his avoidances and his abstentions just as automatically as he dropped them when his *pukimani* period expired. When he became *pukimani*, he punctiliously fulfilled the requirements because if he did not, he was likely to be unsuccessful in his enterprises. Big men simply did not dare to be casual about the requirements lest their reputations suffer and they lose face and influence. Less successful men were occasionally explained as probably being secret violators. "His wives and daughters all seem to die young; he must have broken some *pukimani* restrictions sometime" was a reason often given for somebody's failure to be as successful as he might have been. It was noticeable in such explanations of nonsuccess that the failure, or in our terms the bad luck, was attributed to the violation of the taboos, never to the active displeasure of the spirits. The spirits simply did not figure in the picture.

Apart from the big ceremonial occasions, a Tiwi did not have much concern with religion in his everyday life except through some aspect of the *pukimani* system. It was only through *pukimani* that the sacred world impinged upon him at all for most of the year. Because *pukimani* was a condition that could not be actively sought but "just happened" to a person every so often by such common events as the death of a relative, his wife giving birth, or his sister's son being initiated, the attitude of a Tiwi toward the whole *pukimani* state was essentially a passive attitude. *Pukimani* behavior was something one accepted and conformed to when required; it was in no way an active attempt to change nature, people, food, gods, spirits, or anything else in the universe. It is therefore not unreasonable to conclude that because their *pukimani* system offered them no handle by which to seek actively to alter the universe in which they lived, the Tiwi found that universe to their liking as it was. Unlike the tribes of central Australia who lavished a lot of thought upon magical methods of improving the food supply or the rainfall, the Tiwi believed and acted on the belief that as long as they observed their *pukimani* taboos, the food would continue to be as abundant and the rains as regular as they had always been. The central Australians, by seeking to coerce nature through magic, suggest that they found nature unsatisfactory; the Tiwi, by relying upon passive taboo-observance alone, suggest rather that their relationship to nature was an acceptable equilibrium that they wanted to preserve, not change. And if everybody observed his *pukimani* taboos when required, that equilibrium would remain undisturbed. Hence the antisocial man in Tiwi was not the maker of individual magic (he was unknown, anyway) but the nonobserver of taboo. By his nonobservance he threatened to upset the normally satisfactory equilibrium between man and nature. For a senior Tiwi male to be charged publicly with breaking *pukimani* rules was a disgrace and a blow to his prestige and his position in public opinion. His behavior was possibly a sin against the spirits but it was certainly a shame in the eyes of his fellows. *Pukimani* observance was thus a matter of respectability to a much greater degree than it was a matter of pleasing the spirits.

Death   As was mentioned earlier, death is the natural phenomenon around which the Tiwi had woven their most elaborate web of ritual. The most frequent and most important Tiwi ceremonies were the mourning ceremonies, and they came in three sizes—small, medium, and large—depending on the age, sex, and importance of the dead person. The mourning ceremonies that drew the crowds were not held until some time after the death and burial. All bodies of dead persons were buried within 24 hours of their death by digging a hole near the camp where the death had occurred and placing the body, wrapped in bark, in it. Near most well-used camping spots there was already a graveyard marked by old graveposts, and the latest corpse was buried there or near there. Seldom was the body carried any distance for burial. If a person died even less than a mile from an old burial ground, there was little inclination to carry the body that far. He would be buried, instead, within perhaps a hundred yards of where he died. This had certain awkward repercussions for social organization, because occasionally a person died while away from his home district and, being buried where he died, his ceremonies were held and his posts erected in a district in which his immediate family did not live. Young men often used this to validate a change of residence, giving as their reason for living in a band territory in which they had not grown up, the location there of their fathers' graveposts.

To avoid constant use of the awkward phrase "mourning ceremony," we refer to it as the funeral though it took place some considerable time after the burial of the body. How long a time elapsed between the burial and the funeral depended upon the importance of the dead person. The more important the deceased, the longer it took after his or her burial to prepare for the funeral, both ceremonially and practically. Babies frequently had no funeral ceremonies at all, especially if they died very young and unnamed. Children were given small funerals, held within a month or so after the death, and the people present were merely the members of the local households.

Photo 11. Richard Miller, at Milikapiti in 1980, dancing the Alligator Dance—alligator being his dance group "dreaming"—in honor of his recently deceased relative, the latter being the focus of this mourning ceremony.

Young adult men and all adult women had funerals of medium size, and old men had the biggest funerals of all. Big funerals were rarely held in the wet season because of the height of the grass and bush and the consequent difficulty of travel. The season after the end of the rains (April–May–June) was a favorite time for funerals because by then people were moving again and there was then an accumulated backlog of funerals to be held for people who had died late in the previous dry season or during the wet. The mourning ceremonies of two or more people were sometimes held together; this obviously required that they be buried close together, although they need not have died at the same time. Seeking as usual to increase his importance in the public eye, a man might hold the medium-sized funeral of one of his children at the same time and place as the big funeral of an important elder—provided their graves were close together—even though two or three months had separated the two deaths.

The actual burial of the body immediately after death was usually a small affair attended only by whatever people happened to be in the vicinity. But some Tiwi ancients were on their last legs for months before they finally expired, and it was typical of Tiwi psychology that people should maneuver to be present when a death occurred. Until the anthropologist understood that even death had its political aspects, he could not understand why the Tiwi were always so anxious to hang around the camp of an old man who was taking an awfully long time to die. Because so very little happened at the actual time of death, this desire to be on the spot seemed merely morbid curiosity.[5] But it was not. A death immediately divided the whole tribe into two groups: a small group of relatives who automatically became mourners and therefore in a state of strict taboo, and the rest who were not sufficiently close to the deceased to have to assume a state of *pukimani*. The mourners, being *pukimani*, could do scarcely anything except weep and wail and gash their heads with stone axes. They could not touch the body or wrap it in bark; nor could they dig the grave, nor put the body in, nor fill in the hole. They had to ask nonmourners to carry out these tasks and thus became obligated to those nonmourners for their services. Death, in other words, incapacitated the relatives, so the nonrelatives swarmed in to "help" them— that is, take advantage of their incapacity. A man who could say, "I helped to dig your mother's grave" had a hold for the rest of his life over the man or men to whom he could say it. Such a hold was not as strong, of course, as that of a man who could say, "I helped you get your first bestowed wife," but the difference of obligation was only a difference of degree. The Tiwi were always "helping" each other, but the man who was "helped" therefore "owed" something to his helper. At deaths, mourners mourned and non-mourners did the work; therefore the mourners "owed" the nonmourners, and such debts were carried on the same mental ledgers as other debts, such as marriage debts.

When deaths occurred suddenly and unexpectedly, the mourners had to choose their helpers for the burial from the relatively few people present at the time, and were thus often forced to become obligated to men they did not much relish being under obligation to. At the funerals the same book-keeping mentality prevailed, but because these were not held until months after the death and burial, the chief mourners had time to select their helpers with care and political finesse. Satellites were very useful in this connection, because a man could ask his satellites to perform the necessary ceremonial services and thus get a return from them for the debts of gratitude they already owed him. This was one reason why a skillful Tiwi politician did not by any means select only close kinsmen for satelliteship. A death that made him *pukimani* was likely to make his close kinsmen *pukimani* also, hence he needed some satellites who were not close kinsmen.

In the interval between the burial and the funeral, the chief mourner, on behalf of all the mourners but fairly independently if he were a big man, allocated all the jobs that had to be done in preparation for the funeral. Everybody who came had to be fed by the mourners, and the collection and hoarding of the necessary food devolved on the women of the mourning households. Thus the mourners provided the food, but everything else necessary had to be prepared by nonmourners. The chief item among the ceremonial necessities was the graveposts. The prohibition on mourners ap-

---

[5] How else was one to interpret the reluctance of Hart's party to move on, after spending three weeks waiting for old Tamboo to die, and the old man still lingered on? "Let's wait another day; maybe he'll die tomorrow" was the invariable response to suggestions that we move. "And if he does die, what will happen?" "Nothing; we'll move on then." But this was early in the fieldwork period, before Hart realized the all-pervasive character of Tiwi opportunism.

proaching the body and the grave extended to the posts, and therefore the cutting, carving, erecting on the grave, and painting of these central features of the funeral ceremonies had to be carried out by nonmourners, "asked to cut the posts" by the chief mourner. Here there was much room for influence maneuvers. A big man acting as chief mourner for a dead relative wanted the funeral to be as lavish as possible, to show his own importance. But the more important the nonmourners he selected to cut the posts for him, the more he owed them for their services. Such a request was in the nature of asking a favor, and to ask a favor was to put oneself in a subordinate position, in terms of influence. The Tiwi power orientation was so ingrained that, even when acting as chief mourner, an elder could not avoid making his requests and allocating the ceremonial tasks so as to gain ground if possible, or at least not lose any ground, in the influence and prestige race.

The mourning ceremonies, though prolonged for several days of constant dancing and singing, were rather dull and monotonous,[6] considered as ceremonial. The gaily colored posts erected right on the grave served as a sort of central altar. Every senior male sang and danced in turn "his own dance" and the rest of the men standing in a large circle acted as a major chorus. A large gap was left in the circle of men and into this gap and out again danced the women in a disorderly clump, as a sort of minor chorus.[7] Most of the day was taken up with endless repetitions of these individually owned and individually performed dances, which had no relation whatever to death or the deceased,[8] but which each "owner" used on every ceremonial occasion. In addition, there were a few ritual performances that were special to the fact of death, including the grand finale of every mourning ceremony, when everybody present, led by the mourners, collectively charged the posts and then roared past them into the surrounding bush. This was done to drive the spirits away from the grave finally and forever and thus end the mourners' state of *pukimani*.

We have no space for further details of ceremonial, but enough has been said to indicate that mourning ceremonies, the biggest collective occasions of the Tiwi dry season, were as much political affairs as they were religious occasions. The connecting link was the state of *pukimani* in which death put the relatives. Men in a state of *pukimani* were at a disadvantage in social and political life while that state lasted. They had to ask other people to do things for them. They had to "pay" for these favors. At the same time they could

---

[6] Goodale, who witnessed many funerals and mourning ceremonies at Milikapiti in 1954 and 1980–1981, wrote in 1986 as follows: "I certainly have a different impression."

[7] Goodale, in review of this passage in 1986, pointed out that women did other sorts of dances than these unison choruses. She believed the use of the word "disorderly" did not accurately describe this type of unison dancing by women. She pointed out that in addition to this variety of female dancing, there were/are also personal solo dances performed in much the same vein as the dances by their brothers and other male relatives (Goodale, 1971).

[8] Goodale, who probably has seen more Tiwi mourning dances than Hart, pointed out in 1986 that the individually owned and performed dances, in fact, *do* bear some relation to the deceased. In 1953 and 1954, Pilling also recorded data on the elaborate symbolism involved in these dances and the songs they accompanied, some examples of which are discussed in Pilling's (1970) paper on patterns of change in the Tiwi language.

Photo 12. A corrugated iron house marked as pukimani, *in the Tiwi village at Nguiu, the Roman Catholic Mission, in May 1953. A white flag waving from a cut-down* kwampi *spear has been used as a* pukimani *symbol. This house had been owned by a deceased male. In late June 1954, this building was still so marked. Ultimately, it was to be the subject of a "smoking," that is, the smoke from a cleansing fire would be blown over the house as the focus of a special mourning ceremony for the deceased. The house would later be torn down by the chief mourning male, the man who "paid for" the mourning ceremony, and the individual sheets of corrugated iron would be available for reuse. In 1954, corrugated iron houses and dugout canoes were too valuable to be destroyed or abandoned permanently in mourning for their deceased owners.*

not afford to be niggardly in running their relative's funeral. If they were, they would never live it down. In such an atmosphere we have to conclude that the spiritual welfare of the deceased was relegated to a minor place and that for the mourners the real climax of the days of frenzied grief around the posts came when the spirits were driven away from the grave into the bush and thus their own *pukimani* state, which had been such a political handicap to them for many months, came to an end.

Initiation   Space permits only the barest mention of initiation, which was, together with mourning, the chief vehicle of Tiwi ritual. For females there were no initiation ceremonies, but for males it was a long drawn-out and elaborate affair, marked by successive stages or grades that began with the status of *Marukumarni*, which a boy entered when he was about 14, and did not end finally until he was around 24. Here again we meet the ideology of debt and obligation. The group of men, necessarily older than himself, who initiated a youth thereby put him under obligation to them for the rest of his life. They "did something for him" and years later would bring it up if his subsequent behavior seemed to be directed against their interests. The obligations contracted in initiation, like obligations contracted at burials or mourning ceremonies, were woven into the kinship and influence systems; indeed the relation of a youth to the men who initiated him was often the beginning of a satellite-patron relationship that lasted half his life.

The initiation of a boy had to be undertaken by a group of men who were already fully initiated themselves and who stood to him in the relation of male cross-cousins. Preferably such men were either married to or likely to marry the boy's sisters, an easily met requirement because girls were "married" so much earlier than their brothers. Very senior and successful men did not bother as a rule with initiation sponsorship because it took too much of their valuable time. Hence in practice, most boys at the *Marukumarni* age were taken in hand by a group of men around 40 years of age who were at least betrothed to, if not already married to, the boys' sisters. Such men justified or rationalized their actions by stating that, as the husbands of the boy's sisters, they wanted their little brother-in-law to be made into a man in proper form. In fact, they were usually given the job by the boy's father, who, having bestowed daughters upon them, regarded it as a legitimate request to make of them. It was the duty of male cross-cousins to initiate their wives' little brothers, but in true Tiwi style the father had to request them to do it, and they counted it in their tallies of what they owed him and what he owed them.

Though the father instigated and stage managed the whole affair, he and his household were always thunderstruck when the cross-cousins—armed to the teeth and painted like a war party—arrived at his camp one evening and proceeded to carry off forcibly the yelling 14-year-old.[9] He had to be dragged literally from the bosom of his family, with his mother screaming and trying to hide him and the father pretending to resist the invaders of his household. From then on, until the final stage *(Mikingula)* at age 24–26, the boy was completely under the authority of the men who carried him off. During these approximately 10 to 12 years, he spent much of the time alone with them in the bush where the group lived a monastic existence, as a small band of isolates, speaking to no one (especially not to females) and obtaining their own food. During these phases the tutors guarded the boy as if he were literally a prisoner and taught him all the things—chiefly ritual matters—that grown men should know. At intervals the youth was allowed to go home, on weekend leaves so to speak, but when at home he had to observe all the silences, the modest demeanor, the taboos and the austerities of the isolated life. In monastic language, he was under a strict rule of obedience to his tutors.

Breaking in on the long years of austerity, spent either in seclusion in the bush or in *pukimani* at home, were periodic collective ceremonies when the youth was ritually advanced from one stage of initiation to the next.[10] These

---

[9] See Hart, 1955 for some further details of the tearing away of the boy from the bosom of his family.

[10] A full list of initiation grade names and their duration in years is given in Hart, 1931.

were public ceremonies, witnessed by large crowds, and the more important of such transition ceremonies took place in January and February when the *kulama* yams were ripe. At these ceremonies the youths were handled in batches or classes, all the boys of one grade being ritually advanced to the next grade, and the top grade or final class being formally graduated as fully initiated men. The crucial grade—when the pubic hairs were forcibly pulled out and he was at last allowed to talk back a little to his tutors—was usually reached by a youth somewhere between his eighteenth and twentieth years, but he still had six years to go after that, not finishing the final grade of *Mikingula* until somewhere past the age of 24 or 25.

In contrast with the mainland initiation ceremonies, we think the most interesting point about Tiwi initiation resides not in the formal ceremonies but in the removal from the food-production units, for long periods of the year, of all the young males between the ages of 14 and 25. It is true that they did not spend *all* their time in seclusion and that after the age of 20 they remained mostly in their household camps, where they contributed to the household food production. Nonetheless, it remains clear that only a very well-off tribe could afford to allow so much time off from food production to all its young hunters. Tiwi fathers, it would seem, in arranging for the initiation of their sons to begin just when they were becoming productive hunters, were willing to sacrifice that productivity for less tangible advantages. The youths, secluded and guarded in the bush while getting an education, were not only out of the work force but were also out of the predatory-bachelor force. A Tiwi elder made sacrifices to "send his sons to college" but he breathed easier to know that the sons of the other elders were all there too.

All males without exception had to go through the full initiation cycle, and from the time of their first forcible seizure at the age of 14–15 to their final graduation at 24–26, they were in a state of *pukimani* and their personal names were strictly taboo to everybody in the tribe. Each youth was referred to only by his grade name, *Marukumarni* for the first year, *Mikingula* for the last four years, and so on. And here we return finally to a point that was mentioned much earlier—namely, the complete unimportance in tribal eyes of all males below the age of 25. Until they had completed the final stage of initiation, Tiwi males were still boys; they did not even have names. Occasionally, when collecting genealogies and coming upon a reference to a young man, the innocent anthropologist would ask, "Is he married?" In tones of the deepest contempt the informant would reply, "That kid, how could he be married? He's still *Mikingula*." Though *Mikingula* was the stage typically reached by a man at about 20–21 and lasted for the next four years, to the Tiwi it was still a stage in the life of a boy. Not until he had finished as *Mikingula* could he step out into the world and life of men. How he spent the years immediately after finishing initiation decided how soon some senior man would think sufficiently highly of him to aid him in acquiring his first ancient widow.

5/Friend and Foe
(1600–1928)

On nearly all sides, the emptiness of a great sea surrounded the Tiwi; to the south, the only path that might have led to the outside was blocked by the hostility of their nearest mainland neighbors. The Tiwi retained this isolation until the very end of the last century, even though for several centuries outsiders had been seen by them; ships passed along the coast and occasionally strangers landed or were cast ashore. Changes in the life on the islands were few, however, until about 1900, when the Tiwi began their integration into the modern world.

HOSTILITY TOWARD OUTSIDERS (1600–1900)

Although in June of 1636 the sailor Pieter Pieterszoon in command of the ships *Cleen Amsterdam* and *Wesel* sailed along the western 20 miles of the north coast of Melville Island and named the region Van Diemensland,[1] our first real knowledge of the natives of Bathurst and Melville islands was gained by the Dutch expedition to this region in 1705 under Maarten van Delft. Men from his three ships spent about two weeks in surveying the north coast of Melville Island, the northern two-thirds of Apsley Strait between Bathurst and Melville islands, and the entire west coast of Bathurst Island.[2] They met natives several times and even allowed them aboard their ships.

Following this meeting between islanders and Europeans was a period during which the natives became extremely hostile to outsiders. Tiwi distrust of foreigners probably stemmed from those decades when the Portuguese on Timor were raiding Melville Island for slaves. Although very little has been published concerning this era, such lack of information should not be taken as a refutation of such practices; the Portuguese archives remain today the only major block of libraries concerning a European colonial power important in the East Indies which has not been examined for material relevant to the

---

[1] Heeres, 1899.
[2] Ibid. See also Mander Jones, 1948 for some further data concerning Dutch knowledge of Melville Island.

history of Australia. From what little is known we may conclude that the Portuguese stopped capturing Tiwi as slaves about 1800.[3]

Even before the Portuguese made their last raids on Melville Island, another type of stranger, the "Malays" (or as we would call them today, the Indonesians), began to have encounters with the Tiwi. It was the search for the Chinese delicacy, the trepang or sea slug, which annually caused the Malays to sail past Melville Island eastward to Arnhem Land and the Gulf of Carpentaria. Neither the free-lance trepangers nor those sailing out of Macassar in the fleet of the Radaj of Boni wanted to stop at Melville Island, and they considered their misfortune to be great if their proas happened to be wrecked on its coast. They, like other Indonesians blown in to the homeland of the Tiwi, had little chance of surviving, for the Tiwi normally speared such poorly armed intruders and asked questions later.

The nineteenth century was an era of decreasing isolation for the Tiwi; during it, the outside world was knocking hard and often on their door. In 1802, a French expedition under Baudin mapped the southwestern tip of Bathurst Island, although its members apparently did not make a landing. In 1818, a British ship under P. P. King made a detailed coastal survey of Bathurst Island and all except the southeastern coast of Melville Island. Then on September 26, 1824, the British founded Fort Dundas on northwestern Melville Island, the first European settlement in the tropical part of Australia. The British and the Tiwi did not make friends. The imaginative commander of this outpost of empire, Major John Campbell, tried to capture a Tiwi and teach him sufficient English so that he could tell his tribesmen that the British would shoot them if they did not stop spearing the Englishmen and their buffalo imported from Timor. One Tiwi was captured but escaped within a fortnight under cover of darkness; meanwhile the British mourned for their doctor and storekeeper who had gotten in the way of well-aimed Tiwi spears. No native learned English. The British, disillusioned by their perpetual battle with the Tiwi and with tropical decay, abandoned Fort Dundas on March 31, 1829. Four and a half years of exposure to the British had affected the Tiwi little.

But the Tiwi were not to remain without external intruders. Shortly before 1844 a Dutch ship was wrecked on their coast. In 1858, an English vessel was lost on Melville Island. In 1869, the city now known as Darwin was founded and ships began to pass Bathurst or Melville islands almost daily. In the 1880s two ships, the *Afghan* and *Northern*, went aground off the southern coast of Bathurst Island. In 1886, the Australian government tried to erect channel markers on the southern shore of Melville Island, whereupon the Tiwi immediately "salvaged" both cloth and iron from them. During June and July

---

[3] The following statement from George Windsor Earl's *The Native Races of the Indian Archipelago. Papuans* (London: Hippolyte Bailliere, 1853, p. 210) is probably the most significant passage concerning the Portuguese relations with Tiwi: ". . . According to . . . the older inhabitants of Timor, Melville Island was only less a source of slavery than New Guinea, in proportion to its smaller extent of surface, at the period in which the slave-trade was encouraged or connived at by the European authorities. . . ."

of the same year the ship *Jane Anderson* was stranded on the shoals of first
Melville and then Bathurst Island. Also in 1886, two Malay proas were wrecked
on the north coast of Melville Island. That year was a great one for looting.

Occasionally visitors came ashore on the islands. The Stokes' survey party
landed in the late 1830s, but saw no natives. A government party crossed
Melville Island in 1887; the Tiwi speared its leader. In 1895, a government
tourist party went to look over the ruins of old Fort Dundas; they kept their
eyes open and no one was injured. In 1897, Joe Cooper, a buffalo shooter,
tried to make a living from the Melville Island buffalo; he was speared and
retreated to Darwin.

Tiwi treatment of outsiders prior to 1900 had been to rob them, spear them,
kill them. This is not, however, the picture painted by modern Tiwi when
talking of their past. They claim that their ancestors greeted each new group
of strangers with the cry: *"Pongki! Pongki!"* (meaning, "Peace! Peace!").
But then it should be noted that before 1900 many a Tiwi peacemaker carried
a spear between his toes. Yet under these circumstances the Tiwi world view
did alter. First there were those changes that came from an attempt to understand the new objects that were suddenly thrust into the Tiwi world: the
trade knives and axes given by Dutch navigators, the matchlock guns used
by the Malays and probably the Portuguese, the rice given to Tiwi by the
surveyors under P. P. King, the Indonesian water buffalo introduced by the
British at their short-lived settlement, the coconut palms the English left
behind them, the cups and plates from shipwrecks in the 1880s, and the flour
tossed overboard to lighten foundering vessels. The Tiwi cherished iron knives
and axes, readily recognizing their greater efficiency. The Tiwi begged for
them; they stole them; and, when a spar washed ashore bound round with
iron bands, the natives burned away the wood and took the iron away to
grind into axes. The matchlock gun, and even the later flintlock, could be
coped with; when one saw the flash, one ducked flat, just in case the weapon
worked, and then rushed in to impale the stranger with a spear. Rice was
useless; it looked like the larvae of the termite, which was not good for
anything anyway. Buffalo were to be killed; they kept wallowing in the best
waterholes. Coconut palms were a great disappointment; they were bigger
than the local cabbage palm, but when cut down, did not have the same
succulent interior. Plates were too much bother to carry around, but cups
were worth saving for a while. Flour could be used for white paint, but it was
not as good as the best white pigment near at hand.

Other modifications took place in Tiwi life before 1900 as a result of action
by outsiders. Probably the greatest of these alterations came as a result of
slave raiding, or "black birding" as it is called in the South Seas. The Tiwi
always kept their young women hidden from strangers, even if they were just
visitors from other bands. The old men rarely left camp. Therefore, it was
the young males who went, or were sent, to try to satisfy their curiosity and
to get iron from the Portuguese—and it was these young males who would
make the best slaves in Timor. The anthropologist is left to wonder to what
extent the removal of a disproportionate number of young men from a group

might alter the form of the society. Is it possible that such happenings might be a factor that contributed to the dominance of the old Tiwi men and their near monopoly of wives? Could it be that the politics involved in wife trading were an indirect result of the Portuguese slave raiding? The possibility at least exists, and perhaps research in Portuguese archives will give us some clearer idea of how many young Tiwi men were carried off to Timor during this period. Present-day Tiwi, of course, remember nothing about it.

THE BEGINNING OF FRIENDLY CONTACT
(1900–1928)

Today the Tiwi have been incorporated into the modern world as a part of the Australian nation, yet they came to understand outsiders, including Australians, through persons with many national backgrounds. Individuals who have helped to shape Tiwi views of non-Tiwi have been Indonesians, Filipinos, mainland natives from the Cobourg Peninsula, Frenchmen, and Japanese, as well as Australians from the southern parts of Australia.

The Tiwi were first drawn out of their hostile insularity by curiosity and the desire for iron, the same factors that had attracted them toward the Portuguese a century earlier. Iron looted from shipwrecks, channel markers, and the camps of casual visitors to the islands was not sufficient; the Tiwi desired a permanent avenue by which they could obtain the metal. The oldest Tiwi in the early 1950s stated that during the 1890s the Tiwi began to feel that opportunity was passing them by as they noted ship after ship sail in and out of Darwin; the islanders therefore came to the conclusion that they wanted a permanent European settlement in their midst, like the earlier Fort Dundas, for only in this way could they be guaranteed an uninterrupted source of iron.

About 1895, events began moving toward the establishment of a long-term European center on the islands. The vanguard of the movement was not European, however. In 1885, mother-of-pearl shell of commercial value was found on the bottom of Darwin Harbor. A few years of intensive diving by "Malay," "Manila," and Japanese pearlers soon worked out the Darwin beds, making it necessary for the growing fleet of pearling luggers to go further afield. They stripped the coast north of Darwin, moved on to the south coast of Melville Island, and finally began working the great shoals at the south end of Apsley Strait. Cautiously at first, the pearlers went ashore for water and firewood. Young Tiwi men became curious and paddled out to visit the luggers hove to just off the southern beaches in the neap tides. Aboard the luggers Tiwi youth had occasional meals, smoked tobacco, and were given iron tools. The Mandiimbula of southern Melville Island in particular began to look forward to the periodic visits of the luggers, for they brought a new source of iron and trinkets.

Joe Cooper, the Australian buffalo hunter who had been chased out of the islands on his first attempt in 1897, returned again a few years later having first kidnapped two Tiwi women so that his mainland native helpers of the

Yuwatja (Iwaidja) tribe near Cape Don could learn the language. When they had, he returned with a strong mainland detachment and well equipped with guns and horses. By 1900, European firearms were efficient weapons and a Tiwi spearman no longer could expect to kill a man armed with a modern rifle. Cooper is said never to have gone unarmed in his 15 or so years (from about 1900–1916) as "King of Melville Island."[4]

In retrospect it is apparent that the agent through whom the Tiwi learned of the outside world was not Cooper, the white man, but his companions the Yuwatja (Iwaidja). They were more numerous and more approachable than Cooper, and several of them even had Tiwi wives whom they had captured. Tiwi accounts of these captives are noteworthy. It was the young Tiwi men hanging around Cooper's camp who suggested to the Yuwatja that they go and capture, by force of arms, Tiwi females who had recently become widows. The young men were thus performing their customary role of agents in widow remarriage—but in this case for foreign clients.

Cooper and his Yuwatja camped at various localities on Melville Island until about 1916 when their last base, at Paru opposite the site of the Mission, was abandoned and he and his mainlanders withdrew from the islands. It was this last camp at Paru that was made headquarters by Sir Baldwin Spencer, the well-known Australian anthropologist, when he visited the Tiwi in 1912.[5]

While Cooper was at Paru he was also visited by a young Alsatian priest, Father François Xavier Gsell, M.S.C., who was contemplating establishing a mission on adjacent Bathurst Island. Cooper tried to discourage Father Gsell by telling him that the Bathurst Islanders had guns and were dangerous; apparently Cooper did not want any missionaries around his rough-and-ready establishment. But Father Gsell did not scare easily; in June 1911 he returned and built his mission station on the southeast corner of Bathurst Island, where it still stands today. Cooper left Paru permanently about five years later.

By 1916, five years after its founding, the Mission had two French priests, several French nuns and some Filipino workmen, and a lugger that ran to and from Port Darwin once a month. It was not until the nuns came that the local Tiwi put any trust in the missionaries; they could not understand why a man who claimed to be as important as Father Gsell claimed to be did not have any wives. When the nuns arrived, the Tiwi were more ready to accept the priest as "a big man" and began to bring their women around.

Thus Cooper with his well-armed retinue of mainlanders had made the islands safe for white men and introduced a desire for white men's goods, particularly tobacco. His retirement from Melville Island left the newly established Mission on Bathurst Island as the only source of supply for these goods. After World War I, however, another influence began to grow in importance. Large numbers of Japanese pearling boats came and anchored

[4] Hardly a year goes by without a newspaper in Australia running a Sunday supplement article on Cooper's stay at Melville Island. Such stories often are titled "The King of Melville Island" and are normally extremely romanticized.

[5] Spencer, 1914. Spencer's account of the Tiwi is remarkably inaccurate and confused. On this trip to the Northern Territory in 1912 he was without his usual collaborator, Gillen.

Photo 13. The building at the left was the first Western structure built at Nguiu in 1911. It then served as both a sleeping and eating shelter for the missionaries, thick-walled and secure from rifle fire, and as a storehouse for food to be handed out to adjacent Tiwi. This view from Pilling's 1953–1954 fieldwork shows this same building, then somewhat more than 40 years old, during its period of use as the home of one of the Tiwi families living at the beach village of Nguiu.

Photo 14. The Old Presbytery at Bathurst Island Mission, Nguiu, during the mass for the local saint, on October 25, 1953. This structure was the center of mission life from when it was built before 1916, through the period of Hart's observation in 1928–1929, until about 1949, when a new presbytery was completed. It was in this building that Pilling resided in 1953 and 1954.

off the coasts of southern and southeastern Melville Island, where they traded with the local bands—the Yeimpi and Mandiimbula. These bands got tobacco and European-type food (flour, rice, tea, sugar) from the Japanese in quantities that the Catholic missionaries could not afford to provide; all the Japanese asked in return was access to young native women. Men who controlled many women—as fathers, as husbands, or as brothers—were thus in a favorable position to profit by the traffic with the Japanese.

Whereas the demands made by the Japanese on the Yeimpi and Mandiimbula for women were quite straightforward and uncomplicated, Father Gsell's demands on the bands of south Bathurst Island were somewhat more complex in their consequences. Many aspects of the old pattern of Tiwi life had to be abandoned to make them into Christians. To the missionaries, polygamy was sinful and could not be part of the new Tiwi life. Prenatal and infant bestowal had to be abolished. Marriages should be between age-mates and should be arranged freely and solely by the couple involved. Such changes were the crux of Father Gsell's program, and the story of how he went about it has run in many a Sunday supplement in the cities of Australia under the title "The Bishop With 150 Wives."[6] Father Gsell did not try to convert or dras-

---

[6] Father Gsell became Bishop of Darwin in 1938. He lived on in retirement to 1958, having seen in his lifetime the fulfillment of his dream of the Tiwi as a Catholic tribe.

tically change the behavior of the older Tiwi; he believed that they were too set in their ways. Rather, he built toward a distant day by working among the younger generation. When infant girls became widows, he purchased them from their fathers. Men with young widowed daughters and those with spare young wives sold such girls for axes, flour, tobacco, cloth, and trinkets. Such "Blackies," as they became affectionately called,[7] lived in the convent with the French (and later Australian) sisters. When such a girl reached the age of about 18, she was asked to choose one of the young single men for her husband. For his part in this excellent deal, which provided him with a wife long before he would get one under the old tribal sytem, the young man had only to promise that he would never take another wife. Father Gsell did not require that either party be Catholic. However, the children born of this new union were baptized and reared as Catholics. Later, a few of the girls who had been sold to Father Gsell before they were 10 went through confirmation as did their youthful fiancés. The first nuptial Mass between two such Tiwi took place in 1928.

When between the mid-1920s and the early 1940s the Japanese began to give trade goods to men for sexual access to their wives, Father Gsell's missionzation program ran into competition. The Japanese gave the old Tiwi males a much better deal than did Father Gsell. The Japanese with their continuous payment for access to women poured into the households of these old men the same sort of goods that Gsell provided. But in the case of the Japanese, the goods were paid time and again over a matter of years and the old father or husband was kept permanently in tobacco and food. Thus, oddly indeed, the two chief outside influences that came to bear upon the traditional Tiwi system of marriage, after about 1920, were both agencies that were anxious (for entirely different reasons and ends) to "buy" young girls and pay their ancient husbands or fathers for relinquishing them; temporarily in the case of the Japanese, permanently in the case of the missionaries. The Tiwi could scarcely be expected to cease putting a high value on women, and upon control over women, under these conditions.

---

[7] The Tiwi in 1954 strongly resented being called "African," "Negro," or "nigger"; but they did not seem to mind being called "Blacks." The term "Blackie" for a young female was in general use by Mission school girls for themselves; it was in no sense derogatory.

6/Changing Tiwi Society: 1930 into the 1970s

CHANGES SINCE 1930

There were in 1929 only two year-round settlements of outsiders that were significant to the Tiwi. One was Bathurst Island Mission, by then nearly 20 years old, the only permanent white-man establishment on the islands. It acted as the main exit point for travel to Darwin, the other focus of Tiwi life. There was also the large camp of Mandiimbula and Yeimpi on the south coast of Melville Island, which owed its existence to the sexual arrangement between the Tiwi and Japanese pearlers.

In the 1930s, the centers of Tiwi activity shifted somewhat. The Australian government successfully broke up the camp located on the south coast by transporting nearly all of the Yeimpi to Darwin and by sending patrol boats out to discourage the Japanese from frequenting the area. In about 1935, the Japanese moved their base for contact with the Tiwi north to the region of Garden Point, at the northern end of Apsley Strait, just beyond the ruins of old Fort Dundas. Around the great freshwater pool on the beach at that locality there developed a Tiwi camp like that which formerly had existed on the south coast; however, the native bands involved were no longer the Yeimpi and Mandiimbula but the Malauila, Munupula, Wilrangwila, and Turupula of northern Bathurst and Melville islands. The government again attempted to control sexual activities between Tiwi and Japanese, but to get to this spot a patrol boat from Darwin had to travel along 40 miles of indented coastline, which amplified and seemed to project every throb of an engine toward the ears of the Japanese miles away. The patrol boats found that they could not sneak up on the pearlers unannounced and, therefore, could not catch them in the act of cohabiting with native women.

By the late 1930s, pressure from missionary and other humanitarian circles in the southern part of Australia forced the government to attempt to terminate, or at least to control, the trade pattern that had become established between the northern Tiwi and the Japanese. A government ration depot was founded at Garden Point about 1939, and many of the local Tiwi females were taken by the government to Darwin in order to stop their use by Japanese pearlers. However, by that time many Japanese half-castes had been born to the women.

In 1940, a new Catholic mission was established at Garden Point to care for these half-castes. This Melville Island Mission brought together not only the island part-aborigines, but also other Catholic half-castes from all over the Northern Territory. By late 1940, it became clear that the existence of a government depot for aborigines at Garden Point was incompatible with a policy aimed toward educating the adjacent half-caste children for life as members of the white Australian community. The government ration center was removed to Snake Bay. Also, by 1940, the government had begun to remove lepers from both Bathurst and Melville islands to a leprosarium on Channel Island in Darwin harbor. Here, over the following years, developed a community of Tiwi that often numbered as many as 40 persons. At Channel Island they found themselves forcefully confined among natives from many mainland tribes. Tiwi who returned from Channel Island after years of residence there were more sophisticated in European ways than their fellow-tribesmen and found themselves agents of white Australian culture.

The winter (May–August) of 1941 was the last in which the Japanese came to Garden Point. The Catholic brothers who were there at the time viewed at least one extraordinary event in those months before Pearl Harbor. On this occasion, a man in the uniform of a Japanese naval officer was seen aboard the mother ship of the Japanese pearling fleet that called in at Garden Point; under Australian law neither ship nor officer were allowed within the 3-mile limit. Pearl Harbor occurred a few months later.

The year 1942 brought modern warfare to the Tiwi. An American plane running out of the Philippines lacked enough fuel to get to Darwin; it landed on the small airstrip at Bathurst Island Mission. Then on February 19, 1942, Darwin was bombed. Japanese planes flew over Bathurst Island Mission on their way to commit what became "Australia's Pearl Harbor." Father McGrath, the local priest, recognized the raiders as Japanese and radioed his warning into Darwin 20 minutes before the horror commenced. The message went unheeded and the loss of life and property was great. Bathurst Island Mission was itself strafed, possibly for the attempt to warn Darwin. The bombing of Darwin left the Northern Territory in chaos. The white residents evacuated southward by any means at hand; in one case, two men drove a road grader 70 miles "down the track" before they felt safe enough to stop.

The disruption of the Tiwi community was as great as that of the white settlement at Darwin, although no Tiwi were killed in the bombing and strafing by the Japanese. The Catholic authorities realized that they could not guarantee a food supply to the natives, and the Tiwi families at the Mission were sent to the bush to support themselves. Tipperary, a Tiwi who was by 1942 an old hand in Darwin, told Pilling (1954) of the privation he had endured when he had taken to the bush and had not had a smoke for four months after the attack on Darwin. Many of the older Tiwi who were in Darwin during the bombing did not survive the war; the psychological strain and lack of sufficient food was too much for them. Genealogies show that an unusually large number of deaths occurred among Tiwi between 1942 and 1946.

When Western food supplies again became available, the old Tiwi bush living seems to have departed. The Tiwi suddenly realized their full depen-

Photo 15. The Roman Catholic church at Bathurst Island Mission, Nguiu, as it appeared during early 1954, with a mission banana plot in the foreground. It was this building that a Japanese airman strafed on February 19, 1942.

dence upon the products that only the whites could provide. As the war came to an end and one after another of the temporary military bases were abandoned, the missionaries and the Tiwi salvaged what they could, transporting large amounts of corrugated iron to Bathurst Island Mission for native huts. The Tiwi were drawn together around the Mission in larger numbers than ever before, their camps ranging in a line along the Mission beach. The majority of the Tiwi, about 600, considered Bathurst Island Mission their home, although some of the young adult males spent most of the year in Darwin. About 50 islanders lived adjacent to the half-caste Melville Island Mission at Garden Point. Another 150 were permanently located at the government settlement at Snake Bay. The remaining Tiwi, about 150, were year-round residents of Darwin; over 100 lived at Bagot Native Compound and at an unsupervised native camp at Point Gunn directly opposite the southernmost tip of Melville Island; the rest were inmates at the leper colony. The resulting total population of about 950, in 1954, is only about a hundred less than the figure of 1,062 which Hart obtained in his census of 1928–1929.

MARRIAGE ARRANGEMENTS

We have discussed how, under the traditional Tiwi pattern of life, the greatest energies of mature males were expended in bargaining with each other for new wives. The old social system was one that has as normal features prenatal and early childhood engagements for females, remarriage for all widows, considerable age difference between marriage partners, and polyg-

Photo 16. The Tiwi village at Nguiu, in June 1953. This village was constructed in large part from corrugated iron salvaged from the American air base on the western tip of southern Bathurst Island.

areas of the bands had been depopulated; in fact, nearly all the Tiwi were located around one of four European establishments—those at Darwin, Bathurst Island Mission, Garden Point, or Snake Bay. In each of these areas a centralized village pattern had developed. Within the Tiwi communities at Snake Bay, Garden Point, and Bathurst Island Mission there remained a few of the old large households with a polygamous base. But in all these camps the household heads were well past 60 and in most cases past 70. Polygamous households were dying out by 1953.

But what was replacing them? One might assume that the European pattern of the single family household based upon neolocal residence would have emerged as the new Tiwi system. This was not the case, however. Just as Hart found in 1928–1929 that successful Tiwi men were the heads of large establishments, so in 1953–1954 the younger male leaders had gathered around them impressive collections of females. But these collections included now only one wife.

Let us consider again the case of Cabbagee. It will be remembered that his had been one of Father Gsell's first marriages and, except for a few uncomfortable months, he had been monogamous all his life. There were camped with him in 1954 a number of women and children who were related to him in many ways. There was his wife Polly, now a good Catholic who had taken the Christian name of Carmel, and her ancient mother Rita, who had borne a child long before the white man came to Bathurst Island. Also in "Cabbagee's camp," as the natives referred to it, was Patrick, Cabbagee's only son, and Patrick's wife. Patrick and his wife had three surviving children

Photo 17. Houses built of corrugated iron sheets salvaged from the World War II U.S. air base on western Bathurst Island, as those buildings appeared one morning during late December 1953. In the foreground, 3-year-old females are practicing the Shark Dance used in the Tiwi mourning rite, as 4-year-old boys and girls, as well as a member of the great-grandmother generation and the sole member of the great-great-grandmother generation look on.

between the ages of 4 and 13; they also were raising 14-year-old Fabian, whose deceased father had been a "brother" of Patrick and whose deceased mother had been a "sister" of Patrick's wife. Cabbagee and Carmel (alias Polly) had three daughters, and Cabaggee had arranged with each son-in-law that he reside with Cabbagee and support him in his fights and politics. These daughters and sons-in-law had a total of 10 children. The other members of Cabbagee's camp included the widow and children of Carmel's deceased younger maternal half-brother. Cabbagee had given this "sister" to Carmel's half-brother for his wife and when he died seven years later leaving a number of young children, Cabbagee defended the right of his "sister" not to remarry. With this "sister" of Cabbagee lived her stepmother and occasionally her real mother, until the latter died. Further, living in Cabbagee's camp were two of his full sister's daughters and their husbands, who became members of the camp by reason of the fact that Cabbagee arranged his sister's marriage in such a way that her husband, Babui, accepted Cabbagee as his leader.[1] When Babui arranged his own daughters' marriages, his new sons-in-law became

---

[1] Hart would use the word "patron" in this relationship. Pilling preferred the word "leader." This is itself an indication of a certain subtle change in Tiwi social structure. The patron-satellite relationship of 1928–1929 was by 1953 better expressed as leader-follower. The pairs of men were closer in age than they had been formerly. How the Tiwi themselves expressed the relationship by 1953 is indicated in the next footnote.

subservient to Babui and thereby subservient to Cabbagee. Also resident in Cabbagee's camp at times were his younger paternal half-brother Pawpaw with his two surviving wives, his full brother Tommy's son, and two of their widowed "sisters" and their children.

We have mentioned here only that segment of Cabbagee's camp led by Cabbagee himself and that led by his half-brother Pawpaw, but such a listing is adequate for our purposes. It is noteworthy that the downward alteration in the age of marriage for males has meant that many less women become widows; first marriages of women last longer and, therefore, the system of patronage established at the time of the first marriage is more permanent. Babui's marriage, for example, had made him a henchman of Cabbagee from about 1920 to 1955. When women did become widows, especially if they had daughters, they were protected by their brothers who thereby became the "boss" of their daughters. The father or the "boss" of a girl arranged her marriage with a boy who was willing to become the "worker" of the girl's controller.[2]

From the economic standpoint, the large household in 1954 had much the same function as before the days of the Mission. The younger women went out together and gathered food; old women stayed home with the young children. The younger men brought home choice items, which were trade goods and money from Darwin. The "boss" of the great household was wealthy; he had food, tobacco, clothes, and usually sufficient money to gamble. The composition of the great households had altered, but their function is very much the same. The establishment of the monogamous Cabbagee was even larger than that of the polygamous old pagan, Ki-in-kumi, described in an earlier chapter; Cabbagee, with only one wife, had more women under his "control" than even Ki-in-kumi had, despite his list of 21 wives. The Tiwi had thus been able to retain their large households even under the Mission-imposed system of monogamy.

THE CHANGE FROM PATRILINY TO MATRILINY

In the pre-Cooper era of feuding, the largest significant units among the Tiwi were the bands; the Tiwi never, in that bygone day, acted as a tribe, even in their attacks upon such outsiders as the British. In the 1950s, when informants talked of the old days they commonly mentioned that male members of old bands came together as units to go on war parties. These old bands did not have a strict rule of descent. But, as has already been indicated, the majority of the males were regarded all their lives as members of the band to which their father belonged. That is, the major unit of the old Tiwi social structure was patrilineal in emphasis.

There also existed in the old Tiwi pattern a strictly matrilineal clan orga-

---

[2] By 1953, the terms "boss" and "worker" had come into the local Tiwi dialect to indicate superordinate and subordinate status interrelationships.

nization, related primarily to totemism. One of the totemic animals of a clan stood for a member of that clan in the song composed to commemorate his death; for instance, the first line of the mourning song for a deceased male of the Red Paint Clan might be "I am red paint." Occasionally, several members of a clan helped one of their number in a fight, but this was apparently not very common before the Mission era. This clan-organization pattern prevailed among the Tiwi through about 1930. Then major and most unpredictable changes began.

What does one expect to happen when a society that has a patrilineal emphasis, like the old Tiwi one, comes into contact with a European society where, if there is any emphasis, it is a patrilineal one? Although one would ordinarily expect a strengthening of patriliny, such was not the case among the Tiwi. The old social unit, which was predominantly patrilineal, was a territorial group with its major functions in the system of feuding. When the feuding system departed and the Tiwi community became more centralized, especially around the Bathurst Island Mission, the utility of the old band organization diminished and the underlying clan organization dominated. Suddenly, fighting was no longer in terms of band membership, for the matrilineal clan had become the only social unit of significance.

By the 1950s, young Tiwi often denied that they had any band membership. But it was not unknown for teen-age Tiwi males to lie awake at night counting up the members of their matrilineal clan. According to informants, in the 1940s and 1950s the major fights that occurred at Bathurst Island Mission were interclan skirmishes.

Thus, among the Tiwi, we have an example of how a society with a patrilineal emphasis under strong influence from another society with a patrilineal emphasis may, if there is an underlying matrilineal organization, become a society which is for all practical purposes solely matrilineal. The introductory student of anthropology is thereby warned that characterizations of societies as matrilineal or patrilineal are rarely adequate to form the basis for reconstructing past or predicting future forms of such societies.[3]

THE TIWI AND THE AUSTRALIAN NATION

Finally, let us consider those aspects of modern Tiwi life that have attracted national attention in Australia. What have the newspaper-reading members of the Australian public come to know about the Tiwi?

Probably the best known Tiwi in the 1950s was a man in his thirties, formerly

---

[3] Goodale reported that in 1980 the swing back to patriliny had begun to reassert itself, following the return to Tiwi ownership and control of the lands of both islands through federal legislation in 1976 (see Chapter 7). By 1986 the expression of importance of the traditional (and flexible) patrilineal land-owning sociopolitical groups was even stronger as plans for development outside of the three major townships were discussed. The adoption, as surnames, of the names of deceased paternal ancestors, introduced in the 1960s by the Catholic Mission, has also influenced the swing back to patriliny. This process serves to underscore the last sentence in the preceding paragraph.

Photo 18. Bagot Native Compound, in March 1954. It was there that most of the Tiwi permanently in Darwin resided.

known to other Tiwi and local residents of Darwin as Bobby Wilson. About 1953, an Australian movie producer, Charles Chauvel, went hunting for a "full-blood" aborigine who could act well enough to portray an aboriginal male in what became the Australian movie *Jedda*. In Darwin, the producer found a football star from the Darwin group of Tiwi who could fill the part. Bobby Wilson soon was billed as Robert Tudawali.[4] He went "on location" at several spots in the Territory and finally traveled to Sydney for the studio shooting. The Sydney papers caught his story and spread his bearded face over the country. Bobby Wilson's photo from the local Darwin newspaper was hung up in several native huts at Bathurst Island Mission. After much publicity, he ultimately returned to his wife and their hut in the Bagot Native Compound in Darwin. Again the newshounds caught his story. According to them, he had returned to a life of degradation. The Australian public was shocked that a star of one of their best films should be discarded to live again like every other aborigine in Darwin. It was rumored that Tudawali was going to be "rescued" and given a role in a second Australian film; however, he only played a few episodes of a television series, and returned to Darwin. Tudawali drank heavily in Darwin; in 1967, he died of burns from a grass fire at a drinking spot near the boundary of an aboriginal settlement.

Bobby Wilson was only one of a large number of young Tiwi who have been recognized as fine athletes. There were two football teams in Darwin in the early 1950s that had Tiwi members: the Catholic team, St. Mary's, which often took the local pennant, and the Wanderers, which drew from the permanent native population in Darwin and included such Tiwi as Bobby

---

[4] The last name Tudawali is an attempt to spell the Tiwi word for shark.

Wilson. It was normal for one of these Tiwi players to be considered among the top three in Darwin football circles. In 1969, David Kantilla, a Bathurst Islander, was a South Australian professional football player.

In 1952, Billy Larrakeyah, a Darwin Tiwi, was thought to have Olympic possibilities as a javelin thrower, but strained his arm in the tryouts; he was killed in a brawl in Darwin in the spring of 1959. For a while in 1954, Edmond Johnson, a Tiwi from Bathurst Island Mission, was one of the players on the newly organized St. Mary's basketball team; other Tiwi played on the Bagot Compound basketball team. Edmond Johnson, a road worker when at Bathurst Island, saved his money and attended the 1956 Olympics. In the late 1950s, a group of young Catholic Tiwi were organized into a water polo team called the Seals. National magazines suggested that they might be the best water polo team in Australia, but that was before the team had gone south to play any non-Darwin group. In 1970, Tiwi boys from Bathurst Island's boys' school were flown to Adelaide, where they competed in an athletic championship; in late 1971, four girls from the Mission's St. Theresa's school went to the South Australian schoolgirls' athletic meet.

Tiwi carving and painting have had popularity in Australian art circles. Traditional Tiwi graveposts were finely carved in geometric designs and painted with precise and complex networks of cross-hatching and simple, but effective, motifs. The first modern innovation in Tiwi art occurred about 1945 when a native known as Katu (or Short Katu) made his first attempt to carve a human figure atop a mourning post. When Pilling later asked Katu why he had carved this post, he said, "Me see 'm along Darwin. Me savvy." That is, Katu transferred the concept of Western realistic statuary in the round into Tiwi art. He carved a second realistic post for presentation to Queen Elizabeth II in 1954. More recently, Tiwi carvers at Milikapiti (Snake Bay) have taken to realistic carving. Two figures, both carved by Tiwi at Milikapiti, were given to the Perth Museum in 1958. Sixteen mourning posts from Snake Bay were purchased by the National Art Gallery in Sydney the same year. An art display of Tiwi graveposts was held in Philadelphia prior to 1960.[5] In 1967, the director of the Western Australian Art Gallery witnessed a memorial ceremony on Melville Island and acquired three of the utilized graveposts for his museum. In 1969, this Perth art gallery had a special exhibit on aboriginal art; the institution's Tiwi gravepost collection was featured prominently.

The elaborately decorated *kwampi* spears have also been the focus of interest in some news articles on Tiwi. In 1954, such spears were regularly for sale in one Darwin souvenir shop. On September 3, 1971, when the new hospital at Garden Point was opened, Bob Kerry and Charlie One, both of whom Pilling had known, flanked the doorway as Mr. Fred Chaney, the Administrator of the Northern Territory, entered. Both of these older Tiwi wore elaborate face painting, and Mr. Chaney entered the building beneath

---

[5] In 1984, following review of this section, Goodale wrote that these posts were "carved at Snake Bay (Milikapiti) in 1954 'for your own funeral, Jane' "; and "were exhibited at the University of Pennsylvania Museum among other items of Tiwi art and culture collected by Goodale."

Photo 19. One of Short Katu's neighbors and age-mates doing some of the painting of Short Katu's human effigy carved for presentation to Queen Elizabeth II in 1954.

an inverted "V" of *kwampi* spears, each held by one of these honor guards.

Male Tiwi skill in dancing has attracted wide attention in Australia. When natives from all over the Territory were sent to dance before Queen Elizabeth in Queensland during her 1954 tour, three Tiwi were among the delegation. The Tiwi contingent, directed by the innovator Short Katu, made every news story covering this part of the Royal Visit. In Darwin, when Bagot Compound needed to raise money for native participation in sports, the Tiwi, usually led by Katu, presented a public dance. As a result, Katu's clan, under his direction, invented many new dances for white Australian audiences. In September of 1968, when the Australian national Minister for Aboriginal Affairs wished to fund a new lounge for the Foundation for Aboriginal Affairs in Sydney, he imported nine Bathurst Island Tiwi males to dance on a Sunday afternoon at the federal Admiralty House. In October 1970, when the International

Photo 20. Reproduction of "Our Lady of the Aborigines" from a Roman Catholic religious card. In 1986, Father Tim Brennan, then in charge of all Catholic missions in the Northern Territory, referred to this image as a "Black Madonna."

Dance Spectacular was held in the Sydney Town Hall honoring the Waratah Spring Festival and the Captain Cook Bi-centenary, Bathurst Island Tiwi dancers performed, receiving a special prize for Australian aboriginal dancers. In June 1970, when two white employees of the Bathurst Island Mission were married there, the Bishop attended, local Tiwi gave a corroboree in honor of the event, and the Darwin *Northern Territory News* gave extensive coverage. Similarly, in September 1971, when Mr. Chaney opened the hospital at Garden Point, there was a Tiwi dance with coverage by both the Darwin paper and the national *Australasian Post*.[6]

In June 1970, two Tiwi youngsters, 7-year-old Annalisa Brook and 8-year-old David Mungatopi, both from Snake Bay, lived in Perth while they performed in white Australian Mary Durack's *The Way of the Wind*, a sort of ballet-corroboree. The show later visited Darwin and other towns in the Northern Territory.

Tiwi have been active in other nontraditional arts. In the early 1950s, one of the 30-year-old female Tiwi at Bathurst Island Mission usually took first prize for embroidery at the annual Territorian fair. By 1971, the Tiwi of Bathurst Island, following a development grant from the national Council for the Arts, began producing cloth silk-screen decorated with traditional Tiwi bark painting motifs. Bede Tungutalum, Cabbagee's daughter's son, and Giovanni Tipungwuti, 19-year-old partners, set up Tiwi Designs, with a $2,000 loan from the Bathurst Island Mission. In October 1971, they received national

[6] In a letter to Pilling, dated November 10, 1984, Goodale stated that this new type of ceremonial occasion was continuing "in the 1980's to be a major arena for Tiwi creativity in dance" (see Grau, 1983).

Council of Industrial Design awards for their silk-screen creations and were flown to Sydney for a two-week visit to aid in raising funds for a $100,000 art center at the Mission. At Bathurst Island, Bede was the guitarist in his own pop group "The Expenses."

Tiwi have been active in Northern Territory public affairs, as well as the aboriginal rights movement. Starting about 1936 and lasting until about 1950, one of the sons of Turimpi was the messenger for the main court in Darwin. In the early 1950s, a half-brother of Cabbagee known as "Union," had some reputation in Darwin as an aboriginal spokesman, if not an organizer and agitator. In 1969, Alf Stanislaus, Cabbagee's half-brother's son, was an attendee at a rights conference in Darwin. In 1971, a Tiwi was expected to run for the Arnhem Land seat in the Northern Territory Legislative Council. In September 1971, Dermot Tipungwuti, of Cabbagee's old establishment, was president of the Melville Island Progress Association.[7]

Perhaps we may look forward to the day when American television audiences can enjoy a Tiwi dance or buy Tiwi Designs cloth; a new state of the Northern Territory may one day have a Tiwi cabinet member. Yet, in 1987, there were still a very few ancient Tiwi who could vaguely remember life before the white man came to live on their islands, when those who arrived like Cooper had in 1897, were ferociously chased out.

---

[7] In a 1984 letter, Goodale updated the preceding list by adding that Hyacinth Tungutalum was elected in 1974 to the Northern Territory's Legislative Assembly, and was designated a Justice of the Peace in 1975. "In 1980, Mr. Tungutalum served as advisor to the Chief Minister, Northern Territory Government, as well as [being] a member of the TLC. The Chairman of the TLC in 1980, Cyril Rioli, also was elected" to the Northern Territory's Legislative Assembly. In early 1987, Stanley Tipoloura was a member of the Northern Territory's House of Assembly.

7/The Tiwi Revisited: 1954–1987
by Jane C. Goodale

FIELDWORK AND THE ANTHROPOLOGY OF THE TIWI

It had been a rough night. On the tail end of a cyclone the battered World War II landing barge, with the unlikely name *Triumph*, ventured out of Darwin Harbor and crossed the tricky currents of Clarence Strait separating the mainland of Australia from the Tiwi islands. On board was a crew of two, a dozen Tiwi, the leader of the National Geographic expedition to the land of the Tiwi, C. P. Mountford, a venerable Aussie "guide" W. E. Harney, or as the Tiwi called him "Bilarni," and two young graduate students, including myself. I remember staggering ashore at the Bathurst Island Mission, landing and shaking hands with another young American graduate student, Arnold Pilling, while we paid our respects to the Mission personnel, before climbing aboard the *Triumph* for a slow chug up Apsley Strait to Garden Point, where we had to beach the now obviously sinking *Triumph*. During the following day while the "floatation chambers" were pumped out, I visited the Garden Point Mission and the settlement school where part-aboriginal children from Catholic missions on the mainland as well as from Bathurst and Melville islands, were sent to receive a "European" upbringing and schooling. The expectation of this (now abandoned) policy was that they might then be assimilated into white Australian society with greater ease than were they to remain with their aboriginal mothers and relatives.

By nightfall on the following day, the *Triumph* made its waterlogged landing on the beach at Snake Bay, the Government aboriginal settlement on the north coast of Melville Island.[1] For the next 10 months (March through December 1954), first with Mountford, Harney, and others, I lived on a beautiful beach a mile from this settlement, or in the surrounding bush with my "sister" D., or "mother" N.,[2] her husband, Laurie, and their teenage daughter (my "sister"), Happy. Later I moved to the settlement where I slept on the porch of one of the two European houses, and where I was closer to the 164 Tiwi who also chose the non-Catholic government-run settlement for

---

[1] The *Triumph* sank permanently to the bottom of Clarence Strait on its return to Darwin.
[2] Because, in 1986, both D. and N. had recently died, Goodale has not used their names in deference to the customary Tiwi taboo.

their residence. The fact that I spent a great deal of my time with the women of Snake Bay, learning about hunting, marriage, and ceremony from their point of view, led me into writing about Tiwi culture with this female perspective. Today, this would not be very unusual, but in 1959 it was and even more intriguing were the discussions Pilling and I held subsequently, which convinced me that the views of men and women, particularly regarding their own marriages, were significantly different, yet, like a symphony, only made sense when both (or all) parts were played together. We found other, mostly harmonious, "symphonies" when we compared differences of opinion held by our Tiwi friends at Bathurst Island or Snake Bay regarding historic events, marriage exchanges, and alliances between clans and between countries. Some of these, we found, had their origins in the fact that in most cases, Tiwi preferred to reside at the modern settlement closest to their traditional countries, and as customs had sometimes varied in the traditional country segments of Tiwi society, so did they vary in 1954 (and indeed in the 1980s) among the various modern communities of Bathurst and Melville islands.

When the first anthropologists (Basedow in 1911; Spencer in 1911–1912; and Hart in 1928–1929, to mention only a few), reported on their field study of the people of Melville and Bathurst islands, variation was not as important a question in ethnographic research as it is today. In fact the fieldworker's task was to sift through informants' varying statements, preferably giving weight to cultural "experts" whose knowledge of custom and law was acknowledged by others to be the greatest, in order to discover the "patterns" or "norms" of *the* Tiwi culture and society. In many ways Hart broke away from this pattern of fieldwork, as he focused on variables in the prestige system of Tiwi men, and thus laid the groundwork for future studies of variation between the countries, each led by or inhabited by men of differing prestige and political power.

In the 1940s and 1950s, when the Tiwi were visited by Ronald M. and Catherine H. Berndt, by Pilling in 1953–1954, by Mountford and Goodale in 1954, new questions were in the anthropological "air." While Pilling concentrated on variations in law, resolution of conflict, and political alliance, I emphasized the variation relating to the nearly equal political power of women and men in both daily and ritual activities. The earlier study of the Berndts on social organization was followed up by one of their students, M. Brandl, in 1968. Brandl's study, of the social context of bereavement, provides us with an excellent picture of the community and social structures of the 1960s, and in particular the kinship, clan, and country affiliations that were still being emphasized in the *pukimani* and *kulama* rituals.

But there was one other factor influencing variation that remained largely unexplored and was brought to my attention when I made a very hasty (two-week) visit to Snake Bay in June 1962, and was taken aback (to put it mildly) to see what eight years of intensified "development" had wrought—or brought—to the Tiwi of Snake Bay. The white staff had increased from 2 (superintendent and teacher and their families) to 10. New housing, new community buildings, full "employment," and a forestry/timber industry had both physically and socially transformed the community as I had known it, but I had no time to investigate the deeper cultural effect of these changes.

It was not until 1980 that I had a chance to return to Snake Bay for a 14-month period. In order to do so I first had to gain the permission of the Tiwi Land Council (TLC), a new organization of representatives of all band territories, or as the Tiwi call them in English "countries," on both islands, charged with dealing with all matters relating to their "countries," which had been returned to their traditional owners with the passing of the *Aboriginal Land Rights (Northern Territory) Act of 1976*. Second, I had to receive permission of the Milikapiti Local Council, an elected group of representatives of those Tiwi living at Snake Bay, now known as Milikapiti. No more leaky barges; I flew on one of two daily planes, servicing the three major communities of Nguiu (on Bathurst Island—where the Sacred Heart Mission continues its activities); Pularumpi, the community at Garden Point—no longer a part-aboriginal school and settlement, but where many of those raised there continue to live and raise their own children; and Milikapiti—on the western shore of Snake Bay.

As the plane made each stop, at Nguiu and Pularumpi, I looked in vain for a familiar face. Finding none I was quite unprepared for the reception I received as I stepped off the plane at Milikapiti. The first to greet me was the widow, Polly, whose husband had been a famous political and ritual leader of the community in 1954. Next to Polly stood her son, Richard, and close by, my "sister" Happy and her friend Rosemary, two former teenagers who with their parents had been members of our little beach community in 1954. "Your sister D. will come see you later," they told me, and I climbed into a truck with my cartons of supplies and was driven to my allotted house. That night I wrote in my diary:

> Wow! What a day! It's now past midnight. I'm in my bed in my luxurious little house for the next year. It has a bedroom, bath, laundry with washer/wringer, large kitchen/dining/living room, and a large weed-covered yard sandwiched in between Robert Tipungwuti—the council President and a Forestry person, Jim Weston. As the whole township is located just north of the old settlement, my geography is very badly off. This place is barely recognizable—street lights, lighting many unpaved roads—going every which way! D. and her daughter Agnes, and her children came to call. Such emotions!—So much to bridge—So many years have gone by!—New ties to make, new friends to acquire—I feel as Rip Van Winkle must have felt when he finally woke up after a twenty-year sleep!

This feeling was not to leave me completely for several months. One of the most difficult adjustments I had to make was to realize that I too had aged 26 years—socially and politically I was no longer a "young woman" but a contemporary with those senior women accorded greatest responsibility, and related power in their own society. They shared this power and responsibility with senior men, but because I had been there when these senior people were themselves "youngsters," and because I had "talked with" their own fathers, grandfathers, mothers, and grandmothers, I was considered to have "almost" as much knowledge of (and therefore responsibility to) the Tiwi world as I had of (and to) my own European world. I found it extremely difficult, but also very rewarding, to play a dual role of both "listener" and "adviser" (when asked), in the various debates and decisions affecting both the local Milikapiti community, and the Island districts served by the TLC (Tiwi Land Council) over the 14-month period.

While I concentrated my efforts at Milikapiti, the network of roads connecting the Melville Island communities of Milikapiti, Pularumpi, Pickertaramoor, and Paru, and a trusty Toyota truck for transport, allowed me to visit with frequency all these Melville Island communities, and make boat connections to Nguiu on Bathurst Island. It also gave me and my friends ready access to prime hunting and fishing areas throughout the countryside of Wulirankuwu. Most of my trips to other communities were to aid others in fulfilling their ritual or Land Council obligations. However, when the destination was Pularumpi, I also had the opportunity to talk with another anthropologist, Andree Grau, who was studying Tiwi dance during the same period of time.[3] Our talks frequently involved variations we experienced and noted while in these two communities and while visiting others.

Although most of this chapter is based on my 1980–1981 research, the opportunity to commute by air to Melville and Bathurst islands while teaching in Darwin during the 1986/1987 academic year allowed me to update my observations.

THE OWNERS OF THEIR LAND—AGAIN

The most significant change in government policy concerning aboriginal people was the passage of the *Aboriginal Land Rights (Northern Territory) Act 1976*, which brought the return of all former mission or reserve lands in the Northern Territory to the "traditional owners," and gave the right of other aboriginal people to demonstrate ownership of other lands held by the Crown in the Northern Territory. The effect for the Tiwi was that all land on the two islands was returned to their ownership, excluding only those areas covered by salt water all or part of the time. The Tiwi considered these watery regions to be part of the lands of each "country" as they included the locations of unborn spirit children (the sacred "dreaming" locations). Because these coastal regions were fished in by many non-Tiwi, they were the subject of negotiation with these other users during the 1980s.

What in 1976 were two titles (one for the former Mission controlled area—Bathurst Island—and one for the former Government Native Reserve and settlement—Melville Island), became one in 1981 the result of strong, consistent concern and effort of the Tiwi to express legally the overall unity of Tiwi people, their land and culture. The distinction that Tiwi people feel between their culture and that of mainland aboriginal people was expressed

---

[3] Note Grau, 1983.

Photo 21. A meeting of the Tiwi Land Council at Nguiu in 1981. The meeting place shown is under the mango trees in the old Bathurst Island Mission compound.

earlier, when (in 1977 following the *Act*) the Tiwi declined representation on the mainland based Northern Land Council (NLC), preferring to form their own representative Tiwi Land Council (TLC), because as one delegate, Mr. Kerinaiua, argued, "It was a good idea . . . that affairs on the Island(s) . . . be administered by Tiwi People and not outsiders."[4]

The TLC is made up of the representatives from each "country," elects its own chairman, and employs a manager to keep the minutes, the budget, pay bills, and perform other such tasks.[5] The Council rotates its monthly meetings between the three townships, and interested Tiwi residents, who are not members, often attend. Women may attend. In 1980 some women attended as concerned co-owners of their country with their brothers.

The Council discusses and makes decisions concerning all matters relating to land and affairs outside the area of each township. This includes granting permission to any non-Tiwi who wishes to visit, for short or long terms, and for any reason. With such a right, they can make decisions for or against any exploitation of Island resources or "development" of their lands. However, much of the discussion in 1980–1981 concerned fulfilling the requirement of the *Act* to maintain a list of "traditional owners" and a map showing the boundaries of their land.

[4] *Milikapiti Records* 1975–1977.
[5] During 1980–1981 and 1986–1987, the TLC granted Goodale permission to attend their sessions.

Photo 22. Father Tim Brennan, left, and Cyril Rioli, at the meeting of the Tiwi Land Council, in Nguiu, during late 1980. Father Tim (as he is called by the Tiwi) was the manager of the TLC from its inception until 1986, when he left Bathurst Island to become director of Catholic missions in the NT. Cyril Rioli was the President of TLC in 1980–1981.

For the Tiwi, listing traditional owners required that they make decisions concerning matters which, for two or three generations, had either not been theirs to make, or were matters regarding "ownership" that had been minimized or altered by their "settled" life at the various centers. As Pilling (and I) found in 1954, the most important social groupings were (and had been for some time) the matrilineal clans (see p. 121). Now they were faced with deciding who were owners of what lands. Both questions had ramifications surely felt, if not expressed, by members of the Council, as they showed a reluctance to comply with this requirement.

The TLC decided first to determine how many countries they wished to be represented, and then follow with decisions concerning how ownership should be determined, after which the lists could be made. The first Council had been formed on the basis of 12 "countries": Yimpinari, Turrupwi, Marruwawa, Wulirankuwu, Marrikawiyanga, Murnupi (north and south), Malawu, Wurangkuwu, Tangilimpi, Jikilaruwu, Mantiyupwi, and Rankijarri. These were named and bounded on a map prepared by the Forestry Section of the Government of the Northern Territory, which had been engaged in timber development on Melville Island since the late 1950s.

The 1981 country debate took a number of months to resolve, with separate meetings held at all three townships where all "owners" (male and female) could participate in the discussions resulting in a final (1983) list of seven countries: Mantiyupwi, Tikilaru, Wurangkuwu, Malawu, Murnupi, Wulirangkuwu, Yimpinari. In this final listing a number of formerly recognized "countries" were merged, owners agreeing among themselves to be collectively represented on the Council (and at the same time the spellings of names were adjusted to conform to current standards). Thus they expressed on paper the continuity of a traditional political process of expansion, and amalgamation of land-based units—a process documented by Hart, Pilling, and others who have compiled different lists and maps over the past 80 years or so.

A related question that was strongly debated in 1980 was: Where were these countries? "Our grandfathers didn't have maps, but we should know our place," argued Walter Kerinaiua, an advocate for determining a definable boundary. However, it was not easy for current owners to so bound their lands. Boundaries in one's head were flexible enough to accommodate the political processes of the past, but could not be marked on a map with the definiteness required by European law. Another problem was that for some, their country was isolated from the townships by a lack of roads, and few of the younger owners had lived or hunted over the land frequently enough fully to know it. But this fact did not in any way diminish the strength of their attachment to it. Andree Grau[6] records a *pukimani* for a piece of land that had been reclaimed by the sea in a storm and the two songs that were composed sometime later, referring to the loss:

> Her face was lovely at Teipwi.
> Her face fell down.[7]

> I had lovely legs just like the hills of Teipwi.
> The sea came and washed my legs away.
> I have bony legs now.[8]

The question of who was to be recorded as an "owner" was decided country-by-country by the senior members—both men and women—debating, as they met to decide the matter for their country. The effects of 70 years of Mission and European influence were immediately brought out when, in the discussion among the leaders of Murnupi, Cyril Rioli, the chairman of the TLC at that time, asked, "It comes down to this—do I have any rights in this land of my mother?" The Murnupuwi agreed that he did. Mr. Rioli had been raised at the Garden Point Mission school and settlement, married, and raised his own family there, but his father had not been an aboriginal through whom he could claim land rights.

The traditional marriage arrangement—where every Tiwi woman was *promised* in marriage to a Tiwi husband before her birth—insured that any child born to her had a Tiwi father through whom certain rights in land were passed. But many years of Mission and European negative influence on *promised* marriage has resulted in increasing numbers of children who are born to Tiwi mothers, but whose father has no rights in any aboriginal land to pass on to them. In each of the debates held in 1981, the senior members agreed that such children were to be considered as having rights in their mother's country, and that their names should be added to the list of owners. Although this sounds like a radical change, it did not appear so to me, because in the past a son-in-law was required to reside in his in-laws' country for long periods of time as he fulfilled his obligations to his wife's parents. Sometimes he died and was buried there, and the presence of his grave legitimatized his children's claims in their mother's (his wife's) country. But the presence of the grave

[6] Grau, 1983: 191.
[7] Ibid., p. 286.
[8] Ibid., p. 304.

of one's father or grandfather had long ago ceased to be a marker of land ownership for many Tiwi, because nearly all Tiwi were buried in the designated graveyards of the Mission, settlements or, now, township where they had lived. Only a few families lived close enough to, or in, their own country to be able to bury their relatives in, and hold the required rituals on, their own land.[9]

The TLC accomplished the difficult task of meeting the requirement of maintaining a list of owners; however, during the process strong feelings were expressed by all members of the TLC that the Tiwi should act as a whole concerning all important decisions regarding the future of their islands. It is interesting to note that when Hart first visited these islands (1928), he found that the Tiwi had no name for themselves as a "tribe." He selected the word for "people" in their language to refer to them collectively. In 1954 when Pilling and Goodale visited them, we found that some individuals referred to themselves as "Tiwi" when addressing non-Tiwi, while retaining their country identities within the tribe. What the TLC members were formalizing then was that this unified tribal identity should be theirs when ultimately deciding how any of their lands were to be developed or used by non-Tiwi, while retaining traditional and distinctive country identities in other contexts; for example, when exercising an owner's right "to be asked" when any Tiwi not a co-owner wished to exploit one's country's natural resources. By 1986, the Tiwi were using the English word "tribe" to talk about these separate groups of "countrymen."

THE TOWNSHIPS AND THEIR GOVERNMENT

Local government councils were in existence in the three major communities for a number of years before the TLC was formed. Their power has been substantially increased until in 1981 the councils have full powers over the budget, personnel, and planning for their respective communities. From the very beginning, women have been elected to the local councils. Although to my knowledge none have served as president, at least one woman, Mary Elizabeth Moreen, daughter of a former powerful local leader at Milikapiti, ran for office in 1980 and perhaps would have been elected had not her Mungatopi family vote been split between her and two Mungatopi men.

Decisions in the councils are mainly reached by discussion and consensus, the traditional Tiwi way, even though a vote may be taken. Women, never reticent to voice their opinion when appropriate, continue to be heard in the council debates on all topics, but most particularly on those that relate to housing, health, education, and maintenance of peace and harmony, law and order, matters relating to the quality of domestic life in which they have

[9] The Mungatopi family were such a group and held two large *pukimani* rituals for two of their members who died in the mid-1970s. These rituals were filmed at the request of the family and are available for viewing. *Mourning for Mungatopi* is the filmed ritual for a son, organized by his father (and "country" leader). *Goodby Old Man* is the funeral ritual for the father himself who died a few years after his son.

Photo 23. Scene at Milikapiti, in 1981, in front of the council office.

always shown leadership and concern. The "households," which a number of senior women manage today within the settlements, often translate to the entire township on certain occasions.

The president of the council is often called to represent the township in many different political forums: on the TLC, and in negotiations with the Northern Territory government and its various departments in obtaining grants for township development in addition to approval of township budgets, and at times with the Commonwealth government. At Milikapiti, Pularumpi, and Nguiu, the local council employs a town clerk to manage its daily affairs, but the council president is its chief spokesperson and negotiator. The position of president may or may not fall to a leader in the local land-owning family. For example, in 1981 (and 1986) Robert Tipungwuti from Wurangkuwu (Bathurst Island) was president of the Milikapiti local council, where the Mungatopi and Tipiloura families were the local landowners. At Pularumpi, Cyril Rioli, a former Member of the Legislative Assembly in Darwin, whose rights in Murnupi land came from his mother, led the council, whereas senior men and women from the Puruntatameri and Tipakalippa families were principal Murnupi landowners. At Nguiu Shire, Titus Wommatakimmi was not only the council president in 1980, but also one of the local owners of Mantiyupwi country, which included the township; whereas Stanley Tipaloura, president in 1986, was from Wulirangkuwu.

Tiwi politics does not seem to have changed very much, only the forums in which political skill may be demonstrated have widened to include those of the encroaching European local political scene. Men are still engaged in contract manipulation, where success is often translated into personal prestige and standing, whereas women use their powers to control and improve the standard of life within the local community and "household."

Just as before the advent of Europeans, Tiwi men today make long-term residential decisions based on two primary factors: rights in land and potential for self-advancement. And a third factor, the availability of adequate natural resources for maintenance of physical and mental health, continues to influence decisions resulting in shorter terms of residence. In the past, because Tiwi women were married from birth (or before) to death and were expected to live with their successive husbands, they had less opportunity to make completely independent residential decisions—in the 1980s they do, often on the same bases as men.

As in earlier years, the majority of Tiwi are choosing to reside in the community closest to their own "country." Nguiu, the largest township (approximately 1,300 Tiwi and up to 100 Europeans) is predominantly made up of those whose countries are Tikilaru, Wurangkuwu, Malawu, and Manti-yupwi (whose country extends to both sides of Apsley Strait). Pularumpi (with about 400 Tiwi and 12, sometimes more, Europeans) is the principal residence of those whose country is Murnupi; whereas Milikapiti (with 300 Tiwi, more or less, and up to 30 Europeans) is the residence of choice for those whose country is Wulirangkuwu or Yimpinari.

Employment in the early 1980s was not available for every adult man or woman as it had been in the initial "development" period of the 1950s and 1960s. The worldwide recession and the admission of a formerly cheap aboriginal labor force into the standard wage category had reduced the size of the local wage work force to a minimum. Men could find employment in the Caribbean pine forest development project, in the local primary schools, in the Township Housing, or Electricity and Water/Sewer Departments, or in the general store owned by the Milikapiti Progress Association, in the club, or in the Milikapiti local council work force in a variety of capacities relating to running a modern town. Women are employed by the council, in the general store and club, in the local clinic (which in 1986 was completely aboriginally staffed), and in the local school. Three Tiwi women are kept busy silk screening T-shirts with colorful Tiwi designs.

A similar employment situation is found at Pularumpi, whereas at Nguiu additional opportunities exist in the local industries, including Bima Wear, a dress-making industry with both a local market on the islands and in mainland stores. Tiwi Designs, a silk-screening fabric industry, supplies Bima Wear with the colorful and distinctive materials that make their clothing so popular, and also produces other items such as drapes, tablecloths, and wall hangings, found in many a Darwin office and home. In 1986 on the occasion of the Pope's visit to Darwin, the Tiwi produced for him a complete set of vestments incorporating both papal and Tiwi symbols. Tiwi Pottery is another industry started by a Tiwi youth whose products are extremely well received. Nguiu has a public restaurant, overnight accommodations for visitors and tourists, a general store and repair garage, as well as the basic facilities found at other townships. All townships are actively engaged in developing for their region tourist attractions and accommodations stressing fishing, arts and crafts, sightseeing, and "wilderness" camping.

Still the dominant feature of Nguiu is the Bathurst Island Mission of the

Photo 24. Cover of the travel brochure for Tiwi Tours, 1986.

Sacred Heart order and its affiliated parochial school system. Although board-
ing facilities at the school are no longer available, a few children from the
other communities are sent to live with relatives in order to attend this school,
which is notably distinct from the government-run schools at Milikapiti and

Pularumpi. For instance, the Nguiu school system has a well-established bilingual program based on an increasing number of graded readers, and other literature, written in Tiwi language and produced locally.[10] The Mission presence at Pularumpi is also a vital part of that community, although the same cannot be said for Milikapiti, where in 1980 a priest arrived late Sunday afternoon, to hold a Mass sandwiched in between the day's hunting and fishing excursions and the weekly showing of a popular film. By 1986 television and video had arrived and made a community film night obsolete.

Nguiu and Pularumpi have "clubs" where beer may be bought and consumed during stated hours in the late afternoon and early evening; whereas at Milikapiti, beer sold at the club in late afternoon may be consumed "at home" throughout the evening. Pularumpi is the only township to have policemen in residence and a "lock-up." Two European officers are responsible for maintaining law and order throughout the two islands, helped to a varying degree by "police aides" appointed by each council and trained by the Northern Territory Department. The image that Pularumpi is the most peaceful of the three communities to live in is not unrelated to these facts!

The last major contrast between the three major communities is both geographical and developmental: the variation in the natural resources and the ease of access to them—for example, the availability of roads and vehicles. Here Milikapiti, with its location on a peninsula of land, offering a vast array of beach, mangrove, reef, and open water as well as inland bush, is considered to have local food resource advantages not found at Nguiu or Pularumpi. In addition the Forestry/Conservation Department had developed over 26 years a network of primary and secondary roads so that, with transport, all local areas may be reached with little effort. All townships have departmentally controlled vehicles, which may sometimes be used for hunting. An increasing number of Tiwi have acquired their own vehicles, and more their own boats and outboards, and the Milikapiti women have organized their own club, several times for the purpose of obtaining and operating a vehicle under their own control to use in food-gathering activities.

An important alternative to township living occurred in the early 1980s, when some members of two major family groups of Bathurst Island left Nguiu to form their own separate communities on their own lands: The Munkara resettled at Cape Fourcroy at the extreme western tip of Bathurst Island in Tikilaru country, whereas the Kantilla family settled at Rocky Point on the western shores of Wurangkuwu, Bathurst Island. The Tipaloura of Wulirangkuwu have established themselves close to the waterfall at Tarakumbi,

---

[10] Some idea of the magnitude of this bilingual program may be gained by reference to the sources listed at the end of this edition (Apuatimi, 1977; Brook, 1975; Fernando, 1982; Godfrey, 1985; Godfrey and Apuatimi, 1976, 1977a–b, 1978; Godfrey and Sister Jacinta Mary, 1975a–b; Godfrey and Manning, 1976a–b; Hempel, 1977; Heysen, 1985a–b; David Kantilla, 1984; Donald Kantilla, n.d.; M. Kantilla, 1981; C. Kerinaiua, 1983; L. Kerinaiua, 1981; M. Kerinaiua, 1981; Kilham, 1979; Le Forte, n.d.; Mungatopi, n.d.; Mungatopi and Munkara, 1980; A. Munkara, 1981; H. Munkara, 1975; M. Munkara, 1981; P. Munkara, 1982; V. Munkara, 1982; Nguiu Nginingawila Literature Production Centre, 1982, 1983, 1984; Osborne, 1979; Puruntatameri, 1982; St. Therese's School, 1980; Summer Institute of Linguistics, 1975a–b, 1976; Tipiloura, 1981; Tipungwuti, Tipungwuti, and Tungutalum, 1981; Tungutalum, 1982; Tungutalum and Tipungwuti, 1981).

and the Mungatopi have plans for building at Karslake. The future of these "suburban" (outstation) communities depends very much on obtaining and maintaining a truck and/or boat for contact with the closest township, and permanent water supplies. Paru, Joe Cooper's old base across the strait from Nguiu, is the oldest "outstation" or suburban community continuously maintained and the home for a small group of senior Kerinaiua family members. In 1981, three (of a planned six) new experimental solar-powered houses were officially "opened" at Paru, with the Bishop, Chief Minister, and other officials of the Northern Territory government, and the architect, attending. One of the new house owners, dancing with abandon in front of her house before the officials arrived, was asked if she were drunk so early in the morning. "No," she retorted, "I'm dancing with joy that I have my new beautiful house!" Solar power pumps water to a storage tank at Paru from a stream over 2 kilometers away, and provides hot water in the showers and turns a house light on at dark and off at dawn!

The differences of each community translate into a number of reasons individual Tiwi choose to be residents at one township, visiting in the others for shorter or longer periods of time. But in the long run, land ownership is the overriding reason to maintain permanent residence in or as close as possible to one's own land. Thus we can see the reemergence of the bands, which in 1928–1929 Hart wrote were "the territorial group with which a man most closely identifies himself," but which in the intervening periods were obscured by the settlements and mission.

CONTINUITY AND CHANGE

"Today the Forestry men are burning off the grass at Milikapiti, so tomorrow we will be able to hunt in the bush for possums, wallabies and sugarbag (honey)," my daughter, Agnes, wrote in a May 1984 letter. Even in Pennsylvania I could almost smell the pungent eucalyptus smoke in the air and hear the excited talk of the women as they planned what they would "go for" and eat tomorrow, and my mouth began to water as I recalled the delicious foods of the islands. One of the greatest (and most pleasant) of the surprises I received in 1980 was to note and participate in the increased amount of hunting, fishing, and collecting the natural resources of the bush, mangrove, reef, and sea over that which I had expected or recalled.

Depending on the season, household managers regularly seize every opportunity to supply themselves and dependents with the preferred traditional foods to supplement that which they can buy in the store. For example, in 1981, my mother N. (age 56), together with her husband (69 years), headed a household that included their only daughter Happy (38), and her four children (18, 16, 14, and 9), N's "sister" (FD), Rachael (29) and her husband Paddy Puruntatameri (51) and their five children (16, 12, 11, 9, and 8), also N's widowed "mother" (MZ) Minnie (aged 65). These 15 people were the regular members of the household, which at times also included one or more visiting relatives. Only Happy had a regular salaried job as teaching assistant.

Other adults received pensions of various kinds and amounts, but there was never enough money to supply the needs of this large household from the store alone. Happy's eldest and "unemployed" son was a very successful turtle hunter, regularly supplying his own and related households. Minnie, Rachael, and her husband, Paddy, were consistent suppliers of oysters, crabs, and cockles from reef and mangroves. My "mother" no longer had the strength to walk very far, but her keen eyesight and knowledge allowed her regularly to locate sugarbag (wild honey), and possum holes in the highest trees near the camp, or a sleeping goanna (a foot-long edible lizard) from the back of a moving truck, and she would direct those more able to chop down the tree or stalk and kill the goanna.

Although Laurie had not the strength to hunt, his influence in the household was typical of the role of elderly men in the past as he remained in the township or camp, directing and disciplining the young men and, when the women were all gone, caring for his blind grandson with love and tenderness. He was also the senior representative of his country on the TLC and a former member of the local council.

Other large households are similarly dependent on the hunting and foraging of the adult members in order to maintain a desired quality of life in the township. Both women and men told me they considered hunting knowledge and skills to be essential for their children to learn, and it did not matter whether these children were young or old. Some of the Mission-raised adults, themselves mothers and fathers, expressed their continued dependence on their own elders for transmission of this essential knowledge for the future survival of themselves and their children.

During the week only the unemployed women and youths were free to hunt or fish, but on Sundays nearly the entire Milikapiti community climbed aboard one of the available trucks, or filled the tanks of their motorboats and private vehicles, and dispersed throughout the countryside for a day of greatly appreciated peace, family life, and "real" food. Although the store stocked frozen meats and snack foods such as meat pies, barbecued chickens, ice cream, and "pop," I have seen these fed to dogs or used as fish bait, when an alternative fresh wallaby, dugong, possum, or fish, was at hand. Prepared cycad nut mash was preferred by most adults to hot-cross currant buns, mangrove worms to hot dogs, and if one felt a bit out of health, hot "cheeky" *iwili* mangrove worm broth was considered as beneficial as the proverbial chicken soup is to some Westerners.

Although Saturdays were often a hunting day as well, other scheduled activities frequently competed for attention. With the monsoon season (November–April) came the weekly football league battles between six local teams. Milikapiti and Pularumpi each fielded a team, whereas Nguiu had enough residents to make up four teams. The teams were based on local land-owning divisions, and "home" games were attended by the entire township. With "spirited" support from the onlookers, team players were somehow able to overcome the afternoon humidity, lack of regular practice sessions, and sometimes the effects of too much beer, and played an extraordinarily exciting

Photo 25. Newly carved mourning poles at the final pukimani *ceremony for the mother of Happy Cook, near Milikapiti, in 1986.*

and skilled game. In 1986 Maurice Rioli from Pularumpi made national newspapers as an outstanding member of "Southern" football team as had his father before him and more than a few other Tiwi in earlier years. On Saturdays following the biweekly payday, nearly everyone engaged in the serious business of exchanging money through the many card games taking place under every shady tree or veranda in the community. By means of this redistribution of available money, it was possible (although of course not guaranteed) for playing adults of any age to raise enough cash to purchase motor cars or boats, tickets, or air charters to Darwin and elsewhere, pay off debts at the store, or meet ritual obligations.

Saturdays and Sundays are also days when *pukimani* (funeral) rituals are scheduled at the various communities. Although a number of changes can be seen in the length and elaborateness of these most important rituals, the basic structure and obligatory roles of kin and spouse remained as they have always been. The Catholic church no longer opposes these rituals and although the burial ceremonies of Catholics in all townships begin with a Mass, they are all followed by traditional expressions of ritual grief, and continue to be where kinship, and matrilineal clan (own and father's) and land affiliations are expressed in songs and dances. Poles are commissioned for the subsequent ritual(s), in general fewer and less elaborate than I saw in 1954, but carvers and other "workers" received up to several hundred dollars in payment for this work and for dancing at the ritual. In 1986 a number of men and women at Milikapiti were commissioned to carve poles for display at the National Museum at Canberra—several of these equal or surpass in originality and

Photo 26. The daughter of Happy Cook, dancing at the final mourning ceremony for her mother's mother, near Milikapiti, in 1986.

carving those I saw carved in 1954. The expenses of the close kin and spouse of the deceased are considerable, and rituals are scheduled when both payment and required participants can be brought together. Sometimes certain relatives hold separate rituals, for a variety of reasons. The composing of songs and performing of specific dance routines is still being transmitted to the younger generation, but not with as much emphasis or success as the elders wish. Part of the difficulty, they say, is the decline in language skills among those whose formal education is mainly, if not entirely, in English.

The *kulama* ritual, where special songs are composed by participants, is still being performed by fully initiated men toward the end of the monsoon season, and a few young and middle-aged men are receiving the detailed instruction in the language skills considered necessary to compose and sing their songs with the exactness required by the ritual, so that no illness or death would come to the singer or his family in the succeeding year. During the 1980 season, *kulama* rituals were held at Nguiu and at Pularumpi. Andree Grau[11] recorded the songs, dances, and other events of four rituals in which a total of 13 fully initiated men participated. Some of these men had taken

[11] Grau, 1983: 158–184.

a "short-cut" route to full initiation status, according to Grau's informants, and had begun their training in their mid- to late thirties. One factor that was aiding the task of learning the appropriate song style was the use of tape recorders, and "these tapes are played over and over during the following weeks, not only by the young men who one day may take part in the ritual, but also by young women who one day may 'follow' (help) their husbands and brothers."[12]

It was in ritual that the strength and persistence of the matrilineal clan groupings, and the associated "dreamings" (father's clan affiliation and the patrilineally related dance groups) were still being shown. It was also in ritual that the strength of all kinship categories and relationships were reaffirmed, including that of promised and actual spouse. Because sons-in-law were still being "given" to their mothers-in-law (sometimes, as in the past, even before she had any children), a husband's role at every young female's death rituals was filled, even when everyone knew that the actual marriage might never have taken place should the child have lived to reach "marriageable" age.

Speech taboos between men and their mothers-in-law still prevailed in many of these relationships. For example, two of the most vocal and active members of the Milikapiti Local Council in 1980–1981 were the president, Robert Tipungwuti, who was the promised husband of a 3-year-old daughter of the other very active member, Mary Elizabeth Moreen. That neither could speak directly to the other produced some awkward, but no impossible, situations. Although no one expected that all promised marriage arrangements would take place, many still did, and marriages that were "arranged" by the couple themselves, more often than not, fulfilled traditional exchange obligations between their respective clans and countries. When they do not, and violate a kinship or clan rule of exogamy, considerable discussion and debate take place, far more than when the marriage is to a non-Tiwi aboriginal from the mainland. A few Tiwi women have formed fairly permanent arrangements with European men, legalized with a European marriage ritual; other women have had briefer affairs with non-aboriginal men, but among parents who express a reluctance to see their daughters married to a European, most tell me that they would support their daughters' choice of a member of any aboriginal group for her husband, and as father of their grandchildren. I believe, although I cannot say with certainty, that Tiwi and other aboriginal parents are expressing, in this and in other ways, a regained feeling of pride and cultural identity strengthened by the recognition by the Australian government of land rights of aboriginal peoples. Even though in most aboriginal societies as among the Tiwi, children do receive particular rights in the land of their mothers, to be without rights in one's father's land as well, is to receive an incomplete heritage and identity as an aboriginal Australian.

The patrilineal *aminiyiati* land-based units, which Hart noted in 1929, composed of the descendants of an important and powerful father's father (*amini*), are reappearing as important units in Tiwi society in the 1980s under a dual

12 Grau, 1983: 183–184.

influence of the Mission and of the Land Rights Act. In conferences of Melville and Bathurst administrators in 1968 and 1969,

> "Father Fallon brought up the matter of surnames and mentioned the system organized by Fr. Cosgrove at the Mission . . . making the following points in favor of extending this surname system throughout all communities: . . . [that] use of nicknames would become a thing of the past. Where Tiwi surnames . . . proved somewhat unmanageable—(to Europeans?!)—they should be stabilized on a shortened version . . . Consideration to the Bathurst Island system by other communities could *simplify appreciation of (patrilineal)* relationships."[13]

Brother Pye[14] listed 55 surnames in his history of the Mission and all but eight were names of deceased male ancestors. To use these as surnames was to overlook the taboo on use of a personal name by anyone for some years after the giver or receiver of that name dies. Although some at Milikapiti told me, "We could have surnames too, if we wanted them," and continued to prefer their single and unique name(s), it appeared that patrilineally inherited surnames were there to stay. But the relationship of surname to the particular lands recognized by the TLC was a bit complex, for this relationship was ultimately based on the political events and decisions of the past, some of which had been recorded and described earlier (by Hart, and by Pilling and others), but most of which were to be found only in the memories of the oldest living generation, or had, like the people of earlier generations, been forgotten.

Regardless of the outcome of debates among the descendants of these men, the true balance of affiliation between those related through mothers (the matrilineal clan and its affiliations with other clans), and between those related through fathers—to a shared named paternal ancestor (whose land was "x" and whose grave marked this relationship giving shared rights in the land), was in the process of being revived by 1980.

The 1980s and 1990s should be an extremely interesting period for the Tiwi as they regain individual and collective control over their life and lands in full. In 1980, the Commonwealth Department of Aboriginal Affairs gave up almost all of its jurisdiction over the aboriginal peoples of the Northern Territory, turning over its role to the Territory Department of Community Development. (Health and Education had been under control of Territory departments for a number of years.) After almost 80 years of control and "development" by representatives from foreign and dominating cultures, the Tiwi of the early 1980s were faced once again with the responsibility of self-development. They viewed this challenge of deciding their own future with both anxiety and courage, while they continued to train their children to survive in their land, and at the same time aspired that they would one day be recognized as fully equal by all other citizens in the larger Australian society. With increasing numbers of non-Tiwi as tourists coming to know

---

[13] Emphasis Goodale's. *Milikapiti Records*, 1968, 1969.
[14] Pye, 1977.

the people and country of Melville and Bathurst islands, it is also possible, as one Tiwi told me in 1986, "that white people too will learn to live *with* and survive in the country," clearly expressing the noncommercial educational aspects that underlie Tiwi concepts and benefits of developing tourism.

8/Fieldwork among the Tiwi, 1928–1929

by C. W. M. Hart

GETTING STARTED

Fieldwork among the Tiwi in 1928–1929 was not difficult provided that the fieldworker was young, healthy, undemanding of personal comfort, and unmarried. (I suspect that these four conditions apply universally to fieldwork among the simpler peoples, but there is no space here to argue the point.) At that date the Tiwi were still mostly nomadic, though the Sacred

Photo 27. *Mourning ceremony around carved and painted graveposts, during Hart's 1928–1929 fieldwork.*

desirable. The only trouble was the language. Around the Mission the younger men spoke pidgin English and some like Mariano spoke it well. But in the northern bands nobody spoke anything except Tiwi. So one had to compromise. I went to and joined the northern bands but I took Mariano with me. Otherwise I could not (at first) communicate with the northern bands. Once this decision had been made there was little problem. The pagan bands were glad to have us; with Mariano as interpreter and assorted members of the northern bands as teachers and helpers I could learn the language. I was no longer identified with the Mission nor with the Tiklauila, and in all sorts of small ways (by observing taboos, for example) I could indicate my lack of sympathy for much of the Mission program. Away from the Tiklauila Mariano was not nearly so much a liability as I had expected; the traditional daily living under tribal conditions was quite congenial to him; the Malauila and Munupula respected him even though they did not agree with him in his advocacy of monogamy, and in fact questions concerning the Mission rarely came up for discussion.

In the meantime I was able to learn the language. It did not come easily, but at least it came. I suppose there are places in the world where it is possible to do fieldwork without knowing the language or by working through interpreters; but surely much is missed by working under such conditions. By the time I left the islands I think I spoke reasonably good Tiwi, understood it better than I spoke it, and was never ashamed to ask that something I did not understand be explained or repeated in another way. The biggest factor in facilitating my learning was of course the isolation from other English-speakers that living in Munupi or Malau provided. If I had remained at the Mission, I would have been speaking English every day to the priests and nuns, and would probably never have learned Tiwi. But in Malau or Munupi nobody spoke any English (except Mariano and he only spoke pidgin), so I either spoke Tiwi or did not speak at all.

Living with the Malauila and Munupula meant, of course, living pretty close to nature. In *The Tiwi of North Australia* there is a section called Daily Activities, and for much of my two years with the Tiwi the daily life of the natives was my daily life too. That is, I went where they went, stopped when they stopped, ate what they ate, slept when they slept, and generally was interested and concerned about whatever they were interested and concerned about. It surprised me, who had no boy-scout background, how little in the way of manufactured objects one needed. Since the Tiwi establishments (collections of households) are always moving, and one moves easiest if one moves light, it was instructive to find out how light the baggage could be made. Sneakers, a hat, and a pair of shorts were all the clothing necessary; a shotgun to kill wallaby and wild fowl and plenty of shells for it; pencils and notebooks; soap and toothbrush (even towels were optional); pipe and tobacco; a camera and plenty of film. These seemed to be the only essentials, except that for an Australian, tea and sugar had to be added; and as luxuries, only because they were light in weight, salt, pepper, and Worcestershire sauce, because Tiwi cooking is very tasteless without condiments. For the natives, stores had to include a few simple medicines like iodine (the "burning medicine" which they loved and demanded to have applied raw to all simple cuts), aspirin, and Epsom salts. And lastly, the heaviest and bulkiest item of all, an endless supply of native twist tobacco, a currency that took one everywhere and opened all doors. Everything else was parked at the Mission and except for the shotgun, all the above items could be carried in one or two small sacks. Blankets were not necessary; the Tiwi on chilly nights sleep between two small fires, which can be kept burning all night with twigs that you take to bed with you, and provided you do not roll, the fires give warmth and keep the mosquitoes away. The native food was perfectly adequate and usually abundant, and by lending my shotgun to a native hunter I was able on most days to contribute my share to the total food production of the household with which I was living. One of the objects thankfully left behind was a razor, because beards were prestige symbols for the Tiwi. Older and important men carried luxuriant beards, the bushier the more admired; only "kids" were beardless, and though I never achieved as bushy a beard as that of Father Gsell (an Alsatian by birth), mine was at least as bushy as that of Father McGrath, his second-in-command. Incidentally but importantly, the Tiwi sign of intense anger is to put the right hand behind the beard, sweep it into the mouth and chomp hard on it, a most convincing indication of fury. How can one uphold one's dignity or indicate one's anger in such a culture if one is clean shaven?

This beard business is, I think, part of the day-by-day fieldwork tactics that fieldworkers in any culture have to be thinking about constantly, and the better they know their culture the better their tactics will be. Tact and tactics seem to have the same derivation as words. For a man without a beard to expect to be taken seriously in Tiwi culture was quite simply tactless or a gaucherie, and anthropologists should avoid gaucheries, otherwise they are no different from tourists. Tourists are usually tactless not through ill-will but through ignorance of the local culture; anthropologists thinking out tactics are merely striving to be more tactful as their knowledge of the culture improves.

GETTING INTO THE KINSHIP SYSTEM

In my travels about the two islands I frequently met groups of natives who had never seen me before. Such groups invariably addressed three questions to the men I was with. "How old is he?" "Is he married?" "What clan does he belong to?" As I was only about 23 at the time (and, of course, unmarried), no Tiwi was likely to take me very seriously if told the truth, since, as I said elsewhere (p. 60), "The men between 21 and 30 were the group which the elders were just beginning to take seriously . . . the younger members of this group were almost indistinguishable from the 'kids' (that is, the under 20-year-old group)." But with a beard I looked much older than 24 and in response to such questions my companions could easily up my age to over

30 without provoking disbelief, and my state of unmarriedness could easily be excused as being due to white men having different customs. All of which goes to show that in a culture such as Tiwi, with its great contempt for male youthfulness, an anthropologist of 23 was at a great disadvantage, but at least I was well aware of it and constantly trying to counteract it.

The third customary question—What is his clan?—was much more difficult to deal with. Like all students of Radcliffe-Brown I had been well grounded in the overall importance of the kinship system in all Australian tribes and of how anybody not in the kinship system was considered to be not quite human. One of Radcliffe-Brown's stories had told of how, when he was doing the research that led eventually to "Three Tribes of Western Australia" (Brown, 1913), he had traveled along the Ninety Mile Beach accompanied by a native interpreter named Teacup. Whenever they approached a new group or a strange camp, it was Teacup's duty to go in first and establish some kin connection between himself and the new group. Until such connection was made, no intercourse was possible between them and the point of the story was how on one occasion, Radcliffe-Brown was awakened by Teacup crawling into his sleeping bag announcing that both of them were going to be killed, because after hours of effort, Teacup had been unable to find any kinship link between himself and the group they had just met. I knew the Tiwi were not going to kill me, but after a few weeks on the islands I also became aware that they were often uneasy with me because I had no kinship linkage to them. This was shown in many ways, among others in their dissatisfaction with the negative reply they always got to their third question, "What clan does he belong to?" Around the Mission, to answer it by saying "White men have no clans," was at least a possible answer, but among the pagan bands like the Malauila and Munupula such an answer was incomprehensible—to them everybody must have a clan, just as everybody must have an age. To answer their first question "How old is he?" by saying "White men don't have ages" would be nonsense. To them it was equally nonsense to answer their third question as we did. And by talking such apparent nonsense we made them uneasy, and by extension, hostile or at least unfriendly. If I had a clan I would be inside the kinship system, everybody would know how to act toward me, I would know how to act toward everybody else, and life would be easier and smoother for all.

How to get myself into the clan and kinship system was however quite a problem. Even Mariano, although admitting the desirability, saw no way of getting me in. "These Malauila and Munupula are just wild men," he said privately, "they just can't understand that white people don't have clans and don't use kinship terms when talking to each other and about each other." In common with my generation of "new anthropologists" (1930 vintage), I had laughed derisively when I had heard or read the accounts of late nineteenth-century travelers and amateur anthropologists who claimed that they had been "fully initiated" into some tribe or other, and anyhow it was not initiation that I felt I needed but merely a place in the kinship system.

There did not seem much hope and then suddenly the problem was solved entirely by a lucky accident and solved so easily that it showed how right I had been in feeling the problem to be there. I was in a camp where there was an old woman who had been making herself a terrible nuisance. Toothless, almost blind, withered, and stumbling around, she was physically quite revolting and mentally rather senile. She kept hanging around me asking for tobacco, whining, wheedling, snivelling, until I got thoroughly fed up with her. As I had by now learned the Tiwi equivalents of "Go to hell" and "Get lost," I rather enjoyed being rude to her and telling her where she ought to go. Listening to my swearing in Tiwi, the rest of the camp thought it a great joke and no doubt egged her on so that they could listen to my attempts to get rid of her. This had been going on for some time when one day the old woman used a new approach. "Oh, my son," she said, "please give me tobacco." Unthinkingly I replied, "Oh, my mother, go jump in the ocean." Immediately a howl of delight arose from everybody within earshot and they all gathered round me patting me on the shoulder and calling me by a kinship term. She was my mother and I was her son. This gave a handle to everybody else to address me by a kinship term. Her other sons from then on called me brother (and I should call them brothers); her brothers called me "sister's son" (and I should call them mother's brother); her husband (and his brothers) called me son and I called each of them father and so on. I was now in the kinship system, my clan was Jabijabui (a bird) because my mother was Jabijabui and Tiwi clans were matrilineal.

From then on the change in the atmosphere between me and the tribe at large was remarkable. Strangers were now told that I was Jabijabui and that my mother was old so-and-so and when told this, stern old men would relax, smile and say "then you are my brother" (or my son, or my sister's son, or whatever category was appropriate), and I would struggle to respond properly by addressing them by the proper term. Actually it was usually quite easy because all I needed was the term reciprocal with the term he used for me. If he called me brother I called him brother, if he called me son I called him father, if he called me sister's son then I called him mother's brother. It got a little harder after that.

For the rest of my stay on the islands this framework persisted. Mariano, in his stubborn manner, continued to address me as "Boss" (to show his Europeanization) and a few sophisticates around the Mission persisted in addressing me as "Mistarti," but the average old man or old woman, especially in Munupi and Malau, addressed me by a kinship term, referred to me by a kinship term (for example, question put to Mariano: "When is my sister's son coming to visit me?") and I hope, if they thought about me at all, thought about me in kinship terms. As they certainly thought about everybody else in such context, I infer that they found it easier and more comfortable to think about me in such a context. And because they were more relaxed and comfortable using that context, my fieldwork was made much easier and relations were on a much more friendly and casual basis than before.

How seriously they took my presence in their kinship system is something I never will be sure about. They certainly did not expect me to change my behavior because of it. Though I was now a Jabijabui with numerous relatives, no pressure was put upon me to act like a true clansman of that clan. My fellow Jabijabui did not ask for special favors or for conduct from me that promoted their special clan interest. They called me brother and I called them brother, and except for occasionally bringing it up in order to get a little extra tobacco, that was all there was to it. It seemed that the primary purpose of a kinship system is to promote ease and prevent strain in everyday, face-to-face living, and the other aspects of kinship and clanship are secondary or subordinate to that primary purpose. That was fine with me and I presumed it was fine with them. However, toward the end of my time on the islands an incident occurred that surprised me because it suggested that some of them had been taking my presence in the kinship system much more seriously than I had thought. I was approached by a group of about eight or nine senior men all of whom I knew, drawn from several bands and when they arrived the only point in common that I recognized them as having was that they were all senior members of the Jabijabui clan, that is, I called them all brother or mother's brother. It turned out that they had come to me on a delicate errand. They were the senior members of the Jabijabui clan and they had decided among themselves that the time had come to get rid of the decrepit old woman who had first called me son and whom I now called mother. (Many of them called her mother too, and those who did not call her mother called her sister.) As I knew, they said, it was Tiwi custom, when an old woman became too feeble to look after herself, to "cover her up." This could only be done by her sons and her brothers and all of them had to agree beforehand, because once it was done they did not want any dissension among the brothers or clansmen, as that might lead to a feud. My "mother" was now completely blind, she was constantly falling over logs or into fires, and they, her senior clansmen were in agreement that she would be better out of the way. Did I agree also? I already knew about "covering up." The Tiwi, like many other hunting and gathering peoples, sometimes got rid of their ancient and decrepit females. The method was to dig a hole in the ground in some lonely place, put the old woman in the hole and fill it in with earth until only her head was showing. Everybody went away for a day or two and then went back to the hole to discover, to their great surprise, that the old woman was dead, having been too feeble to raise her arms from the earth. Nobody had "killed" her, her death in Tiwi eyes was a natural one. She had been alive when her relatives last saw her. I had never seen it done, though I knew it was the custom, so I asked my brothers if it was necessary for me to attend the "covering up." They said no and they would do it, but only after they had my agreement. Of course I agreed, and a week or two later we heard in our camp that my "mother" was dead, and we all wailed and put on the trimmings of mourning. Mariano thoroughly disapproved and muttered darkly that the police in Darwin should be informed, but I soon told him that this was Jabijabui business and since he was not Jabijabui, it was none of his affair.

I have gone into some detail about my "mother" because the whole affair shows the all-pervasiveness of the kinship system and how every action, even the choice of a term by which to address me or the getting rid of a decrepit old woman, had to be handled along kinship lines. Even my telling off of Mariano can be seen in that light. He was my friend, but in a crisis I rejected his advice and acted in concert with my brothers and mother's brothers. The lines of friendship (and there were plenty of them in Tiwi) always dissolved or broke at the call of the kinfolk or clan. In times of crisis a Tiwi did not have friends, he only had brothers and mother's brothers and sisters' sons.

So by the end of July 1928 I was away from the Mission, caught up in the kinship system, learning the language, going round from camp to camp in Malau and Munupi, and more or less reconciled to life in the bush. Sleeping on the ground, washing in the creek or waterhole (if any), eating with one's fingers, some days walking from sunrise till sunset and camping (after dark) in an ant's nest, at other times camping for weeks at a time in the same spot, where food and water were plentiful. It was all rather dirty but apart from that very pleasant indeed and certainly helped, I think, to make my point that the role of an anthropologist and that of a missionary were quite different. As a guest I did whatever my Tiwi hosts wanted me to do; if they wanted to move I moved too; if they wanted to stay where they were I stayed too. Never in my life, before or since, have I been so submissive to the will of others, and never before had the Tiwi seen or heard of a white man who was so undemanding.

TIME ON MY HANDS

And therein lay the germ of the next difficulty. I had too much time on my hands. Evans-Pritchard was to tell me, years later, that he had found the same thing when working with the Azande of the Sudan and had only been able to combat it by a rigid determination to take notes, about something, no matter how boring or trivial, every single day he was in the field. But the Azande are a very numerous tribe and there is always something going on in an Azande village or cattle-camp. But Tiwi households (numbering 10, 15, 20 people) spent something like 40 out of every 52 weeks of the year living by themselves with only minimal contact with other households. Frequently households were combined into what I called establishments and of these there were seven in Malau and about nine in Munupi in 1928. But more than half of them were of little use to me because they contained mostly young or middle-aged people who did not have much to add to my general store of anthropological information, and who, in any case, were expected to work all day. During the day only the babies and one or maybe two old wives to look after them would be left in the camp; the rest would be scattered through the bush, the women and children gathering wild fruits, vegetables and nuts, the men hunting. Only at sundown would they all come in and the brief period between sundown and bedtime would be busily taken up by cooking, gossiping, and eating. Encamped with such a household, what was I supposed to do all day? The hunters did not want me. I made too much noise and frightened the game away. The women did not want me because their gathering habits were all business and in any case unmarried men were supposed to stay away from them. Apparently the only daytime activity for me was to stay in camp and help the old women in charge of the babies, but such a role had little appeal.

In bigger establishments, which were those of the older and more prestigeful men, the old men did not hunt but stayed in camp all day, doing very little on most days except eat and sleep. Some of them did a little work like carving ceremonial graveposts or, like Timalarua, making canoes or carving spears, but as a group these Munupula and Malauila elders were not particularly good informants, except for their memories of historical occurrences. On most matters none of these old men was as good an informant as Mariano. They did not have the somewhat detached objective attitude toward their own culture that he had acquired through his contacts with the missionaries and other white men. As the behavior of my Jabijabui brothers was later to show, the senior men of the northern bands were rather naive about their own culture, in the sense that they accepted its logics as self-evident without being able to explain or analyze them. None of the sophisticated Tiklauila around the Mission would have thought for a moment that I might start a blood feud against them if they "covered up" my mother without my knowledge or consent; the more naive Malauila and Munupula thought it likely because that was the only logic of such a situation they knew. That was "the Tiwi way" and they knew no other way to handle it. The white policeman logic that Mariano immediately raised as an alternative logic for me to follow never occurred to them because it was not a Tiwi logic. From which I conclude that the best informants in still functioning native societies are rarely likely to be the pure unsullied primitive old pagans (the "noble savages") but are much more likely to be men who, through contact with another culture, usually European, have been shaken a little in their acceptance of their own culture to the point where they have "to explain it," even to themselves and who, when explaining it to outsiders are therefore able to bring out logics and interconnections that their more primitive seniors are incapable of putting into words.

This, of course, does not imply that I depended on Mariano for everything. Ceremonies came and went, mourning ceremonies and initiation and naming ceremonies, and there I could make my own descriptions and talk to the ceremonial leaders (Tu'untalumi, Enquirio, Ku-nai-u-ua) about the meaning and history and the symbolism of the rituals. Folklore and tribal legends any old man could give me, but they did not vary much in their stories and I did not see much point in listening to and recording the same legend for the fifth or sixth time. Technology bored me. All the young functionalists of those early days had a profound contempt for the type of anthropology book that contained dozens of pages of descriptions of how the people made pots or baskets or cut digging sticks, a contempt that Radcliffe-Brown (and later, after I left the Tiwi, Malinowski) did much to encourage. What else in the culture was there that would or might occupy my abundant spare time? Pondering this question I came to my next moment of truth.

SOME UNANSWERED QUESTIONS ABOUT KINSHIP

I had learned my kinship systems of Australia from Radcliffe-Brown (and there never was a better teacher) and had accompanied Lloyd Warner (as a "learner") on his trip in early 1928 to the Roper River where he gathered up kinship systems (at the rate of six or seven a day) for the tribes on the periphery of his Murngin area. As a result I thought of a kinship system as a diagram of vertical and horizontal lines usually 4 by 5 spaces in size, with the native name of Father's Father at the top left-hand corner and the native name for Daughter's Daughter at the bottom right-hand corner. Tacked on in front of the middle line was a character named Ego, and you really needed two such charts for each tribe, one for Ego (male) and the other for Ego (female). (See Brown, 1913 for such charts.) In this sense I had "got" my Tiwi kinship system even before I left Darwin to go to the islands. Following Warner's methods, a half-hour's discussion with a few Tiwi who happened to be in Darwin at the time, made it clear that the Tiwi system was of the usual Kareira type (Type I in Radcliffe-Brown's classification), with a few special or unusual features added. Nothing to it: Type I with modifications. After arriving in the islands I had been using it for terms of address and of course after my adoption by my old mother was expected to use it for terms of reference also. There did not seem to be much more work to do on that section of the culture.

And yet things kept cropping up that were clearly matters of kinship, but which I did not at all understand. "She is promised to Padimo" somebody would say, pointing to a little girl of 5 or 6. I did not remember anything in class concerning what "promising" a wife meant, or of who had the right to "promise" one. This was a matrilineal society and I already knew that in it sisters, brothers, mothers, and mother's brothers were very close to one another.

Well then, "Who promised her to Padimo? Her brothers?" Loud laughter. "Of course not. Her father. Only the father has the right to promise a girl to her future husband."

"But suppose the father dies. Does his disposition of the girl take place as he wished?"

"Certainly. The new father has to carry out the wishes of the previous father."

"Can the brothers promise their sister?"

"No, because they are too young."

"What do you mean, because they are too young? They are not always too young."

"Well, look at this little girl promised to Padimo. She is only 5 or 6. Her only brother is about two years older than her, that is about 7. How could he promise anything to anybody. He's not dry behind the ears."

"Well, when he grows up can he promise her to somebody?"

"No, because she's already promised to Padimo."

"Look here, I know Padimo, he's a man of about 36. Twenty-five years from now this little girl will still only be around 30 and her little brother will be about 32. But Padimo by that time may well be dead. What then will happen?"

"Well, you can't tell. When Padimo dies her mother will marry again and her new father will rename the little girl."

"Wait a minute, there are two points there. Suppose her mother does not remarry when Padimo dies. What then?"

"Oh, she has to. All women must have a husband all the time."

"Well, well, I didn't know that. No matter how old she is?"

"No matter how old and no matter how young. All Tiwi females have husbands."

"And secondly, what's all this about renaming the child?"

"Well, a father names all his children, but if he dies his widow must marry again, and then her new husband renames all her children."

"And if the second husband also dies?"

"Then she must get a third husband and he will rename all her children."

"And what happens to the old names?"

"They all become taboo."

"I see."

Of course, in the early days I did not see at all, but there was enough in the preceding dialogue and many like it to convince me that I really knew nothing about how Australian kinship systems actually worked and that there seemed to be a great deal to the Tiwi system that was not even mentioned in "Three Tribes of Western Australia." Combing my memory, I could not remember anywhere in the Australian literature any discussion of decision making in marriage arrangement, that is, who decided which girl would marry which man. Apparently as long as a man married his mother's brother's daughter (in Kareira), or his mother's mother's brother's daughter's daughter (in Arunta), there were no other relevant considerations. (Later research when I got back to the libraries showed that my memory was right. Nowhere in the classic literature on Australian tribes does any writer explore the mechanics of how the decision is made by which this particular girl marries this particular man.) This conclusion of mine, is, on the whole, confirmed by a recent treatment of the same matter, apparently stimulated by the 1960 Tiwi publication, by one of the younger Australians, Dr. L. R. Hiatt (Hiatt, 1967).

The conversation reported above, and others like it, reveal an extraordinary number of new leads, all of them unexpected. The compulsory marriage for all females, the naming and renaming rules, the discrepancy in age between Padimo and his child bride of 5 or 6, the implication that although a little boy of 7 could have no say in the disposition of his sister he might have some say by the time he was 32, the intriguing question of how ancient widows of 60 or more got new husbands, all of these questions clearly needed intensive research. But one could not explore such questions very far on a general or abstract level. The discussions kept going around in circles because all the things mentioned and others not brought out yet were interconnected. For instance, I now want to ask why the father of the little girl promised her to

Padimo in the first place. And I also want to know how on earth a man (or woman) ever gets a permanent name if their names are always changed after their mother remarries. And I now see dimly that if all first marriages of girls are of the Padimo type, to a man 30 or more years older than the girls, then Tiwi women as a group are likely to be widowed many times during their lives and will therefore each bear children to quite a number of different husbands. What I needed most to sort out the jumble were some detailed, concrete cases.

How all these things and many others work out and tie together has already been discussed in Chapters 1 through 4. Here, I am only concerned about how I came slowly to understand it all and to put it together as a cultural system. Discussed or explored with the Tiwi at the level of discussion exemplified previously, which is what I called the abstract level of discussion, there are too many loose ends or places where the informants could say (indeed had to say), "Maybe" or "We can't tell," or "Perhaps that will happen, perhaps not." Only by getting hold of some complete details of actual marriages and promises and remarriages of widows could I hope to unscramble the jigsaw. And that meant genealogies.

ANSWERS IN GENEALOGIES

I have always liked genealogies, and still do. There is something clean and structural about them, like blueprints. Rivers had used them extensively when writing *The Todas* (1906), and in some ways my problem was similar to that which he had faced when he discovered that the Todas were practicing both polygyny and polyandry at the same time. Though I was not yet sure what the things were, the Tiwi marriage system seemed to include many different things at the same time. Many years later, Ward Goodenough, studying the Trukese of Micronesia was confronted by another similar problem, that of understanding the complicated land-tenure system of the island of Truk, where inheritance follows several different patterns simultaneously, and like Rivers and me, Goodenough also found that tracing actual cases through genealogies was the only road to understanding (Goodenough, 1951). In all three cases, my own judgment is that the genealogical method was not just useful but absolutely essential for the anthropologist concerned to understand his culture, which makes one wonder why it is not used more often. The interminable disputes about the Murngin, for instance, might readily be settled if Warner had only given us some complete and detailed genealogies. Barnes has written a very elegant and stimulating analysis of the place of genealogies in fieldwork (Barnes, 1967).

In any case, as soon as I showed interest in collecting genealogies, it turned out that "the time on my hands" problem was solved. The experts on genealogical matters were the old women, the older the better, because their memories went back further. And it was just these old veterans who had the most spare time. In the camps of the important men, they were the ones who stayed around the camp all day, keeping an eye on the babies, and attending to the wants of the old men. Their gathering days were past and though they might accompany the younger women into the bush, it was to act as watchdogs over the younger women rather than as energetic participants in the food quest. In practice they enjoyed a great deal of independence and if I asked some of them to stay in camp and supply me with genealogies, they did not have to ask anybody's permission to do so. Some old women, like my "mother" for instance, were quite stupid and senile, but there were plenty whom I could use, and whose memory of long-ago marriages could be checked against each other. So I had my task for all my spare time, the genealogies, and I had my task force, the older women in any camp that I came to. From then on I was always busy.

For the Tiwi genealogies must be the most complicated genealogies that any anthropologist ever sought to collect. Every older woman had at least four and sometimes six or seven husbands in the course of her lifetime, bearing children to at least three of them. Every old man had or had had a number of wives, some now dead, some still living and some bestowed upon him but not yet in residence in his camp. On page 69, I gave a detailed breakdown of the 21 wives of Ki-in-kumi, an elderly Malauila, and he was by no means exceptional. Many of these wives had been married to other men before marrying him and hence their children had to be shown not only in Ki-in-kumi's genealogy but also in the genealogies of their real fathers (now dead), who often were not Malauila at all, and therefore would not only be on a different page but in a different volume. All bestowals and rebestowals and most, if not all, widow-remarriages were parts of deals, and somehow the nature of the deal had to be found and noted in the genealogies. Because deals were often begun years before my arrival and the payoff (or part of it) was only taking place now, it was necessary to get as much genealogical information as possible, not only about the living, but also about the dead. Old Ki-in-kumi had gotten started on his accumulation of 21 wives in his early thirties, which meant in the 1890s, and those deals of the 1890s were themselves the results or partly the results of deals that took place 30 years before that, and now in 1928, Ki-in-kumi, as an old man, was still making deals (that is, bestowing his daughters) according to the commitments of both those earlier sets of deals. (This point is well brought out by the footnote on p. 57.)

THE AGE FACTOR

In addition to these Byzantine complexities of marriage and descent, the age factor was of great importance. All Tiwi young men started their careers by being or seeking to be what I have called "satellites" of older men. But, at some later stage of their lives many of them stopped being satellites and instead tried to attract satellites of their own. The formal kinship relationship of two men would not change with age, but their relationship as partners or rivals in marriage deals would change often. Therefore in making their genealogies, one had to watch carefully for changing ages. The genealogy of Inglis and Tomitari, given on page 79, would be meaningless if the ages of the people concerned were not given. Tomitari was the sister's son of Inglis throughout his life, as much in 1914 as in 1928. But their relationship as participants in a series of marriage deals changed drastically between 1914 and 1928, and the reason for the drastic change was that they were both 14 years older in 1928. This incidentally is a good example of why the formal kinship system of 4 by 5 kinship terms plus Ego was so useless in understanding Tiwi marriage arrangements.

Thus there had to be included in all genealogies, as far as it could be established, the age when a bestowal or remarriage took place of (1) the male partner, (2) the female partner, (3) the bestowing agent (such as the father), or agents (such as a group of brothers), and (4) any satellites or stand-ins who might have been used by any of the parties.

In addition to all these complexities, there were always the dreadful and constant confusions introduced into the genealogies by the endless changing of peoples' names. The personal names of people changed whenever their mother remarried, which was often. Hence a man might appear in one genealogy at the age of 3, under one name; then under a quite different name he would appear in another genealogy at the age of 15; then somewhere else under another name at the age 30; and finally in his own genealogy under the name I knew him by as a senior man. This was often good for a laugh. Getting the genealogy of a man of the last generation I would be told for instance that he had three sons, A, B, and (let us say) Timalamdemiri. "How many of them are still alive?" "Is A still living?" "No, he's dead." "Is B still living?" "No, he's dead." "Is Timalamdemiri still living?" Shouts of laughter. "You went hunting with him last week! He's now called Pingirimini."

So the genealogy project involved not only the collection of the genealogies of everyone in the tribe still living, but also as many of the dead as the old women could remember. It also involved the much more formidable task of editing them, sorting them, sifting them, correcting the people who appeared under different names in different genealogies, and finally cross-indexing them. Much of this could not be done in the field, especially the cross-indexing, but had to wait for my return to civilization where there were electric lights and I could work at night. The whole effort was well worthwhile. Without the genealogies, I could never have written the chapter entitled "The Prestige and Influence System," and even there I only used the genealogies of the Malauila, preferring to stick to one band and cover that band completely rather than jump around from one band to another for random illustrations.

LAMENT

I was very fortunate indeed to have had the chance to do fieldwork under the conditions described above. The Tiwi no longer live their wandering life in the bush, but have now gathered permanently around the mission station or the new government stations, which have been set up on the islands. All over the world the same thing is happening. The true hunting and gathering tribes no longer hunt and gather. Levi-Strauss laments that in South America the lonely savannas are becoming more lonely as man disappears from them. In 1928–1929 the savannas of the Tiwi country were indeed far from being lonely places, and I remain most grateful to the Tiwi for having given me the opportunity to discover what it was like to live their type of life. If only they were still in their savannas and I were 30 years younger, I would love to do it all over again. But alas, nowadays the Tiwi are monogamous, go to Mass every Sunday, and wear pants. Such is progress. How sad and how dull.

Sources for the Case Study and on the Tiwi

Many scholarly publications categorize their terminal bibliographies into lists under such labels as "Books," "Articles," and "Documents." The first edition of *The Tiwi* separated Historical References from Anthropological References. Citations in present-day anthropological publications are usually unsegregated—books, newspaper articles, and bureaucratic publications all being united in one alphabetical list. The sources that follow are assembled in the latter manner.

The list that follows departs from standard anthropological usage, because it not only includes all items referred to in the text, but it has been expanded to include most Tiwi titles a scholar is likely to find in a major research library. Such an expanded bibliography has been included to encourage scholars and students having research libraries available to move from *The Tiwi*, Third Edition, to the preparation of additional scholarly analyses. It is realized that many, if not most, students in anthropology, are at major North American universities, some of which expect students, even freshmen, to take disparate sources and draw from them their own research conclusions.

The list of sources has also been expanded to provide the reader with some idea of the range of topics and types of material that has been issued in the Tiwi language as part of the bilingual program at Bathurst Island: traditional tales, graded readers, a sports account, a newspaper, a story of an angel in the dream-time, cartoon book stories, science fiction, and Tiwi history. An attempt has been made to include at least one work from each of the Tiwi language publishers, and also a work by each Tiwi author. Many readers may find these sources an intriguing mirror of the Tiwi of the 1980s.

The list that follows includes not only anthropological sources and Tiwi publications, but also explorer's accounts, popular travelogues, missionary articles, and other items. This bibliography has been compiled with the aid of the Australian Institute of Aboriginal Studies, Canberra, and its bibliographer Chris Birdsall; their aid has been greatly appreciated. This assembly of sources on the Tiwi is not intended to be exhaustive: It omits many items— especially newspaper accounts—unlikely to be held in the university research libraries of either North America or Australia. Some omitted sources are cited in Beryl F. Craig's 1966 bibliography, included herein.

Apuatimi, Raphael
  1977   Nginingawíla yinkíti [Our Own Food]. Darwin: Summer Institute of Linguistics, Australian Aborigines Branch.
Attenborough, David
  1963   Quest Under Capricorn. London: Lutterworth.

Australia. Parliament. Standing Committee on Public Works

1972a   Minutes of Evidence Relating to the Proposed Construction of Tiwi and Wanguri Schools at Darwin, Northern Territory. Canberra: Government Printer.

1972b   Report Relating to the Proposed Construction of Tiwi and Wanguri Schools at Darwin, Northern Territory. Twelfth Report of 1972. Parliamentary Paper, No. 83 of 1972. Canberra: Government Printer.

Babui, Esther

1972   The Tiwi Story. Bathurst Island, NT.

Barclay, Arthur

1939   Life at Bathurst Island Mission. Walkabout 5 (8):13–19.

Barlow, Captain Maurice

1923   Captain Barlow to Major Owens (dated 19th May 1825). Commonwealth of Australia, Historical Records of Australia, Series III, Despatches and Papers Relating to the Settlement of the States, vol. 6, Northern Territory, August 1824–December 1829. Pp. 645–649. Sydney.

Barnes, John Arundel

1967   Genealogies. *In* The Craft of Social Anthropology, Arnold Leonard Epstein, ed. Pp. 101–127. London: Tavistock Publications. Also available by Hindustan Publishing Company, Delhi, India, 1978, same pagination.

Basedow, Herbert

1913   Notes on the Natives of Bathurst Island, North Australia. Journal of the Royal Anthropological Institute of Great Britain and Ireland 43:291–323.

1925   The Australian Aboriginal. Adelaide: Preece.

Bates, William, and William Hicks

1923   Minutes of Inquiry (dated 3 November 1827): Enclosed in Letter from Major Campbell to Colonial Secretary Macleay (dated November 1827). Commonwealth of Australia, Historical Records of Australia, Series III, Despatches and Papers Relating to the Settlement of the States, vol. 6, Northern Territory, August 1824–December 1829. Pp. 701–705. Sydney.

Berndt, Catherine Helen, and Ronald Murray Berndt

1950   Expressions of Grief Among Aboriginal Women. Oceania 20 (4):286–332.

Berndt, Ronald Murray

1955   "Murngin" (Wulamba) Social Organization. American Anthropologist 57:84–106.

1957   In Reply to Radcliffe-Brown on Australian Local Organization. American Anthropologist 59:346–351.

——, and Catherine Helen Berndt

1964   The World of the First Australian. Sydney: Ure Smith.

Birdsell, Joseph B.

1977   The Recalibration of a Paradigm for the First Peopling of Greater Australia. *In* Sunda and Sahul: Prehistoric Studies in Southeast Asia, Melanesia and Australia, J. Allen, J. Golson, and R. Jones, eds. Pp. 113–167. London: Academic Press.

Borsay, Andrea
  1983   Folkloric: Dance Anthropology. Dance Australia 12:33–34.
Bowler, J. M., R. Jones, H. Allen, and A. G. Thorne
  1970   Pleistocene Human Remains from Australia: A Living Site and
          Human Cremation from Lake Mungo, Western New South Wales.
          World Archaeology 2:39–60.
Brandl, Maria
  1970   Adaptation or Disintegration? Changes in the Kulama Initiation
          and Increase Ritual of Melville and Bathurst Islands, Northern
          Territory of Australia. Anthropological Forum 2 (4):464–479.
  1971   Pukumani: The Social Context of Bereavement in a North Aus-
          tralian Tribe. Ph.D. dissertation. Nedlands: University of Western
          Australia.
  1983   A Certain Heritage: Women and Their Children in North Aus-
          tralia. In We Are Bosses Ourselves: The Status and Role of Ab-
          original Women Today, F. Gaye, ed. Pp. 29–39. Canberra: Aus-
          tralian Institute of Aboriginal Studies.
Brook, Eric
  1975   Táriṅgíni wúta ngárra-púrnayinga = The Snake and His Wife.
          Darwin: Summer Institute of Linguistics, Australian Aborigines
          Branch.
Brown, Alfred Reginald [later known as Radcliffe-Brown, Alfred Reginald]
  1913   Three Tribes of Western Australia. Journal of the Anthropological
          Institute of Great Britain and Ireland 43:143–194.
Brown, Cecil H.
  1983   Where Do Cardinal Direction Terms Come From? Anthropological
          Linguistics 25 (2):121–161.
Campbell, John
  1834   Geographical Memoir of Melville Island and Port Essington, on
          the Cobourg Peninsula. Journal of the Royal Geographical Society
          4:129–181.
  1922a   Major Campbell to Colonial Secretary Macleay (dated 8th April
          1827). Commonwealth of Australia, Historical Records of Aus-
          tralia, Series III, Despatches and Papers Relating to the Settlement
          of the States, vol. 5, Northern Territory, 1823–1827. Pp. 799–808,
          890–891. Sydney.
  1922b   Major Campbell to Colonial Secretary Macleay (dated 9th Novem-
          ber 1827). Commonwealth of Australia, Historical Records of Aus-
          tralia, Series III, Despatches and Papers Relating to the Settlement
          of the States, vol. 5, Northern Territory, 1823–1827. Pp. 821–824.
          Sydney.
  1923a   Major Campbell to Colonial Secretary Macleay (dated 10th Oc-
          tober 1826). Commonwealth of Australia, Historical Records of
          Australia, Series III, Despatches and Papers Relating to the Set-
          tlement of the States, vol. 6, Northern Territory, August 1824–
          December 1829. Pp. 677–687. Sydney.
  1923b   Major Campbell to Colonial Secretary Macleay (dated 7th June
          1827). Commonwealth of Australia, Historical Records of Aus-
          tralia, Series III, Despatches and Papers Relating to the Settlement
          of the States, vol. 6, Northern Territory, August 1824–December
          1829. Pp. 687–695. Sydney.

1923c   Regulations Respecting the Natives, and the Carrying of Firearms (probably dated 1st October 1826): Enclosure M, no. 1, with the Letter from Major Campbell to Colonial Secretary Macleay (dated October 10, 1826). Commonwealth of Australia, Historical Records of Australia, Series III, Despatches and Papers Relating to Settlement of the States, vol. 6, Northern Territory, August 1824–December 1829. P. 676. Sydney.

——, and John Gold

1923   Minutes of an Examination Taken This Twenty-Seventh Day of October, One Thousand Eight Hundred and Twenty Six in Presence of John Campbell, Esqre., and John Gold, Esqre., Two of His Majesty's Justices of the Peace for the Colony of New South Wales and Its Dependencies To Investigate the Particular Circumstances Attending the Death of Julius Campbell, a Prisoner of the Crown Who Was Killed by the Natives of Melville Island on the Morning of Thursday, the Twenty Sixth Day of October, One Thousand Eight Hundred and Twenty Six: Enclosure no. 3 in the Letter from Major Campbell to Colonial Secretary Macleay (dated 20th December 1826). Commonwealth of Australia, Historical Records of Australia, Series III, Despatches and Papers Relating to the Settlement of the States, vol. 6, Northern Territory, August 1824–December 1829. Pp. 685–686. Sydney.

Capell, Arthur

1940   The Classification of Languages in North and North-West Australia. Oceania 10 (3):241–272; (4):404–433.

1965   A Typology of Concept Domination. Lingua 15:451–462.

1967   The Analysis of Complex Verbal Forms: With Special Reference to Tiwi (Bathurst and Melville Islands, North Australia). Papers in Australian Linguistics 2:43–62. Pacific Linguistics, Series A: Occasional Papers, No. 11.

Casey, Dermot A., and Aldo Massola

1957   The Derivation of the Melville and Bathurst Islands Burial Posts. National Museum of Victoria, Memoirs 22 (9):1–7.

Chowning Ann, and Jane Carter Goodale

1965   The Passismanua Census Division, West New Britain Open Election. In The Papua—New Guinea Election 1965, David G. Bettison, Colin A. Hughes, and Paul W. van der Veur, eds. Canberra: Australian National University.

1966   A Flint Industry from Southwest New Britain, Territory of New Guinea. Asian Perspectives 9:150–153.

Collard, G. J.

1935   Bathurst Island, North Australia. Walkabout, October:44–45.

Conigrave, Charles Price

1936   North Australia. London: Jonathan Cape.

Coon, Carleton S.

1963   The Origin of Races. London: Jonathan Cape.

Craig, Beryl F.

1966   Arnhem Land Peninsular Region (Including Bathurst and Melville Islands). Australian Institute of Aboriginal Studies, Occasional Papers in Aboriginal Studies No. 8, Bibliography Series No. 1. Canberra.

Dean, Beth, and Victor Carell
1956   Dust for the Dancers. Sydney: Ure Smith.
Douglas, William Orville
1954   Jiberabu. Colliers 134 (November 26):28–31.
Earl, George Windsor
1853   The Native Races of the Indian Archipelago. Papuans. London: Hippolyte Bailliere.
Elkin, Adolphus Peter, Ronald Murray Berndt, and Catherine Helen Berndt
1951   Social Organization of Arnhem Land. Oceania 30 (4):253–301.
Fernando, Richard Casey
1982   Ngirramini ngini Kapitini Amarika: The Adventures of Captain America. Bathurst Island, NT.: Nguiu Nginingawila Literature Production Centre.
Flynn, Rev. Frank
1947   Distant Horizons: Mission Impressions. Newtown, N.S.W.: A. J. Colley.
Ford, Edward
1942   Medical Conditions on Bathurst and Melville Island. Medical Journal of Australia 2 (11):235–238.
Fry, Henry K.
1949   A Bathurst Island Mourning Rite. Mankind 4 (2):79–80.
1950   A Bathurst Island Initiation Rite. Mankind 4 (4):167–168.
Godfrey, Marie
1985   Repetition of Tiwi at Clause Level. Aboriginal and Islander Grammars: Collected Papers, S. Ray, ed. Pp. 1–38. Darwin: Summer Institute of Linguistics, Australian Aborigines Branch.
——, and Raphael Apuatimi
1976   Ngíningawíla júrra 2. Darwin: Summer Institute of Linguistics, Australian Aborigines Branch.
1977a   Teachers' Guide, Nginingawila, jurra 3. Darwin: Summer Institute of Linguistics, Australian Aborigines Branch.
1977b   Nginingawila, jurra 4. Darwin: Summer Institute of Linguistics, Australian Aborigines Branch.
1978   Nginingawila, jurra 5. Darwin: Summer Institute of Linguistics, Australian Aborigines Branch.
Godfrey, Marie, and Sister Jacinta Mary
1975a   Ngíningawíla júrra, 1. Darwin: Summer Institute of Linguistics, Australian Aborigines Branch.
1975b   Ngíningawíla júrra, 1: Teachers' Guide. Darwin: Summer Institute of Linguistics, Australian Aborigines Branch.
Godfrey, Marie, and K. Manning, eds.,
1976a   Ngirramini ngini karri ngawa ngarimakirri: 'Stories About When We're Frightened,' [in] Tiwi, by Anastasia Kelantumana, et al. Batchelor, NT.: Darwin Community College, School of Australian Linguistics.
1976b   Ngirramini ngini parlingari: 'Stories About Long Ago,' [in] Tiwi, by Anastasia Kelantumana, et al. Batchelor, NT.: Darwin Community College, School of Australian Linguistics.

Goodale, Jane Carter

1955   Melville Island. Philadelphia Anthropological Society, Bulletin 8 (3):2–4.

1957   "Alonga bush"—a Tiwi Hunt. Pennsylvania, University Museum Bulletin 21 (3):3–35.

1959a   The Tiwi Dance for the Dead. Expedition 2 (1):2–13.

1959b   The Tiwi Women of Melville Island, Australia. Philadelphia Anthropological Society, Bulletin 21 (3):13–14.

1959c   Tiwi Women of Melville Island, Australia. Ph.D. dissertation, Philadelphia: University of Pennsylvania.

1960   Sketches of Tiwi Children, Expedition 2 (4):4–13.

1960/1963/1974   Tiwi of North Australia. *In* Funeral Customs the World Over, Robert Wesley Habenstein and William M. Lamers, eds. Milwaukee: Bulfin Printers.

1962   Marriage Contracts among the Tiwi. Ethnology 1 (4):452–466.

1963   Qualifications for Adulthood: Tiwi Invoke the Power of a Yam. Natural History 72 (4):10–17.

1966a   Blowgun Hunters of the South Pacific. National Geographic Magazine 129 (6):793–817. Concerns Passismanua peoples of New Britain.

1966b   Imlohe and the Mysteries of the Passismanua (Southwest New Britain). Expedition 8 (3):20–31.

1970   An Example of Ritual Change among the Tiwi of Melville Island. *In* Diprotodon to Detribalization: Studies of Change among Australian Aborigines, Arnold Remington Pilling and Richard Alan Waterman, eds. East Lansing: Michigan State University Press.

1971   Tiwi Wives: A Study of the Women of Melville Island, North Australia. American Ethnological Society Monographs No. 51. Seattle and London: University of Washington Press.

1981   Siblings as Spouses: The Reproduction and Replacement of Kaulong Society. Association for Social Anthropology in Oceania, Monograph Series 8:275–305.

1982   Production and Reproduction of Key Resources among the Tiwi of North Australia. American Association for the Advancement of Science Selected Symposium 67:197–210. Boulder, CO: Westview Press.

1985   Pig's Teeth and Skull Cycles: Both Sides of the Face of Humanity [Kaulong]. American Ethnologist 12 (2):228–244.

——, and Joan D. Koss

1966   The Cultural Context of Creativity among Tiwi. American Ethnological Society, Annual Spring Meeting 1966, Proceedings, pp. 175–191. Seattle: University of Washington Press.

Goodenough, Ward Hunt

1951   Property, Kin and Community on Truk. Yale Publications in Anthropology, No. 46. New Haven, CT: Yale University Press.

Grau, Andree

1983   Dreaming, Dancing, Kinship: The Study of Yoi, the Dance of the Tiwi of Melville and Bathurst Islands, North Australia. Ph.D. dissertation. Belfast: Queen's University.

Gsell, François Xavier
  1955   "The Bishop With 150 Wives": Fifty Years As a Missionary. Sydney, London, Melbourne, Wellington: Angus and Robertson.
Harney, William Edward
  1957   Life Among the Aborigines. London: Robert Hale Limited.
——, and Aldolphus Peter Elkin
  1943   Melville and Bathurst Islanders: A Short Description. Oceania 13 (3):228–234.
Harris, John
  1985   Contact Languages at the Northern Territory British Military Settlements, 1824–1849, Aboriginal History 9 (1–2):148–169.
Hart, Charles William Merton
  1930   The Tiwi of Melville and Bathurst Islands. Oceania 1:167–180.
  1931   Personal Names among the Tiwi. Oceania 1:280–290.
  1932   Grave Posts of Melville Island. Man 32:18.
  1954   The Sons of Turimpi. American Anthropologist 56:242–261.
  1955   Contrasts between Prepubertal and Postpubertal Education. In Education and Anthropology, George Dearborn Spindler, ed. Stanford, CA: Stanford University Press.
  1970   Some Factors Affecting Residence among the Tiwi. Oceania 40 (4):296–303.
  1974   Fieldwork among the Tiwi, 1928–1929. In Being an Anthropologist: Fieldwork in Eleven Cultures, George D. Spindler, ed. New York: Holt, Rinehart and Winston. Also Chapter 8 of present volume.
——, and Arnold R. Pilling
  1960   The Tiwi of North Australia. New York, Holt, Rinehart and Winston.
Hartley, Humphrey Robert
  1923   Captain Hartley to Colonial Secretary Macleay (dated 8th September 1828). Commonwealth of Australia, Historical Records of Australia, Series III, Despatches and Papers Relating to the Settlement of the States, vol. 6, Northern Territory, August 1824–December 1829. Pp. 751–761. Sydney.
Heeres, Jan Ernest
  1899   The Part Borne by the Dutch in the Discovery of Australia 1606–1765. London: Luzac & Company.
Hempel, Robin
  1977   Pumpuni, Pumpuni! How the Tiwi Learned to Love Their Library. Australian Library Journal 26 (5):95–102.
Heysen, Sue
  1985a   Japini awarra mapurtiti yinuwuriyi kapi Nguiu!!: Yesterday, a Monster Came to Nguiu. Bathurst Island, NT.: Nguiu Nginingawila Literature Production Centre.
  1985b   Kuwanga jikirimi nginaki jarrumuwani? What Made These Tracks? Bathurst Island, NT: Nguiu Nginingawila Literature Production Centre.
Hiatt, Lester Richard
  1967   Authority and Reciprocity in Australian Aboriginal Marriage Arrangements. Mankind 6 (10):469–475.

Hill, Ernestine Hemmings
　1956　The Great Australian Loneliness. Melbourne: Roberston and Mullens.

Hingston, J. P.
　1938　Exploration of Melville Island. Royal Australian Historical Society, Journal and Proceedings 24 (2):157–163.

House, James
　1959　Tiwi Burial Poles as Sculpture. Expedition 2 (1):14–16.

Jones, Frank Lancaster
　1963　A Demographic Study of the Aboriginal Population of the Northern Territory, With Special Reference to Bathurst Island Mission. Australian Institute of Aboriginal Studies, Occasional Papers in Aboriginal Studies, No. 1; Social Anthropology Series, No. 1. Canberra.

Kantilla, David
　1984　Nguiulla Football League: Tapalinga versus Imalu. Grand Final at Nguiu Oval 6th March, 1983–84. [Bathurst Island, NT.: Nguiu Nginingawila Literature Production Centre.]

Kantilla, Donald
　n.d.　Jipiyuka amintiya jipwajirringa: The Carpet Snake and the Wallaby. [Bathurst Island, NT.: Nguiu Nginingawila Literature Production Centre.]

Kantilla, Marita
　1981　Ngirramini ngini awinyirra wulikimaka amintiya nyirramuwaringa: A Story about an Old Woman and Her Daughter. Bathurst Island, NT.: Nguiu Nginingawila Literature Production Centre.

Kerinaiua, Cyril James
　1983　Ngirramini ngirri arlipiwura [in Tiwi]. Bathurst Island, NT.: Nguiu Nginingawila Literature Production Centre.

Kerinaiua, Leah
　1981　Ngirramini ngini pajinga amintiya jinaringa: The Watersnake and the Blind Snake. Bathurst Island, NT.: Nguiu Nginingawila Literature Production Centre.

Kerinaiua, Magdeline
　1981　Ngirramini ngini kijini pulangumwani: A Story about a Little Dog. Bathurst Island, NT.: Nguiu Nginingawila Literature Production Centre.

Kilham, Christine A., ed.
　1979　Four Grammatical Sketches: From Phrase to Paragraph. Darwin: Summer Institute of Linguistics, Australian Aborigines Branch.

King, Phillip Parker
　1827　Narrative of a Survey of the Intertropical and Western Coasts of Australia: Performed between the Years 1818 and 1822. London: John Murray, 2 vols.

Kirk, Robert L. et al.
　1971　Population Genetic Studies in Australian Aborigines of the Northern Territory: The Distribution of Some Serum Protein and Enzyme Groups among Populations at Various Localities in the Northern Territory of Australia. Human Biology in Oceania 1 (1):54–76.

Klaatsch, Hermann
  1907a   Schlussbericht über meine Reise nach Australien in der Jahren
          1904–1907. Zeitschrift für Ethnologie, 39 Jahrgang, Heft iv–v:6,
          pp. 635–687.
  1907b   Some Notes on Scientific Travel amongst the Black Population of
          Tropical Australia, 1904, 1905, 1906. Australian and New Zealand
          Association for the Advancement of Science, Report 11: 577–592.
Kupla, Karel
  1957   Australian Aboriginal Bark Painting. Oceania 27 (4):264–267.
Lee, Jennifer R.
  1983   Tiwi Today: A Study of Language Change in a Contact Situation.
          Ph.D. dissertation. Canberra, Australian National University.
LeForte, Bernard
  n.d.   Ngirramini ngini awarra yirrikirijirti monkey: The Ugly Little Mon-
          key. [Bathurst Island, NT.: Nguiu Nginingawila Literature Pro-
          duction Centre.]
McCarthy, Frederick David
  1945   Fire Without Matches. Australian Museum Magazine 8 (11):368–
          373.
Mander Jones, Phyllis
  1948   The Tasman Map of 1644. Sydney: The Trustees of the Public
          Library of New South Wales.
Milikapiti Records
  1968   Regional Conferences—68–3–12. Record #273. Milikapiti, NT:
          November.
  1969   Regional Conferences—68–3–12. Record #272. Milikapiti, NT: May.
  1975–1977   Regional Conferences—SOC = 03. Record #319. Milikapiti,
          NT.
Mountford, Charles Pearcy
  1955   Expedition to the Land of the Tiwi. National Geographic Magazine
          109 (3: March):417–440.
  1958   The Tiwi, Their Art, Myth and Ceremony. London: Phoenix House.
Mungatopi, Katrina,
  n.d.   Ngirramini ngini kirijini amintiya pula[n]gumwani: A Story about
          a Little Boy and a Dog. [Bathurst Island, NT.: Nguiu Nginingawila
          Literature Production Centre.]
——, and Ancilla Munkara
  1980   Pwanga: Spider. [Bathurst Island, NT.: Nguiu Nginingawila Lit-
          erature Production Centre.]
Munkara, Ancilla
  1981   Ngirramini ngini karri ngurruwariyi warta: Bush Holidays. Bathurst
          Island, NT.: Nguiu Nginingawila Literature Production Centre.
Munkara, Hilary et al.
  1975   Ngíningawíla mirrijíni. [Our Medicine; in Tiwi]. Darwin: Summer
          Institute of Linguistics, Australian Aborigines Branch.
Munkara, Marguerite
  1981   Ngirramini ngini kitirika amintiya tayamini: The Story of a Turtle
          and a Dingo. Bathurst Island, NT.: Nguiu Nginingawila Literature
          Production Centre.

Munkara, Peter Damien
    1982   Kakunukurluwi waliwalinguwi: The Planet of the Giant Ants. Bathurst Island, NT.: Nguiu Nginingawila Literature Production Centre.
Munkara, Valerian
    1982   Ngirramini ngini awarra ngatawa kurumutamini: The Incredible Hulk. Bathurst Island, N.T.: Nguiu Nginingawila Literature Production Centre.
Murdock, George Peter
    1949   Social Structure. New York: Macmillan.
Murphy, J. F.
    1920   Bathurst Island, a Mission Station for the Aborigines. Australia 3 (3):77–80.
National Geographic Society
    1975   Atlas of the World, 4th ed. Washington, D.C.
    1981   Atlas of the World, 5th ed. Washington, D.C.
Nguiu Nginingawila Literature Production Centre
    1982   Karri warniyati amintiya kuwurntingilimiri ngirramini: Jirnani Weekend News. Bathurst Island, NT.
    1983   Ngirramini ngini Fort Dundas—Punta (1824–1829): History of Fort Dundas—Punta. Bathurst Island, NT.
    1984   Ngirramini karri putuwurugi awarra awurankini fort amintiya karri pirripapijingi Tiwi (1824): The Building of the Fort and Further Contact with Tiwi Tribes (1824). Bathurst Island, NT.
Northern Territory
    1976   Aboriginal Land Rights Act. Darwin.
Northern Territory. Department of Health
    1983   Tiwi Foods. Darwin.
Osborne, C. R.
    1974   The Tiwi Language: Grammar, Myths, and Dictionary of the Tiwi Language Spoken on Melville and Bathurst Islands, North Australia. Australian Institute of Aboriginal Studies, Australian Aboriginal Studies, No. 55; Linguistic Series, No. 21. Canberra.
    1979   The Tiwi Language, and Nginingawila Ngapangiraga. Nguiu, NT: Nguiu Nginingawila Literature Production Centre.
Perkins, Very Rev. A.
    1936   Bathurst Island and Palm Island Missions. *In* The National Eucharistic Congress, Melbourne, Australia, December 2nd–9th, 1934, Rev. J. M. Murphy and Rev. F. Moynihan, eds. Melbourne.
Pilling, Arnold Remington
    1957   Law and Feud in an Aboriginal Society of North Australia. Ph.D. dissertation. Berkeley: University of California.
    1958   Australia. Asian Perspectives 2:98–111.
    1961   Six Archaeological Sites in the Detroit Area. Michigan Archaeologist, 7: 13–30, 33–54. Also printed in Selections from the Michigan Archaeologist, Volumes 1–10, James Edward Fitting, ed. Michigan Archaeological Society Special Publications, No. 1, Ann Arbor, 1969.
    1962a   Aborigine Culture History, A Survey of Publications, 1954–1957. Detroit, MI: Wayne State University Press.

1962b A Historical *Versus* a Non-Historical Approach to Social Change and Continuity among the Tiwi. Oceania, 32 (4):321–326.

1965 An Australian Aboriginal Minority: The Tiwi See Themselves as a Dominant Majority. Phylon 26:305–314.

1966 Life at Porter Site I, Midland County, Michigan. Michigan Archaeologist 12:235–248.

1968a Southeastern Australia: Level of Social Organization. *In* Man the Hunter, Richard Borshay Lee and Irven DeVore, eds. Chicago: Aldine Publishing Co.

1968b A Use of Historical Sources in Archaeology: An Indian Earthworks near Mt. Clemens, Michigan. Ethnohistory 15:152–202.

1970 Changes in Tiwi Language. *In* Diprotodon to Detribalization: Studies of Change among Australian Aborigines, Arnold Remington Pilling and Richard Alan Waterman, eds. East Lansing: Michigan State University Press.

1974 Dating Early Photographs by Card Mounts and Other External Evidence: Tentative Suggestions. Image 17 (1):11–16.

1978 Yurok. *In* Handbook of North American Indians 8: California, Robert Fleming Heizer, ed. Washington, DC: Smithsonian Institution Press.

1980 Southeastern Michigan. *In* Phase II Completion Report for Conference on Michigan Archaeology, Major Problem Orientations in Michigan Archaeology 1980–1984, James W. Mueller, ed. Jackson, MI: Gilbert/Commonwealth.

1982a Preface. *In* Chilula: People from the Ancient Redwoods, Robert G. Lake, Jr. Washington, DC: University Press of America.

1982b Chilula War Story on Round Valley. *In* Chilula: People from the Ancient Redwoods, Robert G. Lake, Jr. Washington, DC: University Press of America.

1982c Chilula Concept of Confession and Sickness. *In* Chilula: People from the Ancient Redwoods, Robert G. Lake, Jr. Washington, DC: University Press of America.

1982d Detroit: Urbanism Moves West: Palisaded Fur Trade Center to Diversified Manufacturing City. North American Archaeologist 3 (3):225–242.

——, and Patricia Leslie Marks Pilling

1970 Cloth, Clothes, Hose, and Bows: Nonsedentary Merchants among the Indians of Northwestern California. American Ethnological Society, Annual Spring Meeting 1970, Proceedings, Pp. 97–119. Seattle.

——, and Richard Alan Waterman, eds.

1970 Diprotodon to Detribalization: Studies of Change among Australian Aborigines. East Lansing: Michigan State University Press.

Priest, Charles A. V.

1986 Northern Territory Recollections[:] 1. Life Amongst the Aborigines. 2. Carrying My Sway. Benalla, Victoria, Australia: privately issued by Charles A. V. Priest.

Puautjimi, Florrie et al.

1978 A Tiwi Lady's Tale. Aboriginal Health Worker 2 (4):4–7.

Puruntatameri, Paulina
    1982   Tiwi Amintiya English. Ngali, June, p. 18.
Pye, John
    1977   The Tiwi Islands. Darwin, NT: Coleman Pty. Ltd.
Radcliffe-Brown, Alfred Reginald
    1930   Former Numbers and Distribution of the Australian Aborigines. *In* Official Year Book of the Commonwealth of Australia, 23.
    1930–1931   The Social Organization of Australian Tribes, Oceania Monographs, No. 1. Oceania 1:34–63, 206–246, 322–341, 426–456.
    1956   On Australian Local Organization. American Anthropologist 58:363–367.
Raisz, Erwin
    1962   Principles of Cartography. New York, San Francisco, Toronto, London: McGraw-Hill Book Co.
Raschke, Hans D., and Robert L. Misner
    1977   Commercial and Legal Studies: A Case Study—the Aborigines. [Melbourne:] Victoria, Education Department, Legal Studies Section, Curriculum & Research Branch.
Richards, Eirlys B.
    1978   Papers in Literacy and Bilingual Education. Summer Institute of Linguistics, Australian Aborigines Branch, Work Papers, Series B, Volume 2. Darwin.
Ritchie, Patrick H., and Henry B. Raine
    1934   North of the Never Never. Sydney: Angus and Robertson; London: Burns, Oates & Washbourne Ltd., 1935.
Rivers, William Halse Rivers
    1906   *The Todas*. London, New York: Macmillan.
Robin, Dennis
    1978   Art in Action: An Ancient Culture Brings Beauty to the World of Fashion. Aboriginal News 3 (5):10–13.
Rothmans of Pall Mall Canada Limited
    1974   Art of Aboriginal Australia. n.p.
[St. Therese's School, Bathurst Island]
    1980   Ngirramini ngini kwarikwaringa: [Stories about Butterflies]. [Bathurst Island, NT.: Nguiu Nginingawila Literature Production Centre.]
Simeon, George
    1978   Do Traditional Medicines Work? Aboriginal Health Worker, 2 (4):15–18.
    1980   Tiwi Ethnomedicine and the Concept of Tarni. Anthropos 75:942–948.
Simmons, Roy T., and J. J. Graydon
    1971   Population Genetic Studies in Australian Aborigines of the Northern Territory: Blood Group Genetic Studies on Populations Sampled at the Localities Including Arnhem Land and Groote Eylandt. Human Biology in Oceania 1 (1):23–53.
Simpson, Colin
    1962   Adam in Ochre: Inside Aboriginal Australia. Sydney, London, Melbourne, Wellington: Angus and Robertson.

Sims, Michael John
  1978   Tiwi Cosmology. Australian Aboriginal Concepts, Lester Richard
          Hiatt, ed. Pp. 164–167. Canberra: Australian Institute of Aborig-
          inal Studies. [Atlantic Highlands,] New Jersey: Humanities Press.
Spencer, Baldwin
  1914   The Native Tribes of the Northern Territory of Australia. London:
          Macmillan.
  1928   Wanderings in Wild Australia. London: Macmillan.
Stanislaus, Alfie
  1969   My Life . . . As Told to Stan Smith. Aboriginal Quarterly 2 (1):16.
Stokes, John Lort
  1846   Discoveries in Australia: With an Account of the Coasts and Rivers
          Explored and Surveyed during the Voyage of *H.M.S. Beagle*, in
          the Years 1837–38–39–40–41–42–43 by Command of the Lord Com-
          missioners of the Admiralty. London: Boone.
Summer Institute of Linguistics, Australian Aborigines Branch
  1975a   Ngíningawíla júrra ngíni pankínya = Our First Book. Darwin.
  1975b   Ngáwurníyi wárta! = [Let's All Go Bush]. Darwin.
  1976   Reading Tiwi. Darwin.
Sydney, S.F.B.
  1955   Snake Bay Corroboree. Geographical Magazine 20 (7):261–263.
Tindale, Norman Barnett
  1956   The Peopling of Southeastern Australia. Australian Museum Mag-
          azine 12 (4).
  1974   Aboriginal Tribes of Australia: Their Terrain, Environmental Con-
          trols, Distribution, Limits, and Proper Names. Berkeley, Los An-
          geles, London: University of California Press.
Tipiloura, Barnabus
  1981   Notes on the Tiwi Ngaripuluwamigi, Bathurst Is. COMA 7:14–15.
Tipungwuti, Paul Raphael, B. Tipungwuti, and L. M. Tungutalum
  1981   Wutawamiya kakirijuwi puruwakirimi. Bathurst Island, NT.: Nguiu
          Nginingawila Literature Production Centre.
Tungutalum, Gerardine
  1982   Ngirramini ngini yungumpula piniparirraya kapi tupwalingampi:
          Dreamtime Story of the Angels Descending on Tupwalingampi
          Hill. [Bathurst Island, NT.:] Nguiu Nginingawila Literature Pro-
          duction Centre.
——, and D. Tipungwuti
  1981   Ngirramini ngini kartirrikani: A Story About Timber. Bathurst
          Island, NT.: Nginingawila Literature Production Centre.
U.S. Army Map Service
  1963a   Bobonara (Vila Armindo Monteiro), Portuguese Timor; Indone-
          sia, SC-51-8. Washington, DC.
  1963b   Kupang, Indonesia, SC-51-11. Washington, DC.
  1964   Pante Masassar, Portuguese Timor; Indonesia, SC-51-7. Washing-
          ton, DC.
Verney, N.
  1969   The Visual Care of the Australian Aborigines. Australian Journal
          of Science 32 (5):192–196.

Viner, Robert Ian
    1978   Notice to Establish an Aboriginal Land Council [Tiwi]. Northern
            Territory Gazette 35 (September 1): 3–4.
Ward, Teresa
    1978   Teaching Aids for Tiwi. Papers in Literacy and Bilingual Educa-
            tion, Eirlys Richards, ed. Pp. 31–105. Darwin: Summer Institute
            of Linguistics, Australian Aborigines Branch.
Warner, William Lloyd
    1937   A Black Civilization. New York: Harper & Brothers.
White, John Peter, and James Francis O'Connell
    1982   A Prehistory of Australia, New Guinea and Sahul. Sydney, New
            York, London, Paris, San Diego, San Francisco, Sao Paulo, Tokyo,
            Toronto: Academic Press.
White, Neville Graeme
    1979   The Use of Digital Dermatoglyphics in Assessing Population Re-
            lationships in Australian Aborigines. Birth Defects 15 (6):437–454.
——, and P. A. Parsons
    1973   Genetic and Socio-cultural Differentiation in the Aborigines of
            Arnhem Land. American Journal of Physical Anthropology 38 (1):5–
            14.
Willey, Keith
    1965   Mission to the Islands. Walkabout 31 (12):51–53.
Yengoyan, Aram A.
    1981   Infanticide and Birth Order; An Empirical Analysis of Preferential
            Female Infanticide among Australian Aboriginal Populations. In
            The Perception of Evolution: Essays Honoring Joseph B. Birdsell,
            L. L. Mai, E. Shanklin, and R. W. Sussman, eds. Pp. 255–273.
            Los Angeles: University of California, Los Angeles.

Index

177